D1570130

A SURVEY OF MANUSCRIPTS
USED IN EDITIONS
OF THE GREEK NEW TESTAMENT

SUPPLEMENTS TO
NOVUM TESTAMENTUM

VOLUME LVII

A SURVEY OF MANUSCRIPTS
USED IN EDITIONS
OF THE GREEK NEW TESTAMENT

BY

J. K. ELLIOTT

E.J. BRILL
LEIDEN · NEW YORK · KØBENHAVN · KÖLN
1987

By the same author

The Greek Text of the Epistles to Timothy and Titus (University of Utah Press, 1968) = *Studies and Documents* XXXVI

Studies in New Testament Language and Text (editor) (Leiden, 1976) = Novum Testamentum *Supplements* XLIV

Codex Sinaiticus and the Simonides Affair (Thessalonica, 1982) = 'Ανάλεκτα βλαταδων XXXIII

Questioning Christian Origins (London, 1982)

The New Testament in Greek: III The Gospel According to St Luke (executive editor for the American and British Committees of the International Greek New Testament Project) (Oxford, Part I: Chapters 1-12, 1984; Part II: Chapters 13-24 (1987))

Library of Congress Cataloging-in-Publication Data

Elliott, J. K. (James Keith)
    A survey of manuscripts used in editions of the Greek New Testament.

    (Supplements to Novum Testamentum; v. 57)
    Bibliography: p.
    1. Bible.   N.T.—Manuscripts, Greek.   I. Title.
II. Series.
BS1939.E57   1987   225.4'8   87-6327
ISBN 90-04-08109-7

ISSN   0167-9732
ISBN   90 04 08109 7

PRINTED IN THE NETHERLANDS BY E. J. BRILL

TO ROSAMUND

CONTENTS

PREFACE

Most Greek New Testaments have a critical apparatus. In these apparatuses certain manuscripts recur. But, in addition, other manuscripts appear, due largely to the preferences of the editor. The appearance of some manuscripts is restricted to only one apparatus. The idiosyncrasies of an editor of a Greek New Testament in compiling his apparatus is evidenced not only in his choice of readings but also in the choice of ms. support for those readings he chooses to present.

The bulk of this book is a series of tables setting out how all the available manuscripts are used in over eight testaments, three synopses and one edition of Luke. In an article in *Novum Testamentum* (XXV 1983 pp. 97–132) entitled *The Citation of Manuscripts in Recent Printed Editions of the Greek New Testament* I tried to show how comparative studies of individual apparatuses could yield interesting and sometimes surprising results. With the aid of the tables further comparative work is facilitated, and the monitoring of the printed editions encouraged. When new or revised texts with apparatuses appear these can be reviewed alongside the information presented here. This survey acts not only as a monitor on the printed editions but as a pointer for those who wish to investigate the readings of given mss. (especially those for which collations are available). It should also assist those who are attempting (a) to study certain mss. and (b) to assemble an apparatus.

Much of the painstaking searching of the apparatuses that resulted in the statistical details included in the introductory remarks on each text was undertaken by the Revd. J. I. Miller. I would like to express my warm thanks to him for this work and also for the initial typing of the tables. The secretaries in the department of theology at Leeds University were responsible for additional typing and I should like to convey my thanks to them too. The help and advice of Mr H. Tolson and the University of Leeds Printing Service were much appreciated. Financial assistance from the British Academy and the University of Leeds is also gratefully acknowledged. Appendix II is reproduced with the permission of the editors of *Novum Testamentum*.

I hope all those who have occasion to consult a critical apparatus will find this book to be of assistance, and all who are concerned with the use of New Testament manuscripts will be able to use my tables to examine where certain mss. have, have not yet, or, because of their slight extent or importance or membership of a recognised family, have not been used.

J. K. ELLIOTT
Leeds, 1986

INTRODUCTION

In sections I, II, IV, V each page is divided into fifteen columns. In the first column is given the Gregory-Aland number commonly accepted internationally for each NT Greek ms. Then follow the editions of the complete Greek Testaments in chronological order. Then comes the evidence of three recent Greek synopses where for the most part the mss. used are, as would be expected, gospel mss. When making comparisons between the numbers of mss. used in each of these synopses consideration needs to be given to the use made in each of them of the Fourth Gospel.

Finally comes the evidence of the International Greek New Testament Project's work on Luke, where of course only mss. containing this gospel are to be found.

In the final column come the categories assigned to certain mss. by K. and B. Aland in their *Der Text des Neuen Testaments*.

Details about what to look for in each of these columns appear below.

COLUMN ONE

I.1a: *Gregory-Aland numbers*

The numbers in column one follow the Gregory-Aland, or more accurately the Gregory-von Dobschütz-Aland system of classifying NT mss.[1] The full list of the mss., together with details about their contents, size and location, are to be found in Aland's *Liste* and in the supplementary information to be found in ANTF III and in copies of the Münster *Bericht* as well as in the introductions to the editions themselves. Those editions which make use of Tischendorf's or Hoskier's numeration have had these numbers conformed to the Gregory-Aland system; von Soden's numbers have also been converted.

Numbers in column one have been retained even where the ms. is now lost, or is subsumed under a different number, or when the number for another reason is free. These details are given in the footnotes. Corrections to Aland's *Liste* and its supplements have been made where I have up-to-date information. The tables in this volume are intended to be used in conjunction with Aland's *Liste* and are compiled to supplement not to supplant that work.

---

[1] With the exception of 206α used by Bover-O'C and for which an Aland number seems not to be available, and of 2059s used by BFBS.

1.1b: *Uncials*

In the tables uncials are listed according to their number. As many of these are more commonly known by a letter, the following conversion table is given for convenient cross-reference:

01	ℵ	013	He	025	Papr	037	Δ
02	A	014	Ha	026	Q	038	Θ
03	B	015	Hp	027	R	039	Λ
04	C	016	I	028	S	040	Ξ
05	Dea	017	Ke	029	T	041	Π
06	Dp	018	Kap	030	U	042	Σ
07	Ee	019	Le	031	V	043	Φ
08	Ea	020	Lap	032	W	044	Ψ
09	Fe	021	M	033	X	045	Ω
010	Fp	022	N	034	Y		
011	Ge	023	O	035	Z		
012	Gp	024	Pe	036	Γ		

1.2: *Doublets*

Sometimes one number in the Gregory-Aland system applies to two separate mss.[1] This is done in some cases for historical reasons. In other cases examination of the ms. has revealed that two separate mss. have been bound into one volume or that separate hands from different dates have been responsible for completing a ms. Where one number is used for two mss. the division is shown in column one. For the purpose of the statistics given at the head of each description of an edition in my introduction all these double mss. have been counted as two when the editor has classified them as such in his own introduction.

The mss. concerned are all cursives:

1 eap	1 r	36 e	36 a	189 e	189 ap
2 e	2 ap	94 ap	94 r	209 eap	209 r
4 e	4 ap	180 e	180 apr	429 ap	429 r
7 e	7 p	181 ap	181 r		

Abschriften are included and follow the mss. from which they are said to be derived.

06	06^{abs1} 06^{abs2}	205	205^{abs}	1929	1929^{abs}
9	9^{abs}	1160	1160^{abs}	1983	1983^{abs}
30	30^{abs}	1909	1909^{abs}	2036	2036^{abs}

---

[1] Excluded here are mss. differentiated by a following letter, e.g. 278a, 278b.

1.3: *Subsumptions*

Sometimes examination of mss. subsequent to their initial cataloguing and classification has revealed that two or more separate fragments are in fact from one ms. The term used in this volume for these now theoretically redundant numbers is 'subsumed', i.e. one ms. is now subsumed by another. This should mean that one number only should dominate. In practice for historical and other reasons the original numbers still seem to survive.[1] The redundant number should be free to be used for a new ms.

In column one subsumed mss. are shown with the number by which they should now be known, or under the umbrella of which they should now be placed, in parenthesis, e.g. 090 (= 064). This means that 090 is part of 064. No note is given under 064.

1.4: *Complete manuscripts*

According to Aland and Aland *Text* p. 91 there are sixty complete mss. of the NT (or more accurately sixty mss. that were originally complete insofar as some of the mss. now have lacunae). Their book gives the sigla for the uncials but not the cursives. The complete list is given below. Each of the mss. is noted in column one of the tables with a capital C alongside the Gregory-Aland number.

Uncials: 01, 02, 04
Cursives: 18, 35, 61, 69, 141, 149, 175, 180[2], 201, 205, 205[abs], 209[2], 218, 241, 242, 296, 339, 367, 386, 498, 506, 517, 522, 582, 664, 680, 699, 757, 808, 824, 886, 922, 935, 986, 1072, 1075, 1094, 1384, 1424, 1503, 1597, 1617, 1626, 1637, 1652, 1668, 1678, 1704, 1780, 1785, 2136, 2200, 2201, 2352, 2494, 2495, 2554

The purpose of drawing attention to these manuscripts is to demonstrate that a good proportion have not been included in the introductory list to any edition of the text whether explicitly cited in the apparatus or not. The absence of a complete ms. from the apparatus in an edition that lists the ms. is obviously more surprising than the absence of a small fragment, and requires an explanation.

1.5: *von Soden*

The apparatus to von Soden's historic text[3] has not been searched to determine his use of mss., but the mss. known to him and allocated a distinctive number in his unique classification have been identified in column one by means of a

---

[1] See my review of N-A[26] in *NovT* XXV (1983) p. 103f.
[2] If this is considered as one ms.: 180 apr was written at a different time from 180e. 209 eap was written at a different time from 209 r.
[3] H von Soden *Die Schriften des Neuen Testaments* I (Berlin, 1902–10), II (Göttingen 1913).

dagger to the right of the number, in order to draw attention both to mss. available (or theoretically available) in his day and also to help recognise the likely reason why certain mss. are used by e.g. Merk and Bover-O'Callaghan.

The dagger alongside 1799 is bracketed because of a query in identifying ε610 (see *Liste* p. 367).

1.6: *Tischendorf*

The monumental 8th edition of Tischendorf's text[1] has not been allocated a separate column in the tables. The equally monumental task of monitoring the use of mss. in the apparatuses to this text was not undertaken (although this can perhaps be a challenge to a patient reader!) because it did not seem appropriate to my purpose. It seemed adequate to indicate which mss. were known to Tischendorf or more precisely to Gregory at the time he wrote the *Prolegomena* to that 8th edition[2] between 1884 and 1894. Works of Gregory later than 1894 have not been included as it may be presumed that the mss. newly introduced after 1894 were not available to Tischendorf. Thus in column one mss. included in the *Prolegomena* are represented by an underlining of the Gregory-Aland

---

[1] C. Tischendorf, *Novum Testamentum Graece* (Leipzig, 1869–72).
[2] The Tischendorf cursives numbers in the *Prolegomena* are:

Gospels	1–1287
Acts and Catholics	1–420
Paul	1–487
Rev	1–185
Lectionaries Evv	1–953
Lect Ap	1–268

(About 108 mss. are classified as uncials)

In *Textkritik* I (1900) the quantity is greater; ignoring uncials Gregory records (Tischendorf numbers):

Gospels	1–1420
Acts and Catholics	1–514 (plus ten others)
Paul	1–515 (plus twelve others)
Revelation	1–185 (plus nine others)
Lectionaries	Evv 1–1072
	Ap 1–287 (plus sixteen others)

(About 126 mss. are classified as uncials)

In *Griechischen Handschriften* (1908) by which time the new (Gregory's own) numeration had been adopted the numbers classified are:

Uncials	01–0161
Papyri	P1–P14
Cursives	1–2304
Lectionaries	l1–l1547 (plus five others).

In *Textkritik* III (Nachtrag) the ms. list of 1909 is as follows:

Uncials	01–0168
Papyri	P1–P14
Cursives	1–2318
Lectionaries	l1–l1561 (plus seven others).

number e.g. 313. As with the indication of mss. known to von Soden (q.v.) it is of importance to know which mss. were already available (at least in theory) to the editors of each of the texts included in the tables. Where an underlining is bracketed (e.g. (1302)(2206)) this means there is some doubt that this ms. was known to Tischendorf (cf. *Liste* p. 333).

1.7a: *Lost*

Occasionally the footnotes indicate if a ms. is lost or burnt since it was originally classified. The significance of including such information is twofold. One is to indicate that such a ms. cannot of course be made use of unless a facsimile or microfilm or collation is available. Second, where such a ms. appears in the apparatus of one of the editions in the survey the information cannot be checked unless an independent reproduction of the information has survived.

Some mss. thought to be lost may in fact only be mislaid, and their present location unverifiable. In some cases of course such mss. might come to light.

1.7b: *Illegible*

When this note is attached to a ms. a warning is given that it is unreasonable to expect this ms. to be made use of in an apparatus.

COLUMNS TWO–FOURTEEN

(a) [ ]

Throughout the lists several ticks are enclosed by square brackets. This is to indicate that, so far as I have been able to see, the ms. in question is not to be found in the apparatus to the edition even though it is included in its introduction. Care needs to be exercised in assessing the significance of this. In some editions it is doubtless due to carelessness in assembling the introduction.[1] In the case of Souter, it seems as if the mss. not to be found in the apparatus to the 2nd edition had originally been cited in the 1st edition and this explains their inclusion in an incompletely revised introduction.

In some editions it would be wrong to conclude, as I did in earlier surveys, that non-appearance means non-use. Some mss. represented by [/] in the lists are fragments and it may well be that they yielded no relevant variant for the apparatus, even though the editors consulted the ms. itself, or a facsimile, or a collation. All we should say in these instances is that [/] means there is no explicit

---

[1] P⁵⁸ for instance is cited in UBS³ᴬ (p. 441 as P³³) but is not in the apparatus to UBS¹⁻³.

reference to the ms. in the apparatus. Similarly an editor by using an umbrella under which to gather all the mss. except those explicitly given may have included one or more of the mss. referred to as [/]. Each case will need to be examined, but I thought it worthwhile maintaining this indication if only to alert readers to look into the issue. In the statistics for each edition in this introduction[1] I have however abandoned the practice adopted elsewhere[1] of giving as a percentage the relation of mss. explicitly cited to those represented as [/].

(b) Sundry

   This word has been used to designate a ms. found in the apparatus of one of the editions but not found in its introductory list of mss. In many cases these supplementary or extra mss. have probably been accidentally overlooked when the introductory lists were being compiled. In the case of Souter, it would appear that many of these sundry mss. in the 2nd edition are those mss. added to the apparatus since the first edition without their also being added to the introduction. In the case of BFBS[2] we have not used the term sundry for cursives even though, apparently deliberately, Kilpatrick ignores the cursives in his introductory lists. The situation is somewhat similar with Vogels who includes only a few cursives in his Explanatio Siglorum Apparatus Critici and concludes this list with 'etc.'. For the purpose of comparability these are likewise not shown as 'sundries'.
   The location of the sundries is given in a footnote (or in the case of Huck-Greeven in an appendix) because there is often a possibility than an alleged sundry is a mere typographical error for a ms. that stands in the introduction. By giving the reader the chance to check on the accuracy of the apparatus at such points I hope to have alerted him to exercise caution before accepting that every sundry ought to have appeared in the introductory lists to the edition concerned. This is especially true in the case of Bover-O'Callaghan's and Merk's editions: the apparent irregularities and difficulties in these editions are set out under the appropriate headings.
   The symbol used throughout the lists in this book is S. (S) is found only in Souter's column at 2125 because this apparent sundry is due to a mistake in Souter's introduction, as is explained in the footnote ad loc, and is not a sundry as such.

2: Nestle-Aland[26]

   26th edition of Nestle-Aland *Novum Testamentum Graece* (Stuttgart, 1979). References throughout are to the first printing unless otherwise stated.

---

[1] e.g. *NovT* XXV (1983) 97–132, esp. 130–132 and *Rev Bib* 92 (1985) pp. 539–556.

Manuscripts listed	Papyri	86[1]
	Uncials	225[2]
	Minuscules	206[3]
	Lectionaries	5
	Total	522
Manuscripts listed under M		622[4]

Manuscripts not explicitly cited in the apparatus are:

Papyri: P^{14}, P^{29}, P^{42}, P^{43}, P^{73}, P^{80}, P^{82}, P^{83}, P^{86}, P^{87}.

Uncials: 031, 045, 057, 077, 080, 0118, 0155, 0164, 0166, 0200, 0256, 0259, 0263, 0264, 0268.

Cursives: 4ap, 7p, 42, 51, 63, 76, 94ap, 117, 122, 124, 174, 189e, 209r, 230, 346, 385, 429r, 451, 491, 543, 713, 788, 826, 828, 983, 998, 1012, 1194, 1329, 1448, 1582, 1729, 1735, 1758, 1831, 1845, 1875, 2014, 2027, 2067, 2143, 2148. Several of these mss. occur as part of families 1 and 13.

Lectionaries: *l*32, *l*185, *l*1575.

Symbols used in the N–A^{26} column are:

I   a ms. unbracketed in Appendix I of the edition, i.e. a constant witness.

II   a ms. shown in the Appendix with an asterisk enclosed in square brackets, i.e. constant only in a designated part of the NT.

III   a ms. shown in the Appendix with an asterisk enclosed in round brackets, i.e. cited only when its reading differs from the majority text.

IV   a ms. singled out for special attention on pp. 50*–53* of the introduction to the edition.

A tick in the column without one of the above Roman numerals alongside is used for all other mss. listed in the Appendix. Where a ms. is divided because of its textual type this is shown as e.g. IVa /c (cf. 453) because this ms. is class IV in Acts, unclassified in the Catholic epistle. (It is instructive to compare these categories with the Aland categories given in the final column of my tables.) Where class II and IV mss. are given special attention in only part of the NT this is indicated because the separate sections of the apparatus (e a p c r) have been analysed to see how the ms. has been cited.

M = Majority Text. Occasionally where the same ms. is listed both as a member of the majority text and in the main list of mss. this is shown as /M in the column. M^7 means that this ms. is included in the 7th printing.

The following notes may help clarify my use of the categories II and IV in the Nestle-Aland column of the tables.

Seventeen cursives occur in the list with an asterisk in square brackets to denote that they are used as constants in certain, designated, parts of the

---

[1] Actually 88 separate papyri are listed but two of these are subsumed by other numbers.

[2] Actually 254 separate mss. are listed but 25 of these are subsumed by other numbers. There are also four sundries in the first printing (034, 075, 0129, 0141).

[3] There are in addition two cursives omitted from the Appendix in the first printing (610 and 2060).

[4] 898 in the 7th printing. Some occur in the main list.

New Testament. The fourth column of the list in the N–A Appendix identifies by means of a bracketed asterisk the relevant part(s) of the New Testament so treated. We may divide these Class II mss. into two lists, one containing nine cursives which are only Class II (= (a) below), the other containing eight cursives which are also identified on pp. 50*–53* as worthy of special mention elsewhere in the New Testament (i.e. my category IV mss.) (= (b) below). The two lists are as follows:

(a)	Number	Contents	Constant in
	365	e a p c	p
	1006	e r	r
	1175	a c p	a p
	1424	e a p c r	e
	1506	e p	p
	1611	a c p r	r
	1841	a c p r	r
	1854	a c p r	r
	2495	e a c p r	a c p

(b)	Number	Contents	Category II	Category IV
	104	a p c r	p	a
	323	a p c	a	p c
	614	a p c	a c	p
	630	a p c	p c	a
	945	e a p c	a	p c
	1505	e a p c	c[1]	c[2]
	1881	a p c	p	c
	2464	a p c	p	a c

Of the eight cursives in list (b) 945 is not actually cited in the apparatus to e, 1505 is not found in e a p, 1881 is not cited in a.

The introduction to N–A is confusing. Category II mss. are, according to p. 70*, constants in the same way as category I mss. (i.e. those identified in the Appendix with an unbracketed asterisk) except that they are constant only for part of the New Testament. Thus they differ from those mss. marked with an asterisk within rounded brackets in column one of Appendix IA (i.e. category III). The latter group are said on p. 70* to be cited only when they differ from M. However, pp. 50*, 52* and 53* list mss. which differ from M. One would expect these mss. to be those designated as category III in the Appendix, but in fact the following category II cursives occur as well: p. 50* (gospels) 1424; p. 50* (Acts) 323, 614, 945, 1175, 2495; p. 52* (Pauline epistles) 104, 365, 630, 1506, 1881, 2465 and, again, 1175, 2495; p. 53* (catholic epistles) 323, 614, 630, 2495; p. 53* (Revelation) 1006, 1611, 1841, 1854. A special note on p. 53* concerns

---

[1] According to N–A p. 708. This seems to be correct.
[2] According to N–A p. 53*, but normally category IV mss. are 'important' (sic) elsewhere (cf. N–A p. 50*).

2344, 2377 which are category II as far as it is practicable in Revelation but because of the special character of these mss. they are treated as category IV in my tables. The introductory words on p. 53* prefacing the list of mss. used in Revelation differ from the words introducing the lists for the other sections of the New Testament. Page 53* (Revelation) speaks of and lists the constants (although in practice the list includes 2030, 2050, 2053, 2062, 2329, 2351 listed as category III in the Appendix) whereas the introductory words for e a p c on pp. 50*, 52*, 53* speak of and list those mss. differing from M (i.e. category III) although, as we have seen, some category II mss. are included. With the uncials there also seems to be confusion, e.g. P (025) is, according to Appendix IA, column 4 category II for c, category III for pr and unclassified for a; on pp. 50* ff. 025 is ignored for a as one would expect, listed under the correct heading for p and for c, although for r the heading on p. 53* would have led us to expect an unbracketed asterisk before r on p. 692.[1]

Fifteen cursives appear in the list with an asterisk in rounded brackets (i.e. class III) to denote they are used in the apparatus only where they differ from the majority text (= M). These are 28, 33, 81, 565, 700, 892, 1010, 1241, 1739, 2030, 2050, 2053, 2062, 2329, 2351.

Manuscripts isolated on pp. 51*–53* for special mention have been designated in my review of this text as category IV mss. There are twenty-seven cursives in this category of which eight also occur as Class II cursives in another part of the New Testament. Those eight manuscripts have already been listed above. The others are as follows:

Number	Contents	Where category IV
6	e a p c	a p
36a	a c	a
69	e a p c r	c
189ap	a p c	a
322	a p c	c
326	a p c	a p
424	a p c r	a p
453	a c	a
623	a p c	c
629	a p c	p
1243	e a p c	c
1704	e a p c r	a
1846	a p c	c
1852	a p c r	c
1884	a	a
1891	a p c	a
2298	a p c	c

[1] That a difference is intended for P(025) in column four of Appendix IA between those parts of the New Testament preceded by an asterisk in round brackets and the unbracketed asterisk preceding c does not explain our dilemma with the cursives where all category II mss. have a bracketed asterisk in column four. The rounded brackets there would agree with the wording of pp. 50*–53* but would make these mss. only category III throughout. Nor can it be deduced that the unasterisked parts of the New Testament in column four are the parts treated as category II status. 1881 for example is extant only for a c p: p is supposedly category II and a c IV.

The following are also to be thought of as category IV in view of the natural reservations made on p. 53*f.:

Number	Contents	Where category IV
2344	a p c r	r
2377	r	r

Nine of the nineteen mss. in the above lists are only cited in the apparatus to that portion of the New Testament for which they are singled out in the introduction as being of special importance. They are 189, 322, 424, 453, 623, 1243, 1704, 1846, 2298. In the case of 322, 424, 623, 1243, 1505, 1846, 2298 pp. 52*–53* implies these mss. are category IV because *inter alia* 'they are cited elsewhere' but they seem not to be so used!

It is interesting now to examine how all these category IV mss. are used and how, if at all, they are cited outside the areas where they are so identified. In the case of the hybrid category IV/category II mss. they are not cited in those parts of the NT where they are extant yet in neither category (104 is an exception). The following commentary on the above list should clarify the position:

6	Not found in e. Frequent in a and (particularly) p. Three occurrences only in c (Jas. 1.12; 5.14; Jude 12).
36a	Frequent in a, once only in c (Jas. 4.9).
69	The only category IV ms. to be cited in all five sections. Cited frequently only in c.
189ap	Not found in apparatus to pc and only found twice in a (Acts 15.7; 25.2).
322	Not found in ap. Frequent in c.
326	Frequent in a and p. Once in c (Jas. 1.8).
424	Not found in c r. Three times in a (Acts 9.29; 13.1; 15.37); four times in p (Rom. 1.9; 4.11; Col. 2.1; Heb. 3.14).
453	Not found in c. Frequent in a.
623	Not found in ap. Frequent in c.
629	Twice in a (Acts 4.25; 9.6; 22.12), three times in c (Jas. 1.3; 2.4; I John 5.8). Very frequent in p.
1243	Not found in e a p. Frequent in c.
1704	Not found in e p c r. Infrequent in a.
1846	Not found in a p. Infrequent in c.
1852	Not found in a r. Once in p (Rom. 5.6). Frequent in c.
1884	Only in *inscriptio* to Acts.
1891	Not found in p. Once in c (II Pet. 3.10). Frequent in a.
2298	Not found in a p. Frequent in c.
2344	Not found in a p. Twice in c (Jas. 4.9; Jude 5). Frequent in r.
2377	Frequent in r.

The above survey allows us to note that category IV mss. are cited for that portion of the New Testament where they are singled out on pp. 51*–53* for special mention. Where they are extant outside these portions they are not usually cited at all. (69 is an exception in this regard.) Usually frequent citation occurs in the special portion of the New Testament although in some cases (e.g. 189a, 424ap, 1704a and 1846c) citation is infrequent.

If we bring into our survey the eight mss. discussed earlier we may now provide a commentary on these:

104	Cited once in c (II Pet. 2.20), once in r (Rev. 13.10), more frequent in p (where it is category II) than a (IV).
323	Frequently cited in a (II) and p (IV) but arguably more frequent in c (also IV).
614	As frequent in c (II) as 323 was in c. More frequent in a (II) than p (IV).
630	Very frequent in p (II). Frequent in c (II) but only once in a (IV) (Acts 23.20).
945	Cited regularly in all three portions, a (II), p and c (both IV).
1505	See notes 1 and 2 on p. xviii. It is not clear if this ms. is II or IV in c. Frequent citation.
1881	Very frequent citation in p (II), where it is one of the most cited mss. It is frequently cited in c (IV).
2464	Very frequent in p (II). Fairly frequent in a and c (IV).

The difference between the citation in those portions known here as category IV and those called category II is (with the exception of 630) difficult to determine. Some category IV mss. seem to be cited just as regularly as the so-called constant category II mss. (*pace* p. 50*).

3: Bover-O'Callaghan

5th edition of J. M. Bover's text revised by J. O'Callaghan in *Nuevo Testamento Trilingüe* (Madrid, 1977)

Manuscripts listed	Papyri	73[1]
	Uncials	122[2]
	Cursives	360
	Talismans	8
	Lectionaries	29
	Total	529

The following mss. seem not to have been cited explicitly in the apparatus:

Uncials:
049, 056, 057, 068, 069, 081, 088, 0118, 0120, 0122, 0138, 0142, 0165, 0175, 0182, 0189, 0191, 0197, 0207, 0208.

The cursives apparently not cited are:
16, 59, 91, 114, 175, 185, 229, 265, 314, 321, 336, 406, 461, 473, 479, 610, 616, 617, 639, 726, 757, 824, 827, 849, 899, 941, 983, 986, 1079, 1094, 1099, 1188, 1216, 1223, 1229, 1278, 1354, 1356, 1579, 1588, 1654, 1732, 1829, 1834, 1859, 1908, 1934, 1957, 2018, 2037, 2038, 2041, 2044, 2045, 2051, 2074, 2075, 2093, 2186, 2259, 2344, 2349, 2430.

Talismans: T[8], T[9].

---

[1] This total excludes P[89]. This number refers (Introducción p. xxxvi) to fragments of Matthew published by M. Naldini *Prometheus* I (1975) pp. 195–200. This number has been given by O'Callaghan to these fragments without reference to the official list maintained by Aland in Münster. These fragments are in fact part of P[70] as is shown in N–A[26]. The correct papyrus 89 is a fragment of Hebrews (see R. Pintaudi *ZPE* 42 (1981) pp. 42 ff.) For the purpose of this count P[89] is discounted and its contents considered as part of P[70].

[2] 0121 is counted as two mss.

Lectionaries:

> *l*34, *l*36, *l*184, *l*243, *l*689, *l*720, *l*749, *l*805, *l*806, *l*807, *l*808, *l*844, *l*845, *l*848, *l*961, *l*1276, *l*1345, *l*1347, *l*1348, *l*1353, *l*1354, *l*1485, *l*1566, *l*2071, *l*2072, *l*2073.

Sundry papyri found in the apparatus but not listed either in the Introducción or on the card insert are: P[77] (Mt. 23.30, 51), P[80] (Jn. 3.34). Sundry uncials are: 050 (Jn. 20.11, 16 bis, 21), 095 (Acts 2.47), 0107 (Mk. 5.14), 0115 (Lk. 10.15), 0133 (Mk. 1.15; 5.34), 0153[1] (Mk. 5.40; 9.18; Lk. 22.42, 43–44, 52 bis, 57, 61, 64; Jn. 5.18; 18.20), 0156 (2 Pet. 3.10 bis), 0163 (Rev. 16.17).

There is a difficulty in collecting together a comparable list of sundry cursives with any certainty. There are several cursive numbers throughout the apparatus that are not referred to in the Introducción or the card insert. Some on the face of it could be sundries; others are clearly incorrect as they are cited *extra sectionem*. Of the latter some are typographical slips that can be corrected, with the help of other apparatuses, to refer to mss. that may or may not be used in Bover-O'Callaghan. Many of these errors go back to the apparatus in Bover's first edition. In private correspondence O'Callaghan has admitted that he was not able to undertake a thorough revision of Bover's apparatus although he was able to confirm suggested corrections where there were proofreading slips in his own revision. The following list of dubious references is intended as an aid to readers puzzled by apparent faults in this apparatus. Column one gives the ms. as it appears in Bover-O'Callaghan, column two gives the reference(s), column three gives my suggested correction where appropriate (a 'C' preceding my suggestion means this has been verified by O'Callaghan, 'L' preceding means that Bover seems to have taken the reading from Legg's apparatus — but this does not imply Legg's reading is correct), in column four 'S' means that this manuscript should probably be added to the list of mss. cited by Bover-O'Callaghan but not listed, i.e. a true sundry ms. Where no S stands the suggested correction is to a ms. that appears in the list and (with the exception of 1219) is used elsewhere correctly.[2]

15	Mk. 8.20	C 115	
48	Mt. 5.22		S
56	Mt. 21.2	?565	
57	Jn. 10.7	C 157	
73	Mk. 1.4	L	S
109	Lk. 10.12	C 209	
118	Acts 2.36	?1108 or ?218	
122	Mt. 10.3; Mk. 13.33	L	S
127	Mk. 2.18; 16.4	L	S
198	Mt. 5.22 (cf. 48 above)		S

---

[1] Consistent with his separate listing of talismans, O'Callaghan refers to 0153 as a collection of ostraca but illogically only does so at John 18.20! As number 0153 it appears in the apparatus elsewhere, separated from other uncials except at Luke 22.52 (sec) and 22.64.

[2] In view of this long list one hesitates to use the word 'correctly'. Readers of this apparatus would be advised to cross-check on the attestation of witnesses adduced in support of a given reading. The mss. in my list here have merely been taken from the apparatus because of their apparent incongruity *ad loc.* Other mss. ostensibly correctly cited may equally well be misprints for other mss. — or be falsely cited.

205	Rev. 6.8, 13; 8.7; 10.6; 11.11 bis; 12.3, 18; 15.6; 18.12; 21.3; 22.12		S
225	Jn. 18.24	N–A²⁶	S
225	2 Pet. 2.21	C 255	
238	Mk. 4.8	L	S
247	Mt. 10.23		S
253	2 Jn. 6	?255	
259	Mt. 27.3		S
272	Jn. 8.6		S
274	Mk. 16.20	Merk & L	S
282	Mk. 15.20	L	S
300	Tit. 1.5	?307	
318	Col. 4.12	?218	
355	Mt. 7.28		S
363	Eph. 6.16		S
367	Rev. 3.17; 5.20; 6.13; 9.10; 11.11; 18.2; 21.4 bis; 22.12		S
379	Jn. 12.4	?579	
387	1 Cor. 14.8		?
402	2 Cor. 10.14	C 462	
404	Rom. 11.25		S
419	Acts 24.15		?
456	Rev. 3.17, 20; 21.4		S
481	Mt. 12.4		S
533	Mt. 5.39		S
570	Lk. 9.25 (cf. 379 above)	?579	
613	Mk. 1.15		?
723s	Acts 18.2	C 623s	
739	1 Cor. 16.6	N–A²⁶ = 1739	
821	Jn. 14.20 (on card insert)		S
837	Mk. 1.10	L	S
838s	Rom. 8.34	C 1838s	
947	Acts 5.16	C 927	
1210	Jn. 21.25	C 1219	
1365	Mt. 8.18; 15.39; 19.16		S
1517	Mt. 4.4		S
1578	Rev. 6.4		S
1626	Rev. 2.7, 15; 3.7; 4.7; 5.6, 11, 12, 13; 6.4		S
1729	Rom. 4.9	?1739	
1777	Rev. 1.3		S
1801	Acts 14.17	?1891	
1819	Over forty times in John		S
2006s	1 Th. 1.9		?
2034	Rev. 3.14; 11.10		S
2052	Rev. 1.19	?2050	
2066	Rev. 1.19; 2.13		S
2104	Rev. 2.20	?2014	
2254	Rev. 4.4, 9; 8.13; 16.3 (on card insert)		S
2324	Twenty-seven times in Mt., Mk., Lk.		S
2326	Lk. 8.28		S
2346	Mt. 19.3; 20.23; 27.11		S
2768	Thirty-one times in John cited as 053 (on card insert)		S
2916	Rev. 9.12		?
2917	Rev. 22.11	?2017	

Over thirty sundry cursives appear in the above list although I am dubious that these represent in all cases the correct reading of that ms. Where a number is identified as a typographical error it seems to refer to a ms. actually listed and correctly used elsewhere, and it may well be that many of these alleged sundries are similarly mere printing errors.

4–6: UBS³, MC, UBS¹ = UBS²

UBS: *The Greek New Testament* edited by K. Aland, M. Black, B. M. Metzger, A. Wikgren and (since the second edition) C. M. Martini (United Bible Societies. UBS¹ = the edition of 1966; UBS² = 1968; UBS³ = 1975)[1]

MC: B. M. Metzger *A Textual Commentary on the Greek New Testament* (United Bible Societies). Reference is to the edition of 1971 containing the Appendix pp. 771–5.

It is suggested that these editions are to be considered together. For the purpose of this survey UBS¹ and UBS² are identical, MC refers to many new mss., some of which are listed in the Appendix to the 1971 edition and most of which are included in the expanded introductory lists of mss. in UBS³.

(a) UBS³	Manuscripts listed	Papyri	52
		Uncials	179
		Cursives	525
		Lectionaries	149
		Total	905

The lectionaries are separated into those systematically cited (fifty-two) and the remaining ninety-seven. The fifty-two are identified in the tables with a Roman numeral I. This siglum (I) is also used for the sixty-two cursives that are listed separately in the introduction as having been 'systematically' cited.

(b) MC	Manuscripts listed	Papyri	1
		Uncials	7
		Cursives	258
		Total	266

In addition the following sundries appear in MC (i.e. mss. listed neither by UBS¹⁻², UBS³ or MC Appendix):

Papyri	P^{29}, P^{35}, P^{53}, P^{56}, P^{57}
Cursives	7e, 36e, 141, 209r, 314, 365, 612, 643, 909, 1905, 1907, 1915, 2040 (= 911), 2043
Lectionaries	*l*1604.

---

[1] A revised edition of UBS³ (to be known as UBS³ᴬ) was issued in 1983. However, it has been ignored for the purpose of this survey because the introductory lists of mss. remain the same as in UBS³. A brief analysis of the changes between UBS³ and UBS³ᴬ may be seen in my review in *Nov T* XXVI (1984) pp. 377–9.

Explanatory Notes: (a) UBS

Papyri

UBS³ does not cite the following: P³⁶, P⁵⁸ although P⁵⁸ (as P³³) is cited in UBS³ᴬ (p. 441). (P³⁶ is erroneously given on p. 331 and has been corrected in UBS³ᴬ cf. N–A²⁶ 7th printing.)

Uncials

UBS¹⁻² lists 170 uncials (including Dᵃᵇˢ¹). UBS³ added nine further uncials, seven of which were taken from MC. The seven are 027, 035, 045, 075, 0150, 0151, 0211 and these do not occur in the apparatus to UBS³. (060 and 0175 used by MC had appeared in the lists in UBS¹⁻² but are not used in any UBS edition). The sundry 0192 (now identified as *l*1604) found in MC p. 119 needs to be added to MC and UBS³. 0150 and 0151 are used by MC in the discussion on p. 661 about the position of Hebrews in the canon and do not appear in an apparatus. The other two mss. added are 014 (The Modena Acts) and 091.

UBS³ does not cite the following explicitly: 0182.[1]

Cursives

In the primary list of cursives (= class I) in the introduction to UBS¹, ², ³ 62 mss. occur. In UBS¹, ² 204 cursives occur in the secondary list. In UBS³ 463 cursives occur. Cursive 94 is class I for r, but not for a c p, 181 is I for a c p, not for r. In making these calculations 429 is taken to be two mss. (as set out in UBS¹, ²)[2] and so too are 180 and 209.

The majority of extra cursives represents those originally included in the Appendix to MC. Two hundred and fifty mss. were added to UBS³ for this reason (none of these was in UBS² except 2386). There are in addition ten cursives in UBS³ which are neither in UBS² nor in the Appendix to MC: 209r, 365, 636, 911, 914, 918, 1333, 1907, 2318, 2768. Thus UBS³ has 259 more cursives listed than UBS². In point of fact 209r *is* used by MC, so too are 365, 1907. 911 appears in MC as 2040. 2318 and 2768 are not used in the apparatus to UBS³; 636 and 918 seem only to have been used in the expanded apparatus at the Comma Johanneum.

Forty-one cursives listed in UBS³ seem not to have been used in the apparatus; 8*, 31, 37, 39*, 53, 55*, 75*, 80, 94ap, 98*, 111*, 134*, 137, 180e*, 224*, 236*, 317*, 429r, 437*, 484*, 569, 571*, 1012, 1077, 1178*, 1215, 1217, 1270*, 1288*, 1295*, 1346*, 1829*, 1849*, 1893*, 2038, 2048, 2050, 2256*, 2318, 2595, 2768 (mss. asterisked are listed but not used in MC and UBS³; those not asterisked are listed in UBS³ not MC). To these we ought to add the 190 cursives listed in UBS³ but used in MC not UBS³.

The following twenty-one cursives appeared in the lists in UBS² but were not used in the apparatus to that edition: (these mss. also appear in the list in UBS³ and although they are not used in the apparatus there they are found in MC) 73,

---

[1] In my *NovT* XXV article (op. cit.) I stated, erroneously, that seven uncials were not cited.

[2] UBS² is ambiguous; 94ap;r means 94r is class I, 181ap;r means 181ap is class I, but 429ap;r refers to two mss. neither of which is class I. 180e;apr and 209eap;r are as 429ap;r.

142, 174, 181r, 235, 328, 441, 618, 627, 635, 983, 1093, 1321, 1689, 1835, 1898, 1923, 2058, 2069, 2074, 2193. These mss. should not have appeared in UBS² but could have been added to the list in the Appendix to MC (cf. 2386).

(b) MC

The first printing of Metzger's *Commentary* included an Appendix listing those mss. apparently used in the discussions but absent from UBS². Two hundred and fifty-eight cursives were added to the lists in UBS² (taking 180e and 180apr as separate mss.) although 2386 was added needlessly as it is in the list in UBS². Of these, only 250 are repeated in the secondary list in UBS³. The expanding of the list in UBS³ when compared with UBS² seems to have been intended to include those mss. originally listed in MC's Appendix: indeed printings of MC later than the appearance of UBS³ deleted the Appendix. The missing eight are 23, 598, 807, 1341, 1884, 1932, 2321, 2322. One peculiarity of these eight is that six of them are incorrectly cited in MC.[1] 1932 appears only in the *subscriptio* to Romans and not as part of a discussion proper. Nevertheless the reason for their absence from UBS³ is unclear.

In fact more than 258 extra cursives have been used in the discussion in MC. There are fourteen sundries, which ought to have appeared in the Appendix to MC. These are:

7e	cited at John 17.7 (p. 249)
36e	cited at Mt. 20.16 (p. 51)
141	(cited by its Tischendorf number 75) at Acts 13.18 (p. 405)
209r	at Rev. 16.16 (p. 757)
314	(cited by its Tischendorf number 23) at I Pet. 1.7 (p. 687)
365	at I Tim. 3.16 (p. 641) and Heb. 9.19 (p. 669)
612	(cited by its Tischendorf number 134) at Acts 1.14 (p. 284)
643	at I John 2.7 (p. 710)
909	(cited by its Tischendorf number 2257) at Acts 10.9 (p. 370)
1905	at Heb. 7.13 (p. 667)
1907	at I Thess. 5.27 (p. 634)
1915	at Rom 1.7 (p. 505)
2040	at Rev. 14.3 (p. 752, and also on pp. 753, 755, 756, 760, 762)
2043	at Rev. 14.20 (p. 755)

Lectionaries

UBS³ does not cite the following explicitly:
*l*1, *l*164, *l*230, *l*241, *l*276, *l*331, *l*574, *l*952, *l*961, *l*983, *l*1014, *l*1291, *l*1300, *l*1311, *l*1610, *l*1635.

There are certain peculiarities in MC: 8, a gospel ms., appears at Acts 12.6 (p. 393); 10, a gospel ms., appears at Gal. 2.14 (p. 593) and Col. 4.13 (p. 626); 23, a gospel ms., appears at I Pet. 1.7 (p. 687); 236, a gospel ms., appears at Heb. 1.3 (p. 662); 437, a ms. of Acts, appears at Luke 18.25 (p. 169); 598 contains Luke but appears at Rev. 14.8 (p. 753); 807, a gospel ms., appears at Jas. 4.5 (p. 683); 1288, a gospel ms., appears at Rom. 15.15 (p. 537); 1341, a gospel ms., appears at Rev.

---

[1] Further see below.

19.13 (p. 764); 2131, containing e a p, appears at Rev. 14.5 (p. 753); 2321, a gospel ms., appears at Rev. 11.18 (p. 749), Rev. 18.3 (p. 760) and Rev. 19.13 (p. 764); 2322, a gospel ms., appears at Rev. 11.18 (p. 747) and Rev. 13.10 (p. 749). N, a gospel uncial, appears at Acts 7.36 (p. 350). *l*883 is now known as *l*1761 but the old number occurs at Luke 18.11 (p. 168). (UBS$^{1-2}$ uses *l*1761; UBS^3 *l*883.)

Other apparent errors, especially in the misplaced use of ms. symbols, can be solved by reading the symbols as belonging to Tischendorf's system of classification.

Occasionally Metzger in the additional ms. attestation given in his Commentary uses the Tischendorf numeration rather than the conventional Gregory numbers, without warning and often interspersed with the Gregory numbers. The following conversion table may be useful to readers to avoid confusion when consulting MC. In the statistics used here the Gregory numbers have been taken into account for those mss. which do not occur with their Gregory number elsewhere. This applies to the mss. asterisked below:

Tischendorf number	Gregory number	Ref.	MC page
E	051	Rev. 16.16	757
		Rev. 21.3	765
G	095	Acts 3.1	305
		Acts 3.3	306
I	065	John 19.14, 20	253
I	096	Acts 2.6	291
		Acts 2.17	295
M	0121a	I Cor. 16.19, 23	570
		II Cor. 1.1	573
M	0121b	Heb. 1.3	662
		Heb. 13.21	676
N	0122	Gal. 5.20	597
O	081	II Cor. 2.9	577
S	049	Acts 2.7	292
		Acts 2.17	295
		Acts 6.3	337
		Acts 6.8	339
		Acts 7.30	347
		Acts 9.25	366
		Acts 15.25	439
		Acts 19.16	471
23	314*	I Pet. 1.7	687
28	110	Acts 2.44	303
31	104	II Thess. 3.18 *subscriptio*	638
37	69	II Thess. 2.8	636
55	0142	Rom. 16.27	540
75	141*	Acts 13.18	405
98	101	Acts 2.7	292
134	612*	Acts 1.14	284
224	876	Jude 12	727
225	909*	Acts 10.9	370

7: *Merk*[9]

A. Merk *Novum Testamentum Graece et Latine* (Rome, 9th edition, 1964)

Manuscripts listed   Papyri   51
                          Uncials   104[1]
                          Cursives   385[2]
                          Lectionaries   3
                          Total   543[3]

Manuscripts not explicitly cited in the apparatus:

Papyri   P[51]
Uncials   066, 0122, 0178, 0179
Cursives 17, 103, 209r, 398, 421, 429r, 480, 757, 783, 824, 1075, 1328, 1626, 1740, 1828, 1849, 1913, 1934, 2054, 2180, 2200, 2352 but some of the allegedly missing mss. may be included within the composite system of grouping mss. under inclusive sigla such as ^r, ^s, or rel or a hyphen to join two mss. within the same (von Soden) grouping.

In addition to the use (or non-use) of mss. listed in the Catalogus, Merk includes several mss. in the apparatus that are not in the lists. As with Bover-O'C it may well be that some of these apparent sundries are in effect typographical errors for mss. listed. Some, however, may be genuine sundries accidentally omitted from the Catalogus: this observation probably applies to those mss. found only in the Pericope Adulterae. Obvious errata are listed separately below. The apparent sundries are as follows:

0149   (= 0187) Mark 6.40
0173   Jas. 1.26 (bis)

———

51   Rom. 1.3
56   John 19.34
57   I Cor 2.6 (? or Gregory 218)
68   John 19.34 (cf. 56 above)
90   1 Cor. 2.6 (cf. 57 above) (?or Gregory 451, also a sundry)
96   John 1.13
139   John 1.3
148   John 8.2

———

[1] M^P is counted as two mss. (0121a and 0121b).
[2] This includes 2768 and 566 but not 70. The apparent division of 368 into von Soden ε521 and α571 is falsely described in Catalogus I p. 31*. Although Merk seems to cite this ms. only in Revelation, the ms. contains e a r according to Aland's *Liste*. ε521 refers to Gregory 70 but Merk should have here ε531 which is the gospel section of 368. This total also takes into account that Merk intends 181 to be a double ms. (although with 94 and 180 which the *Liste* also describes as double mss. Merk states that he uses them only for Revelation).
[3] G Nolli, *Novum Testamentum Graece et Latine* (Vatican City, 1981) reproduces Merk's list of continuous text mss. to which he adds the lectionaries from UBS[3] (combining the two lists there into one). Nolli (probably accidentally) omits *l*963 before, and probably because of, *l*983. The apparatus to this text is very limited and although a search of its apparatus has not been undertaken, it is very unlikely that many of the mss. in its Catalogus I are to be found there. The lectionaries are excluded from his Catalogus III which seems to reproduce Merk's Catalogus II.

158	Luke 24.13 (confirmed by independent search)
164	John 7.53
223	Acts 21.28
247	John 8.2
274	Mark 16.20
282	John 8.7
296	Rom. 6.21; 1 Cor. 6.15; Eph. 5.16; Col. 1.18 etc. (?or Gregory 1610)
319	Rom. 7.15, 10.1, 13.3; 1 Cor. 14.16; 2 Th. 2.12 (on card insert i.e. Catalogus II)
331	John 8.8
343	John 5.1 (?or 348)
347	John 8.33 (?or 348)
364	John 8.8
457	2 Pet. 1.2 (?or 453)
458	Acts 22.20 (?or 453)
491	Frequent in Acts and Paul (on card insert)
570	John 4.49
875	John 8.11
1100	Acts 4.34
2069	Rev. 2.13
2305	Rev. 2.8

Some mss. may appear with a pre-Gregory number. The following conversions are suggested:

38	Rev. 13.3	= Gregory 2020
214	Rev. 1.6	= Gregory 1704: Sundry
217	Rev. 6.1	= Gregory 2258: Sundry
300	Acts 13.45	= Gregory 1251: Sundry

If all the sundries on the above lists are correct and valid we have two sundry uncials and over thirty sundry cursives.

The following mss. are cited *extra sectionem*. Suggested corrections are offered where possible but these have not been independently verified and it may well be that they ought to remain as mere errata. None of the suggestions is a sundry:

67	Rev. 19.6: [2]67 i.e. 2067
264s	Acts 7.39
310	2 Cor. 13.6
337ss	Rev. 2.2: [2]37ss i.e. 2037ss
353sss	Acts 5.34, 39: 283ss
362	Matt. 22.34: 372
365ss	Acts 14.8
376	Rev. 1.3: 336
465	Luke 4.38: 265
470	Acts 3.11
520	Rev. 22.20: 620
552	Heb. 9.16: 522
691s	Matt. 3.12
802	Luke 8.28: 892
1083	Luke 7.19: 1093
2278	Acts 14.18, 15.7: 2298
2321	Rev. 18.21: 2329
2339	Rev. 18.14: 2329

In view of the dubious nature of the alleged sundries, it may also be wise to be cautious in accepting Merk's citation of mss. that are not used in other editions or whose readings cannot be confirmed. It is likely that the evidence of these (and doubtless other) mss. is taken over unchecked from older editions, especially that of von Soden.

8: *Vogels*[4]

H. J. Vogels *Novum Testamentum Graece et Latine* (Freiburg and Barcelona, 4th ed., 1955)

Manuscripts listed	Papyri	4
	Uncials	46[1]
	Cursives	274[2]
	Total	324

In addition, twelve extra uncials are to be found in the apparatus: 016, 031, 047, 081, 097, 099, 0112, 0122, 0124, 0141, 0142, 0179. One uncial seems not to be cited explicitly in the apparatus: 042.

There are some cursives which could refer to mss. now no longer identifiable and taken by Vogels from older apparatuses. These are 8 (ac), 10 (p), 11 (r), 15 (p), 42 (e), 45 (p), 88 (e), 91 (e), 453 (e). These have not been included in the statistics or the tables.[3]

9: *BFBS*[2]

H ΚΑΙΝΗ ΔΙΑΘΗΚΗ (British and Foreign Bible Society, 2nd edition, 1958)

Manuscripts listed	Papyri	37
	Uncials	78[4]
	(Cursives	238*)
	Total	353

* Cursives are not in fact printed in the introductory lists and could formally be included in my tables under the siglum S = Sundry. This has not been done, and the cursives have been given as if they were printed in an introductory list — including the peculiar ms. 2059s.

Sundries in the other categories are:

Papyri	P^{12}
Uncials	023
Lectionaries:	l6, l1184.

---

[1] Taking M^P as two mss. 0121a and 0121b.
[2] Only seventeen are listed. The rest could formally be classed as sundries, but, as with BFBS, are in the tables as if they were listed.
[3] For details see my 'The Citation of Greek Manuscripts in Six Printed Texts' *Rev Bib* 92 (1985) pp. 539–556.
[4] Counting M as two mss. known now as 0121a and 0121b.

Manuscripts listed but not cited explicitly in the apparatus are:

Papyri	P^{24}, P^{25}, P^{43}
Uncials	034, 045, 047, 048, 049, 096, 0142, 0188, 0189

10: *Souter*

A. Souter *Novum Testamentum Graece* (Oxford, 2nd edition, 1947)

Manuscripts listed	Papyri	23
	Uncials	76[1]
	Cursives	243
	Total	342

In addition, certain other mss. are to be found in the apparatus. These sundries are:

Papyri	P^{27}, P^{30}, P^{51}, P^{52}
Uncials	060, 095, 0109, 0141, 0169, 0206, D$^{abs\ 1}$
Cursives	4 ap, 7 p, 627, 629, 844, 1006, 1841, 2051, 2062
Talismans	T^{9} (cited as P Oxy 1151)

These mss. were added for the 2nd edition.

The following mss. seem not to have been used in the apparatus, and are bracketed in this survey:

Uncials	010, 013, 031, 052, 071, 079
Cursives	4e, 7e, 29, 31, 74, 91, 118, 121, 172, 205, 220, 230, 250, 258, 327, 543, 618, 788, 826, 828, 876, 983, 1689, 1709, 2021, 2023, 2039, 2059, 2322

Some of these mss. are not explicitly given in the apparatus because their readings are concealed under a family siglum (e.g. 118 under fam. 1, and 1709 under fam. 13). Many of the mss. occur in the apparatus to the 1st edition (1910); when the references were deleted in the 2nd edition the mss. were not removed from the Introduction.

Some apparent errors in the apparatus may be resolved if one reads an apparently erroneous number as a number from a pre-Gregory system.

Some errors remain unresolved. 88 occurs at John 19.14. A particular problem concerns 31, frequently (i.e. over 30 times) to be found in the apparatus to Paul. An analysis of these readings with Harley ms. 5537 (numbered 104 by Gregory, and known as 31 pre-Gregory) shows that Souter cannot always mean 104; besides which at 2 Cor. 3.1; 8.7 he quotes both 31 *and* 104 for the same *v.l.*! 3 occurs at Rev. 1.14: this cannot be Gregory or Hoskier but could theoretically be Stephanus τ$\overline{\varsigma}$ (now lost). 2125 is found in 1 Tim. 1.17: this looks as if it is cited *extra sectionem* according to Souter's Introduction which states that this cursive contains only a, but this information is at fault. 2125 according to Aland's *Liste* contains ap. The uncial said by Souter's Introduction p. xii to be 0170 is in fact

---

[1] Including Fp 010 bracketed (p.x).

0171: 0170 is the Gregory number for the ms. listed by Souter as Oxyrhynchus 1169. The apparatus to Luke 22.62 needs to be adjusted accordingly.

11: *Synopsis*[10]

K. Aland *Synopsis Quattuor Evangeliorum* (Stuttgart, 10th edition 1978). Occasionally reference is made to K. Aland *Synopsis of the Gospels* 3rd edition (United Bible Societies 1979) = Greek-English Syn[3].

Where additional or different information is to be found in *Synopsis* 12th edition this is indicated in the footnotes. Editions of the Greek Synopsis beyond the 12th edition, and editions of the Greek-English Synopsis beyond the 6th edition are likely to contain significant changes in the apparatus.[1] This work is in preparation in Münster.

Manuscripts listed	Papyri	41[2]
	Uncials	167[3]
	Cursives	136
	Lectionaries	6
	Total	350

Several mss. occur as part of the majority text K (= Koine). Under this siglum are:

	Uncials	8
	Cursives	175
	Total	183[4]

The following sundries occur:

	Ostraca	0153
	Uncials	0249
	Cursives	2ap, 58, 175, 257, 301, 569, 1325[5]
	Lectionaries	*l*1602.

The following mss. are not explicitly cited in the apparatus:

Papyri:	P[7], P[42], P[62], P[83], P[86]
Uncials:	080, 092a, 0118, 0164, 0200, 0216, 0238, 0260, 0263, 0264, 0268, 0269
Cursives:	2e, 7, 138, 597, 899, 1346, 2386
Lectionaries:	*l*118, *l*181.

---

[1] cf. *Bericht* 1979–81 pp. 17–18. My review of Synopsis 13th ed. (which was not available in time to be included in this book) will appear in *Nov T* XXIX.
[2] 42 in Syn[12].
[3] 171 in Greek-English Syn[3] and Syn[12].
[4] Of these 272, 399, 945, 998, 1229, 1604 also occur in the main list of mss. They are noted in the tables as /K.
[5] Cursive 254 at John 15.8 seems to be an error. This ms. contains only pr.

12: *Huck-Greeven*[13]

Albert Huck *Synopsis of the First Three Gospels* 13th edition by H. Greeven
(Tübingen, 1981)

Manuscripts listed   Papyri   37
                      Uncials   166
                      Cursives   61
                      Lectionaries   1
                      Total   264

This total represents for the most part mss. given special attention by
Greeven. In addition there are some three hundred and seventy sundries.[1]

Ostraca   0153
Uncials   0267
Cursives   2e, 3, 4e, 6, 11, 15, 16, 17, 18, 19, 20, 21, 25, 29, 34, 37, 38, 39, 40, 44,
             45, 46, 47, 49, 50, 51, 52, 53, 54, 56, 57, 59, 60, 61, 63, 64, 66, 67, 68,
             70, 72, 73, 74, 76, 77, 80, 81, 86, 90, 96, 98, 106, 107, 108, 111, 114,
             116, 122, 125, 126, 127, 130, 137, 138, 139, 142, 145, 156, 158, 161,
             162, 185, 205, 213, 217, 220, 225, 226, 229, 234, 235, 237, 238, 239,
             240, 241, 242, 243, 244, 245, 247, 248, 249, 251, 252, 253, 258, 259,
             262, 270, 271, 272, 273, 274, 280, 281, 282, 291, 299, 300, 301, 330,
             331, 340, 345, 348, 372, 382, 397, 399, 406, 407, 409, 410, 433, 435,
             440, 443, 448, 449, 462, 470, 471, 472, 473, 474, 475, 476, 477, 478,
             481, 482, 483, 484, 485, 487, 488, 489, 495, 506, 551, 566, 569, 575,
             597, 655, 660, 661, 697, 713, 716, 726, 808, 821, 837, 850, 998, 1009,
             1012, 1028, 1038, 1047, 1064, 1075, 1079, 1092, 1093, 1154, 1170,
             1187, 1193, 1195, 1200, 1201, 1216, 1229, 1242, 1279, 1295, 1296,
             1302, 1321, 1344, 1346, 1352, 1354, 1355, 1365, 1375, 1396, 1515,
             1537, 1542, 1546, 1547, 1555, 1573, 1574, 1579, 1588, 1610, 1635,
             1642, 1646, 1654, 1661, 1739, 1790, 1831, 1838, 1891, 1898, 2145,
             2148, 2355, 2533.
Lectionaries *l*1, *l*2, *l*3, *l*4, *l*5, *l*6, *l*7, *l*8, *l*9, *l*10, *l*11, *l*12, *l*13, *l*14, *l*15, *l*16, *l*17, *l*18, *l*19,
             *l*20, *l*21, *l*22, *l*24, *l*26, *l*27, *l*28, *l*29, *l*30, *l*31, *l*32, *l*33, *l*34, *l*36, *l*37, *l*38,
             *l*39, *l*40, *l*42, *l*44, *l*46, *l*47, *l*48, *l*49, *l*50, *l*51, *l*52, *l*53, *l*54, *l*55, *l*60, *l*63,
             *l*64, *l*67, *l*68, *l*69, *l*70, *l*72, *l*76, *l*77, *l*80, *l*88, *l*108, *l*124, *l*130, *l*134, *l*135,
             *l*148, *l*150, *l*158, *l*181, *l*183, *l*184, *l*185, *l*187, *l*195, *l*196, *l*211, *l*219,
             *l*238, *l*241, *l*246, *l*251, *l*253, *l*258, *l*259, *l*260, *l*299, *l*302, *l*303, *l*305,
             *l*309, *l*313, *l*331, *l*333, *l*360, *l*374, *l*382, *l*490, *l*543, *l*823, *l*845, *l*850,
             *l*854, *l*861, *l*871, *l*883 (= *l*1761), *l*932, *l*950, *l*952, *l*956, *l*997, *l*1043 (=
             *l*1596), *l*1084, *l*1127, *l*1231, *l*1345, *l*1346, *l*1347, *l*1348, *l*1349, *l*1350,
             *l*1353, *l*1354, *l*1355, *l*1536, *l*1564, *l*1578, *l*1579, *l*1599, *l*1602, *l*1604,
             *l*1623, *l*1627, *l*1629, *l*1632, *l*1634, *l*1642, *l*1663, *l*1693, *l*1749, *l*1837,
             *l*1963.

Manuscripts listed but not explicitly to be found in the apparatus are:

Papyri   P[6], P[36], P[55], P[73], P[86]
Uncials   058, 060, 064, 069, 072, 080, 0100, 0101, 0105, 0110, 0114, 0118, 0125,
             0126, 0132, 0134, 0143, 0144, 0145, 0146, 0147, 0148, 0154, 0155,
             0161, 0170, 0184, 0196, 0200, 0204, 0213, 0215, 0218, 0231, 0233,
             0234, 0235, 0239, 0249, 0253, 0255, 0263, 0265, 0269
Cursives   2191 (= part of group sigma, see Huck-Greeven, p. xviii).

---

[1] Appendix I gives details about the location of the sundry cursives and lectionaries.

The following sundries occur in the apparatus and are not apparently gospel mss.: 42 (Mk. 14.68; Lk. 19.4; 24.3), 88 (Lk. 24.43), 91 (Mk. 12.4, 21; 13.9; Lk. 5.2, 33; Jn. 19.6), 255 (Mk. 2.18, 21; 3.13; 10.6; Lk. 4.38), 256 (Mk. 3.35). 254 at Lk. 11.53, Jn 15.20 is the Tischendorf number for Gregory 238. (At Lk. 20.26 both 238 and 254 stand in the apparatus!) At Mt. 20.30 1254 should read 1354. At Mk. 1.31 1970 should read 1790.

The following lectionaries are to be deleted: *l*62 (Lk. 12.59), *l*1485 (Mt. 12.40). *l*1596 (unassigned in Aland's *Liste*) found at Mk. 6.21, 22, 24, 27 bis, 29; Lk. 2.2, 5, 15 bis should read *l*1043. *l*1633 at Lk. 8.16 should read *l*1663. *l*1692 at Lk. 19.4 should read *l*1642.

13: *Orchard*

J. B. Orchard *A Synopsis of the Four Gospels in Greek* (Edinburgh, 1983)

There is no introductory list of mss. but the following appear in the apparatus:

Papyri	12
Uncials	84 (including 0153)
Cursives	29
Total	125

14: *IGNTP*

The New Testament in Greek III, *The Gospel According to St Luke* edited by the American and British Committees of the International Greek New Testament Project, Part One chapters 1–12 (Oxford, 1984), Part Two chapters 13–24 (Oxford, 1987)

Manuscripts listed	Papyri	8
	Uncials	62
	Cursives	128
	Lectionaries	41
	Total	239

The lectionaries are divided into those representative of the dominant text (ten) and the remainder which are identified individually. The former group is designated I in the tables.

In many editions in this survey, with the possible exception of Huck-Greeven and N–A²⁶, the use of mss. in the apparatus seems to be fairly arbitrary. N–A²⁶ has its constants and one knows where one stands with these. Huck-Greeven's listed mss. are somewhat similar. IGNTP is unique in citing every ms. it lists for every reading either explicitly when it betrays a text at variance with the collating base (the Oxford 1873 reprint of the Textus Receptus) or implicitly when it agrees with the TR.

COLUMN FIFTEEN

Aland categories

In Aland and Aland *Text* pp. 106–111, pp. 117–137, pp. 140–164 and pp. 167–170 certain mss. are given a number from I–V to indicate the quality attached to them by the Münster Institut. These categories have been translated into letters (A = I, B = II etc.) and these are given in the final column. Not all the mss. which have been assigned a category have yet been included in a Münster text (e.g. 1910, 1942, 2197, 2374, 2516 or even the complete ms. 2200). 2110 has been categorised but is a ms. which according to the *Liste* should be deleted! It is instructive to compare where available these categories with the classification of the same ms. in N–A²⁶.

Brackets around and queries with the classification letters reflect the doubts expressed by Aland and Aland *Text* in their description of the separate mss.

SECTION III

Talismans and Ostraca

These categories appear in a separate section (III). The Münster Institut is proposing not to extend this classification beyond those already known and used as 0152 and 0153. 0152 = T¹ in E. Nestle, *Einführung⁴* ed. E. von Dobschütz p. 86: 0153 = 0¹⁻²⁰ in E. von Dobschütz, *ZNW* 32 (1933) p. 188.

SECTION V

Lectionaries

In 1933 Donald W. Riddle in an article entitled 'The Use of Lectionaries in Critical Editions and Studies of the New Testament Text'[1] wrote 'The fact is quickly perceived, as one investigates critical editions and studies of the Greek New Testament, that slight and incompetent use has been made of lectionary mss.' The position has hardly changed after over 50 years. Aland's *Liste* catalogues over 2000 lectionary texts, and only a few of these find their way into the apparatus of recent printed editions as will be evident in Section V of this present volume. Gregory also catalogued a large number of lectionaries but Tischendorf⁸ made only occasional use of lectionary citations in his apparatus. Only a handful of lectionaries are referred to by von Soden (and these are indicated in Section V). Riddle (*op. cit.* p. 73) claims that von Soden's failure to use lectionary mss. in his text is an 'inexplicable enigma'.

As the bulk of the lectionaries included in the *Prolegomena* to Tischendorf⁸ have not been used in any edition of the Greek New Testament it was convenient to include these in a separate list rather than as mere underlinings to a list in a table for which all the columns would be blank. Hence there is a separate

---

[1] In E. C. Colwell and D. W. Riddle (eds.) *Prolegomena to the Study of the Lectionary Text of the Gospels* (Chicago 1933) p. 67.

list of Tischendorf's lectionaries within Section V. By contrast von Soden's lectionaries are given within the tables as there are few of these and only a couple are not represented in other apparatuses.

Only the IGNTP apparatus correctly displays the evidence of the lectionaries by including in the citation an indication of the lection to which the variant belongs. Such information is essential for understanding the significance of the lectionaries (see Riddle *op. cit.* pp. 72, 77).

SUMMARY OF ABBREVIATIONS

Aland and Aland *Text*	K. Aland and B. Aland, *Der Text des Neues Testaments* (Stuttgart, 1982).
Aland, *Repertorium*	K. Aland (ed.), *Repertorium der Griechischen Christlichen Papyri* I Biblische Papyri (Berlin, New York, 1976).
ANTF III	*Arbeiten zur Neutestamentlichen Textforschung* Vol III *Materialien zur Neutestamentlichen Handschriftenkunde* ed. K. Aland (Berlin, 1969).
Bericht	*Bericht der Stiftung zur Förderung der Neutestamentlichen Textforschung* (Münster). Issued about every two years.
C	A ms. containing the complete NT.
F1	A member of family 1 (Lake group of cursives) or a ms. assigned to this group for only part of the NT.
F13	A member of family 13 (Ferrar group of cursives) or a ms. assigned to this group for only part of the NT.
Gregory, *Griechischen Handschriften*	C. R. Gregory, *Die Griechischen Handschriften des Neues Testaments* (Leipzig, 1908).
Gregory, *Prolegomena*	C. Tischendorf, *Novum Testamentum Graece* 8th edition Vol. III *Prolegomena* by C. R. Gregory (Leipzig, 1894).
Gregory, *Textkritik*	C. R. Gregory, *Textkritik des Neuen Testamentes* (Leipzig, I 1900, II 1902, III 1909).
K	Koine. A composite siglum used in Aland *Synopsis* to indicate certain uncials and cursives.
l	lectionary.
Liste	K. Aland, *Kurzgefasste Liste der Griechischen Handschriften des Neuen Testaments* (Berlin, 1963).
M	Majority Text. A composite siglum used in N–A^{26} to indicate cursives supporting the majority text.
P	Papyrus.
S	Sundry.
van Haelst	J. van Haelst, *Catalogue des Papyrus littéraires Juifs et Chrétiens* (Paris, 1976).

The abbreviations for Biblical books are normal and should be obvious. Parts of the NT are abbreviated as

> e — Gospels
> a — Acts
> p — Pauline epistles
> c — Catholic epistles
> r — Revelation.

Page references in the footnotes to the tables are to the editions of the NT to which the footnote belongs.

SECTION I

PAPYRI

Gregory-Aland Number	Editions of the Greek New Testament									Synopses			Luke	Aland Categories
	Nestle-Aland26	Bover-O'Callaghan	UBS3	MC	UBS1 = UBS2	Merk9	Vogels4	BFBS2	Souter2	Synopsis10	Huck-Greeven13	Orchard	IGNTP	
P 1 †	/I	/	/		/	/		/	/	/	/			A
P 2 †	/I	/	/		/					/	/			C
P 3	/I	/	/		/			/	/	/	/		/	C
P 4 †	/I	/	/		/	/		/	/	/	/	/	/	A
P 5 †	/I	/	/		/	/		/	/	/	/	/		A
P 6 †	/I	/	/		/				/	/	[/]			B
P 7¹ †	/									[/]	/		/	(E)
P 8 †	/I	/	/		/	/		/	/					B
P 9 †	/I	/							/					(A/E)
P 10 †	/I	/	/		/	/		/	/					A
P 11 †	/I	/	/		/	/		/						B
P 12 †	/I							S²						(A/E)
P 13 †	/I	/	/		/	/	/	/	/					A
P 14 †	[/] I													B
P 15 †	/I	/	/		/	/		/	/					A
P 16 †	/I	/	/		/	/		/	/					A
P 17 †	/I	/						/	/					B
P 18 †	/I	/	/		/	/		/	/					A

¹ Lost. ² Sundry at Heb 1.1.

Gregory-Aland Number	Editions of the Greek New Testament									Synopses			Luke	Aland Categories
	Nestle-Aland²⁶	Bover-O'Callaghan	UBS³	MC	UBS¹ = UBS²	Merk⁹	Vogels⁴	BFBS²	Souter²	Synopsis¹⁰	Huck-Greeven¹³	Orchard	IGNTP	
P 19 †	/I	/	/		/					/	/			B
P 20 †	/I	/				/		/	/					A
P 21	/I	/	/		/					/	/	/		C
P 22	/I	/	[/]		[/]	/		/		/	/			A
P 23	/I	/	/		/	/		/						A
P 24	/I	/	/		/	/		[/]						A
P 25	/I	/	/		/	/		[/]		/	/			(E)
P 26	/I	/	/		/									A
P 27	/I	/	[/]		[/]	/		/	S¹					A
P 28	/I	/				/				/	/			A
P 29	[/]I	/		S²		/		/						D
P 30	/I	/	/		/	/		/	S³					A
P 31	/I	/												B
P 32	/I							/	/					A
P 33	/I	/	/		/				/					B
P 34	/I	/												B
P 35 †	/I	/		S⁴						/	/			A
P 36 †	/I	/	[/]		[/]					/	[/]			C

¹ Sundry at Rom 8.34, 38; 9.3 as P Oxy 1355.   ² Sundry at p 259.   ³ Sundry at 1 Th 5.9, 10 as P Oxy 1598.   ⁴ Sundry at p 63.

Gregory-Aland Number	Editions of the Greek New Testament									Synopses			Luke	Aland Categories
	Nestle-Aland[26]	Bover-O'Callaghan	UBS[3]	MC	UBS[1] = UBS[2]	Merk[9]	Vogels[4]	BFBS[2]	Souter[2]	Synopsis[10]	Huck-Greeven[13]	Orchard	IGNTP	
P 37	/I	/	/		/	/		/	/	/	/	/		A
P 38	/I	/	/		/	/		/	/					D
P 39	/I	/	/		/	/				/		/		A
P 40	/I	/	/		/	/		/						A
P 41	/I	/	/		/	/		/	/					C
P 42	[/] I	/								[/]	/		/	B
P 43	[/] I	/					[/]							B
P 44	/I	/				/				/	/			B
P 45	/I	/	/		/	/	/	/	/	/	/	/	/	A
P 46	/I	/	/		/	/	/	/	/	/	/	/		A
P 47	/I	/	/		/	/	/	/	/					A
P 48	/I	/	/		/	/		/	/					D
P 49	/I	/	/		/	/		/						A
P 50	/I	/	/		/			/						C
P 51	/I	/	/		/	[/]		/	S[1]					B
P 52	/I	/				/		/	S[2]	/	/			A
P 53	/I	/	S[3]		/		/			/	/			A
P 54	/I					/		/						C

[1] Sundry at Gal 1.3, 4, 6, 8 (misprinted as 2147), 17, 18 as P Oxy 2157.   [2] Sundry at Jn 18.37 as P Ryl 457.   [3] Sundry at p 369.

Gregory-Aland Number	Editions of the Greek New Testament									Synopses			Luke	Aland Categories
	Nestle-Aland[26]	Bover-O'Callaghan	UBS[3]	MC	UBS[1] = UBS[2]	Merk[9]	Vogels[4]	BFBS[2]	Souter[2]	Synopsis[10]	Huck-Greeven[13]	Orchard	IGNTP	
P 55	/I	/				/				/	[/]			B
P 56	/I	/		S[1]										B
P 57	/I	/		S[2]										B
(= P 58 / P 33)	/I /I	/ /	[/][3] [/][3]		[/] [/]									B B
P 59	/I	/	/		/	/				/	/			C
P 60	/I	/	/		/					/	/			C
P 61	/I	/	/		/									B
P 62	/I					/				[/]	/			B
P 63	/I	/	/		/	/				/				C/E
P 64	/I		/		/	/	/			/	/			A
P 65	/I	/	/		/	/								A
P 66	/I	/	/		/	/	/			/	/	/		A
(= P 67 / P 64)	/I	/	/		/	/				/	/	/		A
P 68	/I	/	/		/	/								C
P 69	/I	/		/	/					/	/	/	/	A/?D
P 70	/I	/	/		/	/				/	/			A
P 71	/I	/	/		/	/				/	/			B
P 72	/I	/	/		/	/								A

¹ Sundry at p 282.   ² Sundry at p 326.   ³ Cited in UBS[3A].

Gregory-Aland Number	Editions of the Greek New Testament									Synopses			Luke	Aland Categories
	Nestle-Aland²⁶	Bover-O'Callaghan	UBS³	MC	UBS¹ = UBS²	Merk⁹	Vogels⁴	BFBS²	Souter²	Synopsis¹⁰	Huck-Greeven¹³	Orchard	IGNTP	
P 73	[/]										[/]			E
P 74	/I	/	/		/	/			،					A
P 75	/I	/	/		/	/				/	/	/	/	A
P 76	/I	/	/		/	/¹				/				C
P 77	/I	S²								/	/			A
P 78	/I													A
P 79	/I													B
P 80	[/]	S³					·			/				(A/E)
P 81	/I	/												B
P 82	[/] I	/								/	/		/	B
P 83	[/]									[/]				C
P 84	/									/				C/E
P 85	/I	/												B
P 86	[/] I	/								[/]	[/]			B
P 87	[/]⁴													A
P 88	/I	/								5	/	/		C
P 89	6	/7												
P 90														

¹ Mistyped as P 78 on p 857 (and repeated by Nolli p XVIII. See p. xxviii fn. 3 above).   ² Sundry at Mt 23.30, 37.   ³ Sundry at Jn 3.34.   ⁴ Designated I in the 7th printing.   ⁵ Used, however, in the 12th Edition.   ⁶ Used and designated I in the 7th printing.   ⁷ Not the true P 89, but the Mt section of P 70.

Gregory-Aland Number	Editions of the Greek New Testament									Synopses		Luke		Aland Categories
	Nestle-Aland[26]	Bover-O'Callaghan	UBS[3]	MC	UBS[1] = UBS[2]	Merk[9]	Vogels[4]	BFBS[2]	Souter[2]	Synopsis[10]	Huck-Greeven[13]	Orchard	IGNTP	
P 91														
P 92	I													
P 93														
P 94														
P 95														
P 96														
P 97														
P 98														
P 99														
P 100														
P 101														
P 102														
P 103														
P 104														
P 105														
P 106														
P 107														
P 108														

[1] Used and designated I in the 7th printing.

SUNDRY PAPYRUS

N–A²⁶ and BFBS²: P Egerton 2 cited at Jn 5.39 (Aland, *Repertorium* p 376; van Haelst, Catalogue, p 207).

SECTION II

UNCIALS

	Gregory-Aland Number	Editions of the Greek New Testament									Synopses			Luke	Aland Categories
		Nestle-Aland²⁶	Bover-O'Callaghan	UBS³	MC	UBS¹ = UBS²	Merk⁹	Vogels⁴	BFBS²	Souter²	Synopsis¹⁰	Huck-Greeven¹³	Orchard	IGNTP	
C	01 †	/I	/	/		/	/	/	/	/	/	/	/	/	A
C	02 †	/I	/	/		/	/	/	/	/	/	/	/	/	C (e)/ A (ap cr)
	03 †	/I	/	/		/	/	/	/	/	/	/	/	/	A
C	04 †	/I	/	/		/	/	/	/	/	/	/	/	/	B
	05 †	/I	/	/		/	/	/	/	/	/	/	/	/	A/D
	06¹ †	/I	/	/²		/²	/²	/₃	/	Ṣ³	/	/²			B
	07 †	/	/	/		/	/	/	/	/	/K	/	/	/	E
	08 †	/I	/	/		/	/	/	/	/	/	/	/		B
	09 †	/	/	/		/	/	/	/	/	/K	/	/	/	E
	010 †	/I	/	/		/	/	/	/	[/]	/	/	/		C
	011 †	/	/	/		/	/	/	/	/	/K	/	/	/	E
	012 †	/I	/	/		/	/	/	/	/	/	/	/		C
	013 †	/	/	/		/	/	/	/	[/]	/K	/	/	/	E
	014 †	/	/	/			/	/	/	/					E
	015 †	/I	/	/		/	/	/	/	/					C
	016 †	/I	/	/		/	/	S⁴	/		/				B
	017 †	/III	/	/		/	/	/	/	/	/	/	/	/	E
	018 †	/III	/	/		/	/	/	/	/					E

¹ D^{abs2}† has not been seen.   ² D^{abs1}† also used.   ³ D^{abs1} can also be found, assuming that D^{abs1} is the explanation for E found at Rom 13.3, a symbol taken over from Tischendorf in Souter's and Vogel's apparatus.   ⁴ Sundry at 1 Cor 16.2; Tit 1.10.

Gregory-Aland Number	Editions of the Greek New Testament									Synopses			Luke	Aland Categories
	Nestle-Aland[26]	Bover-O'Callaghan	UBS3	MC	UBS1 = UBS2	Merk9	Vogels4	BFBS2	Souter2	Synopsis10	Huck-Greeven13	Orchard	IGNTP	
019 †	/I	/	/		/	/	/	/	/	/	/	/	/	B
020 †	/III	/	/		/	/	/	/	/					E
021 †	/	/	/		/	/	/	/	/	/	/	/	/	E
022 †	/III	/	/		/	/	/	/	/	/	/	/	/	E
023 †	/	/	/		/	/	/	S[1]	/	/	/	/		E
024 †	/III	/	/		/	/	/	/	/	/	/	/	/	E
025 †	/II c(r) /III p / a[2]	/	/		/	/	/	/	/	/	/			C (pc) E (ar)
026 †	/III	/	/		/	/	/		/	/	/	/	/	E
027 †	/I	/	[/]	/		/	/		/	/	/	/	/	E
028 †	/	/	/		/	/	/	/	/	/K	/	/	/	E
029 †	/I	/	/		/	/	/	/	/	/	/	/	/	B
030 †	/	/	/		/	/	/	/	/	/	/	/	/	E
031 †	[/]	/	/		/	/	S[3]	/	/	/K	/	/	/	E
032 †	/I	/	/		/	/	/	/	[/]	/	/	/	/	C
033 †	/	/	/		/	/	/	/	/	/	/	/	/	E
034 †	S[4]	/	/		/	/	/	[/]	/	/K	/	/	/	E
035 †	/I	/	[/]	/		/	/	/	/	/	/	/		C
036 †	/III	/	/		/	/	/	/	/	/	/	/	/	E

[1] Sundry at Mt 23.25.   [2] On r cf. N–A[26] p 53* and p. 692.   [3] Sundry at Lk 6.26; 13.15.
[4] Sundry at Mt 20.27 but listed in the 7th printing.

Gregory-Aland Number	Editions of the Greek New Testament									Synopses			Luke	Aland Categories
	Nestle-Aland[26]	Bover-O'Callaghan	UBS[3]	MC	UBS[1] = UBS[2]	Merk[9]	Vogels[4]	BFBS[2]	Souter[2]	Synopsis[10]	Huck-Greeven[13]	Orchard	IGNTP	
037†	/III	/	/		/	/	/	/	/	/	/	/	/	C
038†	/I	/	/		/	/	/	/	/	/	/	/	/	B
039†	/	/	/		/	/[1]	/	/	/	/	/	/	/	E
040†	/I	/	/		/	/	/	/	/	/	/	/	/	C
041†	/	/	/		/	/	/	/	/	/	/	/	/	E
042†	/	/	/		/	/	[/]	/	/	/	/	/		E
043[2]†	/	/	/		/	/	/	/	/	/	/	/		E
044†	/I	/	/		/	/	/	/	/	/	/	/	/	C
045†	[/]	/	[/]	/		/		[/]		/K	/	/	/	E
046†	/I[3]	/	/		/	/	/	/	/					E
047†	/	/	/		/	/	S[4]	[/]	/	/	/	/	/	E
048†	/I	/	/		/	/		[/]	/					B
049†	/	[/]	/		/	/		[/]						E
050†	/I	S[5]	/		/		/			/	/			C
051†	/I	/	/		/			/	/					C
052†	/I	/	/		/			/	[/]					E
053†	/I		/		/	/[6]				/	/		/	E?
054†	/I	/	/		/	/				/	/			E?

[1] cf. 566 and 2149.   [2] Part Lost. cf. Krodel, *JBL* 91 (1972) pp 232–8.   [3] III according to the 7th printing.   [4] Sundry at Lk 6.42.   [5] Sundry at Jn 20.11, 16bis, 21.   [6] Styled X^b. X^b is found, however, only in Jn where it is cursive 2768 (see ANTF III p 29).

Gregory-Aland Number	Editions of the Greek New Testament									Synopses			Luke	Aland Categories
	Nestle-Aland²⁶	Bover-O'Callaghan	UBS³	MC	UBS¹ = UBS²	Merk⁹	Vogels⁴	BFBS²	Souter²	Synopsis¹⁰	Huck-Greeven¹³	Orchard	IGNTP	
055¹											/			
056 †		[/]	/		/	/	S²							E
057 †	[/] I	[/]												A
058 †	/I	/	/		/				/	/	[/]			C?
059 †	/I	/	/		/	/			/	/	/			C
060 †	/I	/	[/]		[/]	/			S³	/	[/]			C
061 †	/I		/		/			/	/					E
062⁴ †	/I	/	/		/	/		/						C
063 †	/I	/	/		/				/	/	/		/	E
064 †	/I	/	/		/	/			/	/	[/]			E
065 †	/I	/	/		/	/			/	/				E
066 †	/I	/	/		/	[/]			/					C
067 †	/I	/	/		/	/				/	/	/		C/E
068 †	/I	[/]	/		/					/	/	/		C
069 †	/I	[/]								/	[/]			C
070 †	/I	/	/		/	/			/	/	/	/	/	C
071 †	/I	/	/		/				[/]	/	/	/		B
072⁴ †	/I									/	[/]			C

¹ Not a continuous text ms. Therefore to be deleted. See H. Bachmann, Münster *Bericht* 1982 pp 69 f.   ² Sundry at Eph 4.4 as Tischendorf 19; at Jas 4.16; 1 Pet 3.5; 2 Pet 1.14; 3.2 as Tischendorf 16.   ³ Sundry at Jn 14.14.   ⁴ Lost.

Gregory-Aland Number	Editions of the Greek New Testament									Synopses			Luke	Aland Categories
	Nestle-Aland²⁶	Bover-O'Callaghan	UBS³	MC	UBS¹ = UBS²	Merk⁹	Vogels⁴	BFBS²	Souter²	Synopsis¹⁰	Huck-Greeven¹³	Orchard	IGNTP	
073 †	/I	/	/		/		/			/	/	/		B
074 † (= 064)	/I	/	/		/	/				/	/	/		C
075 †	S¹		[/]	/										B
076 †	/I	/	/		/	/			/					B
077 †	[/]I													B
078 †	/I	/	/		/	/				/	/	/		C/E
079 †	/I	/	/		/	/		/	[/]	/	/			C
080 †	[/]									[/]	[/]			(E)
081 †	/I	[/]	/		/	/	S²							B
082 †	/I	/	/		/	/								C
083 †	/I	/	/		/	/		/	/	/	/	/		B
084 † (= 073)	/I	/	/		/	/			/	/	/	/		B
085 †	/I	/	/		/	/		/	/	/	/	/		B
086 †	/I		/		/				/	/	/	/		C
087 †	/I	/	/		/					/	/			B
088 †	/I	[/]	/		/	/			/					B
089 †	/I	/								/	/			B
090 † (= 064)	/I	/	/		/	/				/	/	/		E

¹ Sundry at 1 Cor 15.16 and frequently elsewhere, but listed in the 7th printing.   ² Sundry at 2 Cor 2.2 as Tischendorf O (= O p).

Gregory-Aland Number	Editions of the Greek New Testament									Synopses			Luke	Aland Categories
	Nestle-Aland[26]	Bover-O'Callaghan	UBS[3]	MC	UBS[1] = UBS[2]	Merk[9]	Vogels[4]	BFBS[2]	Souter[2]	Synopsis[10]	Huck-Greeven[13]	Orchard	IGNTP	
091 †	/I	/	/		/				/	/	/			B
092a (= 089)[1]	[/] I									[/]	/			B
092b (= 087)†	/I		/							/	/			B
093 †	/I		/		/									E
094 †	/I									/	/			B
095 †	/I	S[2]	/		/		/		S[3]					C
096 †	/I	/	/		/	/	[/]							C
097 †	/I		/		/		S[4]							C/E
098 †	/I													A
099 †	/I	/	/		/	/	S[5]	/	/	/	/			C
0100[6] †	/I		/		/					/	[/]			
0101 †	/I									/	[/]			B
0102 †	/I		/		/					/	/	/	/	B
0103 †	/I									/	/			E
0104 †	/I									/	/	/		E
0105 †	/I		/		/				/	/	[/]			C/E
0106 †	/I	/	/		/	/		/		/	/	/		C
0107 †	/I	S[7]	/		/					/	/			C
0108 †	/I	/	/		/					/	/		/	B

[1] See H. Bachmann Münster *Bericht* p 70.   [2] Sundry at Ac 2.47 (cited as Tischendorf G). [3] Sundry at Acts 2.47.   [4] Sundry at Ac 13.45 (cited as Tischendorf Ia).   [5] Sundry at end of Mk 16.   [6] Now known as *l* 963 (not so listed by H. Bachmann, Münster *Bericht* 1982 although he does recognize the subsumption of 0195 by 0100).   [7] Sundry at Mk 5.14.

Gregory-Aland Number	Editions of the Greek New Testament									Synopses			Luke	Aland Categories
	Nestle-Aland[26]	Bover-O'Callaghan	UBS[3]	MC	UBS[1] = UBS[2]	Merk[9]	Vogels[4]	BFBS[2]	Souter[2]	Synopsis[10]	Huck-Greeven[13]	Orchard	IGNTP	
0109 †	/I		/		/	/			S[1]	/	/			C
0110 (=070)[2] †	/I		/		/					/	[/]			C
0111 †	/I		/		/									B
0112 (=083)[3] †	/I	/	/		/	/	S[4]			/	/	/	/	B
0113 (=029)[5] †	/I		/		/					/	/	/	/	B
0114 (=l965)[6] †	/I									/	[/]			B
0115 †	/I	S[7]	/		/					/	/	/	/	C
0116 †	/	/	/		/	/		/		/	/	/	/	E
0117 (=063)[8] †	/I		/		/					/	/	/	/	E
0118 †	[/]I	[/]								[/]	[/]			A
0119 (=0106)[9] †	/I		/		/					/	/	/		C
0120 †	/I	[/]	/		/				/					E
0121a †	/I	/	/		/	/[10]	/[11]	/						C
0121b †	/I	/	/		/	/[12]	/[13]							C
0122 †	/I	[/]	/		/		[/]		S[14]					C
0123 (=095)[15] †	/I													C
0124 (=070)[16] †	/I	/	/		/	/	/		S[17]	/	/	/	/	C
0125 (=029)[18] †	/I	/	/		/	/				/	[/]	/		B
0126[19] †	/I		/		/					/	[/]			C

[1] Sundry at Jn 16.33.   [2] See H. Bachmann, Münster Bericht 1982 p 70.   [3] See Note 2.
[4] Sundry at end of Mk 16.   [5] See Note 2.   [6] Bachmann, loc cit, does not refer to this.
[7] Sundry at Lk 10.15.   [8] See Note 2.   [9] See Note 2.   [10] Cited as Mp.   [11] Cited as M except at 2 Cor 11.6.   [12] See Note 10.   [13] Cited as M.   [14] Sundry at Gal 5.14, 19, 20, 23; 6.1.
[15] See Note 2.   [16] See Note 2, and cf also F-J Schmitz Münster Bericht 1982 p 83 for inclusion of 0194 therewith.   [17] Sundry at Lk 23.34, 53; 24.17. Jn 8.57.   [18] See Note 2.   [19] Lost.

Gregory-Aland Number	Editions of the Greek New Testament									Synopses			Luke	Aland Categories
	Nestle-Aland²⁶	Bover-O'Callaghan	UBS³	MC	UBS¹ = UBS²	Merk⁹	Vogels⁴	BFBS²	Souter²	Synopsis¹⁰	Huck-Greeven¹³	Orchard	IGNTP	
0127 †	/I									/				C
0128 †	/I		/		/					/	/			C
0129¹ †	S²		/		/									
0130 †	/I	/	/		/	/				/	/	/	/	C/E
0131 †	/I	/	/		/	/		/	/	/	/	/		C
0132 †	/I		/		/					/	[/]			C/E
0133 †	/	S³								/	/	/		E
0134 †	/I		/		/					/	[/]			E
0135 †	/I									/	/		/	E
0136 †	/I		/		/					/	/			E?
0137⁴ † (= 0136)	/I									/	/			E?
0138⁴ † (= 0102)	/I	[/]	/		/	/		/		/	/	/		B
0139⁴ † (= 029)	/I	/					/			/	/		/	B
0140 †	/I													C
0141 †	S⁵	/	/		/	/	S⁶	/	S⁷	/	/	/		C
0142 †		[/]	/		/	/	S⁸	[/]	/					E
0143 †	/I		/		/					/	[/]			C
0144⁹ †											[/]			

¹ Together with 0203, now forms part of *l*1575. See H Bachmann, Münster *Bericht* p 70.
² Sundry at 1 Cor 1.28 but listed in the 7th printing.   ³ Sundry at Mk 1.15; 5.34.
⁴ Bachmann, loc cit.   ⁵ Sundry at Jn 7.53f; 8.14; 9.14; 11.45 but listed in the 4th printing.
⁶ Sundry at Jn 5.3 (where cited as Tischendorf 314).   ⁷ Sundry at Jn 1.50; 2.12; 5.3; 11.53; 14.34; 16.36 (where cited as Tischendorf 314).   ⁸ Sundry at 1 Cor 8.6; Col 4.12 (where cited as Tischendorf 55) and at 1 Pet 1.3 (where cited as Tischendorf 46).   ⁹ Lost.

Gregory-Aland Number	Editions of the Greek New Testament									Synopses			Luke	Aland Categories
	Nestle-Aland²⁶	Bover-O'Callaghan	UBS³	MC	UBS¹ = UBS²	Merk⁹	Vogels⁴	BFBS²	Souter²	Synopsis¹⁰	Huck-Greeven¹³	Orchard	IGNTP	
0145¹†	/I									/	[/]			C
0146¹†	/I		/		/					/	[/]			C
0147¹†	/I									/	[/]		/	C
0148†	/I		/		/					/	[/]			C
0149² (= 0187)												/		C
0150†		[/]	/											C
0151†		[/]	/											E
0152³		/							S⁴					
0153⁵		/								S⁵	S⁵	/		
0154¹†											[/]			
0155¹†	[/]		/		/					/	[/]			B
0156¹†	/I	S⁶	/		/	/								B
0157¹†														
0158¹†														
0159¹†	/		/		/									C
0160†	/I	/								/	/			C
0161†	/I									/	[/]			C/E
0162†	/I	/	/		/	/				/	/	/	/	A

¹ Lost.   ² See H Bachmann, Münster *Bericht* 1982 p 70.   ³ Talisman 1 — see von Dobschütz *ZNW* 32 (1933) p 188 and see Section III below.   ⁴ See Section III below.   ⁵ Ostraca 1–20 — see von Dobschütz loc cit and Bachmann loc cit pp 69f.   ⁶ Sundry at 2 Pet 3.10 ᵇⁱˢ.

Gregory-Aland Number	Editions of the Greek New Testament									Synopses			Luke	Aland Categories
	Nestle-Aland[26]	Bover-O'Callaghan	UBS[3]	MC	UBS[1] = UBS[2]	Merk[9]	Vogels[4]	BFBS[2]	Souter[2]	Synopsis[10]	Huck-Greeven[13]	Orchard	IGNTP	
0163 †	/I	S[1]							/					C
0164 †	[/] I									[/]	/			C
0165 †	/I	[/]	/		/	/			/					D?
0166 †	[/] I													C
0167	/I									/	/			C
0168[2]														
0169 †	/I	/				/			S[3]					C
0170 †	/I	/	/		/				S[4]	/	[/]			C
0171 †	/I	/	/		/	/	/	/	/[5]	/	/	/	/	D
0172 †	/I		/		/		/							B
0173 †	/I				S[6]									B
0174[2]	/I													(E)
0175	/I	[/]	[/]		[/]	/								B
0176	/I		/		/									C
0177	/I	/	/		/	/				/	/		/	B
(= 070) 0178[7]	/I	/			[/]					/	/		/	C
(= 070) 0179[7]	/I	/	/		/	[/]	S[8]			/	/		/	C
(= 070) 0180[7]	/I	/	/		/					/	/	/		C

[1] Sundry at Rev 16.17. [2] Lost. [3] Sundry at Rev 3.20, cited as P Oxy 1090 (sic) (= 1080). [4] Sundry at Mt 6.13, cited as P Oxy 1169. [5] Cited as 0170. [6] Sundry at Jas 1.26. [7] See H Bachmann, Münster Bericht 1982 p 70. [8] Sundry at Lk 22.62.

Gregory-Aland Number	Editions of the Greek New Testament									Synopses			Luke	Aland Categories
	Nestle-Aland²⁶	Bover-O'Callaghan	UBS³	MC	UBS¹ = UBS²	Merk⁹	Vogels⁴	BFBS²	Souter²	Synopsis¹⁰	Huck-Greeven¹³	Orchard	IGNTP	
0181	/I	/	/		/					/	/	/	/	B
0182	/I	[/]	[/]		[/]					/	/		/	C
0183	/I													C
0184	/I	/								/	[/]			B
0185	/I													B
0186	/I		/		/									C
0187 †	/I		/		/	S¹				/	/			C
0188	/I	/				/		[/]		/	/			C
0189	/I	[/]	/		/	/		[/]						A
0190² (= 070²)	/I	/	/		/					/	/	/	/	C
0191² (= 070²)	/I	[/]	/		/					/	/		/	C
0192 (= l1604)²				S³										
0193⁴ (= 070⁴)	/I		/		/					/				C
0194² (= 070²)														C
0195⁵ (= l983⁵)														
0196	/		/		/					/	[/]		/	
0197	/I	[/]	/		/					/	/			E
0198	/I							/						C

¹ Sundry at Mk 6.40 (cited as 0149).   ² See H Bachmann, Münster *Bericht* 1982 p 70.
³ Sundry at Mk 15.34.   ⁴ See Note 2, also F-J Schmitz *op cit* p 83 for inclusion with 0124.
⁵ See Note 2, and cf 0100.

Gregory-Aland Number	Editions of the Greek New Testament									Synopses			Luke	Aland Categories
	Nestle-Aland[26]	Bover-O'Callaghan	UBS[3]	MC	UBS[1] = UBS[2]	Merk[9]	Vogels[4]	BFBS[2]	Souter[2]	Synopsis[10]	Huck-Greeven[13]	Orchard	IGNTP	
0199	/I											/		C
0200	[/] I									[/]	[/]			C
0201	/I		/		/									B
0202[1] (= 070)	/I		/		/					/	/	/	/	C
0203[2]														
0204	/I									/	[/]	/		B
0205[3]														B
0206	/I		/		/	/		/	S[4]					C
0207	/I	[/]	/		/	/		/						C
0208	/I	[/]	/		/			/						C
0209	/I		/		/									C/E
0210	/I		/		/					/	/			C
0211 †			[/]	/						/	/	/	/	E
0212[5]	/									/	/			(E)
0213	/I									/	[/]			C
0214	/I		/		/					/	/			C
0215 (= 059)[1]	[/] I									/	[/]			C
0216	/I		/		/			/		[/]	/			C

[1] See, eg H Bachmann, Münster *Bericht* 1982 p 70. [2] Together with 0129, now forms part of *l*1575, cf Bachmann, loc cit. [3] Lost. [4] Sundry, cited as P Oxy 1353 at 1 Pet 5.6, 10. [5] Diatessaron fragment.

Gregory-Aland Number	Editions of the Greek New Testament									Synopses			Luke	Aland Categories
	Nestle-Aland²⁶	Bover-O'Callaghan	UBS³	MC	UBS¹ = UBS²	Merk⁹	Vogels⁴	BFBS²	Souter²	Synopsis¹⁰	Huck-Greeven¹³	Orchard	IGNTP	
0217	/I		/		/					/	/			C
0218	/I									/	[/]			C
0219	/I													C
0220	/I		/		/		/							A
0221	/I		/		/									C
0222	/I													C
0223	/I		/		/									B
0224¹ (= 0186)	/I													B
0225	/I		/		/									B
0226	/I		/		/									C
0227	/I													C
0228	/I													C
0229²	/I		/		/			/						C
0230	/I		/		/									(E)
0231	/I							/		/	[/]			C
0232	/I		/		/									B
0233	/										[/]	/		C
0234² †	/I		/		/					/	[/]	/		B

¹ See H Bachmann, Münster *Bericht* 1982 p 70.   ² Lost.

Gregory-Aland Number	Editions of the Greek New Testament									Synopses			Luke	Aland Categories
	Nestle-Aland[26]	Bover-O'Callaghan	UBS[3]	MC	UBS[1] = UBS[2]	Merk[9]	Vogels[4]	BFBS[2]	Souter[2]	Synopsis[10]	Huck-Greeven[13]	Orchard	IGNTP	
0235[1] (= 083)	/I		/		/					/	[/]			B
0236	/I		/		/									C
0237 †	/I		/		/					/	/	/		C
0238	/I		/		/					[/]				C
0239	/I									/	[/]		/	C
0240	/I													B
0241	/I													C
0242	/I		/		/					/	/	/		C
0243	/I		/		/									B?
0244	/													B
0245	/I													B
0246	/I		/		/									C
0247	/I													B
0248														E
0249	/I									S[2]	[/]			C/E
0250	/		/		/					/	/	/	/	C
0251	/I													C
0252	/I													C

[1] See H Bachmann, Münster *Bericht* 1982 p 70.   [2] Sundry at Mt 25.4[bis], 6, 7, 9.

Gregory-Aland Number	Editions of the Greek New Testament									Synopses		Luke		Aland Categories
	Nestle-Aland[26]	Bover-O'Callaghan	UBS[3]	MC	UBS[1] = UBS[2]	Merk[9]	Vogels[4]	BFBS[2]	Souter[2]	Synopsis[10]	Huck-Greeven[13]	Orchard	IGNTP	
0253[1]	/I									/	[/]		/	E
0254[1]	/I													A
0255[1]	/I									/	[/]			E
0256	[/] I									/				C
0257									·					E
0258[1]														
0259	[/] I													C
0260	/I									[/]	/			C
0261	/I													C
0262	/I													C
0263	[/] I									[/]	[/]			(E)
0264	[/] I									[/]				(E)
0265	/I									/	[/]		/	E?
0266	/I									/	/		/	C
0267	/I									/	S[2]	/	/	(E)
0268	[/] I									[/]				(E)
0269	[/]									[/]	[/]			C/E
0270	[/]													B

[1] Lost.   [2] Sundry at Lk 8.20.

Gregory-Aland Number	Editions of the Greek New Testament									Synopses			Luke	Aland Categories
	Nestle-Aland[26]	Bover-O'Callaghan	UBS[3]	MC	UBS[1] = UBS[2]	Merk[9]	Vogels[4]	BFBS[2]	Souter[2]	Synopsis[10]	Huck-Greeven[13]	Orchard	IGNTP	
0271	/I									I				B
0272	/I									I				E
0273	/I									I				E?
0274	/I									I	/	/		B
0275	2													
0276	2													
0277														
0278														
0279														
0280														
0281														
0282														
0283														
0284														
0285														
0286														
0287														
0288														

[1] Cited, however, in the twelfth edition, also in the third edition of the Greek-English Synopsis.
[2] Added in the 7th printing as I.

SECTION III

[A] TALISMANS
and
[B] OSTRACA

[A] *TALISMANS*
(see 0152)

Bover-O'Callaghan lists and uses the following:[1]

T 1 (Mt 6.13) = 0152 according to Nestle, *Einführung* 4th Edn,
H Bachmann, Münster *Bericht* (1982) p 69
Aland, *Kurzgefaßte Liste.*

T 2 (Mt 4.24[bis]).
T 3 (Mt 6.10, 12).
T 4 (Mk 1.1).
T 6 (Mt 6.12, 13).
T 10 (Mk 1.1).

Souter cites (as P Oxy 1151):
T 9 (Jn 1.3).

[B] *OSTRACA*
(see 0153)

a) Bover-O'Callaghan's Introducción (p XXXVII) lists 0153 as Ostraca, and uses 0153 at Mk 5.40; 9.18. Lk 22.42, 44, 52bis, 57, 61, 64. Jn 5.18; 18.20.
b) Syn[10] (Sundry) at Lk 22.52, 61, 64, 68.
c) H–G (Sundry) at Mk 5.40; 9.22. Lk 22.45, 50bis.

---

[1] T8 and T9 are listed on p XXXVII but are not found in the apparatus.

SECTION IV

CURSIVES

Gregory-Aland Number	Editions of the Greek New Testament									Synopses			Luke	Aland Categories
	Nestle-Aland²⁶	Bover-O'Callaghan	UBS³	MC	UBS¹ = UBS²	Merk⁹	Vogels⁴	BFBS²	Souter²	Synopsis¹⁰	Huck-Greeven¹³	Orchard	IGNTP	Aland Categories
1 eap † / F1 / 1 †	/ /	/ /	I/ I/		I/ I/	/ /	/ /	/ /	/ /	/	/	/	/	C(e) E(apc)
2 e † / ap †	M⁷ /M	/	/		/	/	/		/ /	[/] S¹	S		/	
3 †	M⁷		/	/			/		/		S			
4 e † / ap †	/ [/]	/ /	/ /		/ /	/ /	/ /	/ /	/ S²	[/]	S	/		
5 †		/	/		/	/	/	/	/				/	C(ap) E(e)
6 †	/IV ap /[e] c	/	/	/		/	/	/	/		S		/	C(cp) E(ea)
7 e † / p †	/ [/] M⁷	/	/	S³	/	/	/	/ /	[/] S⁴	[/]	/		/	
8 †			[/]	[/]										
9 † / 9ᵃᵇˢ †	M⁷						/			/				
10 †			[/]	/						/				
11 †	M⁷						/		/		S			
12 †	M⁷						/							
13 † / F13	/	/	I/		I/	/	/	/	/	/	/	/	/	C
14 †	M⁷						/							
15 †	M⁷										S			
16 †		[/]	[/]	/			/				S		/	
17 †	/	/	/		/	[/]	/	/	/	/	S			
C 18 †	M		/		/	/	/	/	/		S			

¹ Sundry at 1 Cor 11.23.   ² Sundry at Ac 4.1; Jas 1.26.   ³ Sundry at p 249.   ⁴ Sundry at Heb 10.1.

Gregory-Aland Number	Editions of the Greek New Testament									Synopses			Luke	Aland Categories
	Nestle-Aland²⁶	Bover-O'Callaghan	UBS³	MC	UBS¹ = UBS²	Merk⁹	Vogels⁴	BFBS²	Souter²	Synopsis¹⁰	Huck-Greeven¹³	Orchard	IGNTP	
19 †							/		/		S			
20 †	M⁷							/		/	S			
21 †	/ M⁷	/	[/]	/		/	/	/	/	/	S	/	/	
22 † (F 1?)	/	/	/		/	/	/	/	/	/	/	/	/	
23 †	M⁷			[/]										
24 †	M⁷													
25 †	M⁷		[/]	/			/			/	S			
26 †									/					
27 †	M⁷	/				/	/	/			/		/	
28 †	/ III	/	I/		I/	/	/	/	/	/	/	/	/	C
29 †	M⁷		[/]	/			/		[/]	/	S			
30 † / 30^abs †	M⁷													
31 †			[/]		[/]				/¹					
32 †	M⁷						/		/					
33 †	/ III	/	I/		I/	/	/	/	/	/	/	/	/	A (ap) B (e)
34 †	M										S			
C 35 †		/	/		/	/	/	/						
36 e † / ac †	M⁷ / IVa /c	/	/	S²	/	/	/	/	/					B (a) C (c)

¹ See above p. xxxi.   ² Cited p 51.

Gregory-Aland Number	Editions of the Greek New Testament									Synopses			Luke	Aland Categories
	Nestle-Aland[26]	Bover-O'Callaghan	UBS[3]	MC	UBS[1] = UBS[2]	Merk[9]	Vogels[4]	BFBS[2]	Souter[2]	Synopsis[10]	Huck-Greeven[13]	Orchard	IGNTP	
37 †	M[7]		[/]		[/]		/				S			
38 †		/	/		/	/	/	/	/	/	S			
39 †	M[7]		[/]	[/]							S			
40 †	M[7]						/		/		S			
41														
42 †	[/]	/	/		/	/	/	/	/					
43 †		/	[/]	/		/	/	/						
44 †	M[7]						/				S			
45 †	M[7]										S			
46 †	M[7]										S			
47 †	M[7]		[/]	/			/			/	S			
48 †		S[1]					/							
49 †	M[7]						/		/		S	/		
50 †	M[7]						/		/		S			
51 †	[/]	/	[/]	/		S[2]	/	/			S			
52 †	M[7]										S			
53 †	M[7]		[/]		[/]						S			
54 †	M[7]						/				S			

[1] Sundry at Mt 5.22.   [2] Sundry at Rom 1.3.

Gregory-Aland Number	Editions of the Greek New Testament									Synopses			Luke	Aland Categories
	Nestle-Aland²⁶	Boyer-O'Callaghan	UBS³	MC	UBS¹ = UBS²	Merk⁹	Vogels⁴	BFBS²	Souter²	Synopsis¹⁰	Huck-Greeven¹³	Orchard	IGNTP	
55†	M⁷		[/]	[/]										
56†	/		/		/	S¹	/	/	/	/	S			
57†	M		/		/	S²	/		/	/	S			
58†	M⁷		/		/					S³				
59†		[/]	[/]	/			/	/		/	S			
60†	M⁷	/	[/]	/		/	/		/		S	/		
C 61†	/	/	/		/	/	/	/	/	/	S	/		C (cpr) E (ea)
62†			/	/										
63†	[/] M⁷		/		/		/	/	/	/	S			
64†	/					/	/	/	/	S				
65†	M⁷													
66†	M⁷								/		S	/		
67†						/					S			
68†	M⁷		[/]	/		S⁴	/				S			
C 69† F13	/ IVc / eapr	/	/		/	/	/	/	/	/	/	/	/	C (epcr) E (a)
70†	M⁷					[/]⁵					S			
71†		/	/		/	/	/	/	/	/	/		/	
72†			[/]	/			/	/	/	/	S			

¹ Sundry at Jn 19.34.   ² Sundry at 1 Cor 2.6.   ³ Sundry at Jn 6.22.   ⁴ Sundry at Jn 19.34.   ⁵ (= 368e). Bracketed in *Catalogus* p 31*.

Gregory-Aland Number	Editions of the Greek New Testament									Synopses			Luke	Aland Categories
	Nestle-Aland[26]	Bover-O'Callaghan	UBS[3]	MC	UBS[1] = UBS[2]	Merk[9]	Vogels[4]	BFBS[2]	Souter[2]	Synopsis[10]	Huck-Greeven[13]	Orchard	IGNTP	
73 †	M[7]	S[1]	[/]		[/]		/				S			
74 †	M[7]		[/]	/					[/]		S			
75 †	M[7]		[/]	[/]										
76 †	[/] M[7]		/		/	/	/				S			
77 †	M[7]						/		/		S			
78 †	M[7]													
79 †														
80 †	M[7]		[/]		[/]		/				S			
81 †	/III	/	I/		I/	/	/	/	/		S			B
82 †	M		[/]	/		/	/	/	/					
83 †	M[7]					/			/	/			/	
84 †	M[7]													
85 †														
86 †							/		/		S			
87 †							/							
88 †	/	/	I/		I/	/	/	/	/					C
89 †	M[7]		[/]	/										
90 †	M[7]		[/]	/		S[2]	/		/		S			

[1] Sundry at Mk 1.4.   [2] Sundry at 1 Cor 2.6 (unless this is the Tischendorf number for 452).

Gregory-Aland Number	Editions of the Greek New Testament									Synopses			Luke	Aland Categories
	Nestle-Aland²⁶	Bover-O'Callaghan	UBS³	MC	UBS¹ = UBS²	Merk⁹	Vogels⁴	BFBS²	Souter²	Synopsis¹⁰	Huck-Greeven¹³	Orchard	IGNTP	
91 †		[/]				/	/		[/]					
92 †	M⁷													
93 †						/	/		/					
94 ap r †	[/] /	/ /	[/] I/		[/] I/	/	/	/	/					C (ac) E? (p) C? (r)
95 †	M⁷													
96 †						S¹	/				S			
97 †	/M⁷		/		/		/	/	/					
98 †	M⁷		[/]	[/]							S			
99 †	M⁷													
100 †	M⁷													
101 †			[/]	/			/	/	/					
102² †			/		/	/	/	/	/					
103 †	/		/		/	[/]	/	/	/					E
104 †	/ IVa / IIp / cr	/	/I		/I	/	/	/	/					C (apc) E (r)
105 †	M		[/]	/					/³					
106			[/]	/				/			S			
107 †	M⁷										S			
108 †	M		/		/		/			/	S			

¹ Sundry at Jn 1.13.   ² Lost.   ³ As 1611.

Gregory-Aland Number	Editions of the Greek New Testament									Synopses			Luke	Aland Categories
	Nestle-Aland²⁶	Bover-O'Callaghan	UBS³	MC	UBS¹ = UBS²	Merk⁹	Vogels⁴	BFBS²	Souter²	Synopsis¹⁰	Huck-Greeven¹³	Orchard	IGNTP	
109 †	M⁷													
110 †	/M		/		/	/	/	/	/					
111 †	M⁷		[/]	[/]			/				S			
112 †	M⁷													
113 †			/		/		/							
114 †		[/]	[/]	/							S			
115 †		/				/	/		/	/	/		/	
116 †	M⁷						/				S			
117 †	[/]													
118 † F 1	/	/	/		/	/	/	/	[/]	/	/		/	
119 †	M⁷		/		/									
120 †	M⁷													
121 †	M⁷						/		[/]					
122 †	[/] M⁷	S¹	/		/		/	/	/	/	S			
123 †	M⁷		[/]	/					/				/	
124 † F 13	[/]	/	/		/	/	/	/	/	/	/		/	
125 †	M⁷										S			
126 †							/	/	/	/	S			

¹ Sundry at Mt 10.3; Mk 13.33.

Gregory-Aland Number	Editions of the Greek New Testament									Synopses		Luke		Aland Categories
	Nestle-Aland[26]	Bover-O'Callaghan	UBS³	MC	UBS¹ = UBS²	Merk[9]	Vogels[4]	BFBS[2]	Souter[2]	Synopsis[10]	Huck-Greeven[13]	Orchard	IGNTP	
127†	M	S¹	/		/		/	/			S			
128†	M													
129†	M													
130†			/		/		/				S			
131† F1	/	/	/		/	/	/	/	/	/	/		/	
132†	M													
133†	M													
134†	M		[/]	[/]										
135†	M²									K				
136†	M⁷			.										
137†	M⁷		[/]		[/]		/				S			
138†	M⁷	/	/		/	/				[/]	S			
139†	M					S³					S			
140†	M													
C 141†	M			S⁴		/	/		/					
142†	M		[/]		[/]		/	/			S			
143†	M													
144†	M									K				

¹ Sundry at Mk 2.18; 16.4. ² Deleted in the 7th printing. ³ Sundry at Jn 1.3. ⁴ Sundry cited as Tischendorf 75 at p 405.

Gregory-Aland Number	Editions of the Greek New Testament									Synopses			Luke	Aland Categories
	Nestle-Aland[26]	Bover-O'Callaghan	UBS[3]	MC	UBS[1] = UBS[2]	Merk[9]	Vogels[4]	BFBS[2]	Souter[2]	Synopsis[10]	Huck-Greeven[13]	Orchard	IGNTP	
145 †											S			
146 †	M													
147 †	M													
148 †	M					S¹								
C 149 †						/	/							
150 †	M													
151 †	M		[/]	/			/		/	K				
152 †														
153 †														
154 †														
155 †	M													
156 †											S			
157 †	/	/	/		/	/	/	/	/	/	/	/	/	C
158 †						S²	/				S		/	
159 †														
160 †											/			
161 †							/	/	/	/	S		/	
162 †	/		/		/	/	/	/		/	S			

¹ Sundry at Jn 8.2.   ² Sundry at Lk 24.13.

Gregory-Aland Number	Editions of the Greek New Testament									Synopses			Luke	Aland Categories
	Nestle-Aland[26]	Bover-O'Callaghan	UBS[3]	MC	UBS[1] = UBS[2]	Merk[9]	Vogels[4]	BFBS[2]	Souter[2]	Synopsis[10]	Huck-Greeven[13]	Orchard	IGNTP	
163 †														
164 †					S[1]									
165 †														
166 †														
167 †	M													
168 †														
169 †														
170 †	M													
171 †	M													
172 †	/	/	/	/		/	/	/	[/]					
173 †														
174 † F 13	[/]	/	[/]		[/]	/			/		/[2]		/	
C 175 †		[/]				/	/			S[3]				
176 †														
177 †	M	/	[/]	/		/								
178 †														
179 †		/	/		/	/						/	/	
C 180 e † apr			[/] [/]	[/] /	/[4] /				/					E (e pcr) c (a)

¹ Sundry at Jn 7.53.   ² According to Greeven p XVII, not pp XXVIII and XXX.   ³ Sundry at Mt 21.19.   ⁴ Cited in gospels even though e is bracketed in column 5 of the *Catalogus* implying non-use (cf. 368 below).

Gregory-Aland Number	Editions of the Greek New Testament									Synopses		Luke		Aland Categories
	Nestle-Aland[26]	Bover-O'Callaghan	UBS[3]	MC	UBS[1] = UBS[2]	Merk[9]	Vogels[4]	BFBS[2]	Souter[2]	Synopsis[10]	Huck-Greeven[13]	Orchard	IGNTP	
181 apc † / r	/ /	/ /	/I [/]		/I [/]	/ /	/	/ /	/						C (apc) E (r)
182 †			/		/									
183 †	M													
184 †														
185 †	M[7]	[/]	/		/	/		[/]		/	S			
186 †	M													
187 †	M[7]													
188 †														
189 e † / ap	[/] / IVa [/] pc													E (e) E (ap)
190 †	M													
191 †														
192 †	M													
193 †	M													
194 †	M													
195 †	M[7]													
196 †	M													
197 †	M[7]													
198 †	M	S[1]												

¹ Sundry at Mt 5.22.

SECTION IV

Gregory-Aland Number	Editions of the Greek New Testament									Synopses		Luke	Aland Categories
	Nestle-Aland²⁶	Bover-O'Callaghan	UBS³	MC	UBS¹ = UBS²	Merk⁹	Vogels⁴	BFBS²	Souter²	Synopsis¹⁰	Huck-Greeven¹³	Orchard	IGNTP	
<u>199</u> †	M⁷													
<u>200</u> †	M													
C <u>201</u> †	M		[/]	/		/	/	/	/					
<u>202</u> †	M⁷													
<u>203</u> †	M	/	[/]	/		/			/					
<u>204</u> †	M													
C <u>205</u> † C <u>205</u>ᵃᵇˢ †		S¹	/		/	/		/	[/]		S		/	C (er) E (apc)
<u>206</u> †		/ apc / r²	/			/	/	/	/					C (c) E (ap)
<u>207</u> †	M⁷													
<u>208</u> †	M													
C <u>209</u> eap † F r I	/ [/]	/	/	S³	/	/ [/]	/	/	/	/	/		/	C (er) E (apc)
<u>210</u> †	M													
<u>211</u> †														
<u>212</u> †	M													
<u>213</u> †	/	/	[/]	/		/	/	/		/	S		/	
<u>214</u> †	M													
<u>215</u> †	M⁷													
<u>216</u> †		/	/		/	/	/		/					

¹ Sundry at Rev 6.8, 13 etc.   ² This ms is styled by the Hoskier number 206 α (no Aland number).   ³ Sundry p 757.

Gregory-Aland Number	Editions of the Greek New Testament									Synopses			Luke	Aland Categories
	Nestle-Aland26	Bover-O'Callaghan	UBS3	MC	UBS1 = UBS2	Merk9	Vogels4	BFBS2	Souter2	Synopsis10	Huck-Greeven13	Orchard	IGNTP	
217 †	M7										S			
C 218 †		/	/	/		/	/		/					C (cp) E (ea)
219 †	M7													
220 †	M7						/	[/]			S			
221 †	/ M7	/	[/]	/		/								
222 †														
223 †	M		[/]	/	S1		/							
224 †	M7		[/]	[/]										
225 †	/	S2	/		/		/	/	/	/	S			
226 †	M	/	[/]	/		/	/	/			S			
227 †	M7													
228 †														
229 †	/	[/]				/	/	/	/	/	S		/	
230 † F13	[/]	/	/		/	/			[/]		/		/	
231 †	M7													
232 †	M7													
233 †														
234 †			/		/		/		/		S			

¹ Sundry at Ac 21.28. ² Sundry at Jn 18.24.

	Gregory-Aland Number	Editions of the Greek New Testament									Synopses			Luke	Aland Categories
		Nestle-Aland26	Bover-O'Callaghan	UBS3	MC	UBS1=UBS2	Merk9	Vogels4	BFBS2	Souter2	Synopsis10	Huck-Greeven13	Orchard	IGNTP	
	235 †	M7		[/]		[/]	/	/		/	/	S			
	236 †	M7		[/]	[/]			/							
	237 †	/		/		/		/			/	S			
	238¹ †	/	S²	/		/	/	/	/	/	/	S	/		
	239 †			/		/		/				S			
	240 †	M		/		/		/		/		S			
C	241³ †	/	/	/		/	/	/	/	/	/	S			
C	242 †		/	/		/	/	/	/	/		S			
	243 †			[/]	/			/	/		/	S			
	244 †	M		/		/		/		/		S			
	245 †	/ M7	/	/		/	/	/	/	/	/	S			
	246 †	M									K				
	247 †	M	S⁴			S⁵		/				S			
	248 †	M7		/		/		/	/	/		S			
	249 †		/	/		/	/	/		/	K	S			
	250 †	M	/				/			[/]					
	251 †	/	/				/	/	/	/	/	S			
	252⁶ †											S			

¹ Part lost.   ² Sundry at Mk 4.8.   ³ Lost.   ⁴ Sundry at Mt 10.23.   ⁵ Sundry at Jn 8.2.   ⁶ Lost.

Gregory-Aland Number	Editions of the Greek New Testament									Synopses			Luke	Aland Categories
	Nestle-Aland[26]	Bover-O'Callaghan	UBS[3]	MC	UBS[1] = UBS[2]	Merk[9]	Vogels[4]	BFBS[2]	Souter[2]	Synopsis[10]	Huck-Greeven[13]	Orchard	IGNTP	
253[1] †			/		/		/		/	/	S			
254 †		/	/		/	/		/	/					C (c) E (apr)
255[1] †	/	/	/		/	/		/	/					
256 †		/	/		/	/								C (p) E (acr)
257[1] †	/	/	/	/		/		/		S[2]				
258 †			/	/			/		[/]	/	S			
259 †	M[7]	S[3]	/		/						S			
260 †	M[7]													
261 †	M									K				
262 †	M[7]	/	[/]	/		/	/	/	/	/	S		/	
263 †		/	/		/	/	/	/	/					C (p) E (eac)
264 †	/ M[7]						/		/	/				
265 †		[/]	[/]	/		/							/	
266 †	M[7]													
267 †	M[7]	/	[/]	/		/				/	/		/	
268 †														
269 †	M									K				
270 †		/	[/]	/		/	/				S			

[1] Lost.   [2] Sundry at 1 Cor 11.23.   [3] Sundry at Mt 27.3.

Gregory-Aland Number	Editions of the Greek New Testament									Synopses			Luke	Aland Categories
	Nestle-Aland²⁶	Bover-O'Callaghan	UBS³	MC	UBS¹ = UBS²	Merk⁹	Vogels⁴	BFBS²	Souter²	Synopsis¹⁰	Huck-Greeven¹³	Orchard	IGNTP	
$\underline{271}$ †							/		/		S			
$\underline{272}$ †	M	S¹					/			K /	S			
$\underline{273}$ †		/	/		/	/	/			/	S			
$\underline{274}$ †	/	S²	/		/	S³		/		/	S			
$\underline{275}$ †	M						/			K				
$\underline{276}$ †	M													
$\underline{277}$ †	M													
$\underline{278}$a † b †	M M⁷									K				
$\underline{279}$ †														
$\underline{280}$ †	M⁷	/				/	/				S			
$\underline{281}$ †	M⁴										S			
$\underline{282}$ †	M⁷	S⁵				S⁶	/				S			
$\underline{283}$ †	M⁷													
$\underline{284}$ †	M⁷													
$\underline{285}$ †	M⁷													
$\underline{286}$ †	M⁷													
$\underline{287}$ †	M⁷													
$\underline{288}$ †	M⁷													

¹ Sundry at Jn 8.6.   ² Sundry at Mk 16.20.   ³ Sundry at Mk 16.20.   ⁴ Deleted in the 7th printing.   ⁵ Sundry at Mk 15.20.   ⁶ Sundry at Jn 8.7.

Gregory-Aland Number	Editions of the Greek New Testament									Synopses			Luke	Aland Categories
	Nestle-Aland²⁶	Bover-O'Callaghan	UBS³	MC	UBS¹ = UBS²	Merk⁹	Vogels⁴	BFBS²	Souter²	Synopsis¹⁰	Huck-Greeven¹³	Orchard	IGNTP	
289 †	M⁷													
290 †	M⁷													
291 †	M⁷	/	/		/	/				/	S			
292 †	M⁷													
293 †														
294 †														
295 †														
C 296 †		/	/		/	S¹	/	/						
297 †														
298 †														
299 †			/		/		/		/	/	S			
300 †	M						/				S			
301 †			/		/					S²	S			
302 †	M													
303 †														
304 †	/ M⁷		/	/						/		/		
305 †														
306 †	M													

¹ Sundry at Rom 6.1 et passim.   ² Sundry at Mt 16.5.

Gregory-Aland Number	Editions of the Greek New Testament									Synopses			Luke	Aland Categories
	Nestle-Aland²⁶	Bover-O'Callaghan	UBS³	MC	UBS¹ = UBS²	Merk⁹	Vogels⁴	BFBS²	Souter²	Synopsis¹⁰	Huck-Greeven¹³	Orchard	IGNTP	
307 †	/	/	/		/	/	/	/	/					C
308 †	M													
309 †	/ M		/		/		/		/					
310 †														
311														
312 †							/							
313 †	M⁷													
314 †	M	[/]		S¹		/	/	/	/					
315 †														
316 †	M⁷													
317 †		/	[/]	[/]		/	/							
318 †														
319 †	M		[/]	/		S²			/					
320 †	M⁷													
321 †	/	[/]	[/]	/		/	/	/	/					
322 †	/ IVc [/] ap		/		/		/	/	/	/				B (c) C (ap)
323 †	/ IVpc / IIa	/	/		/	/	/	/	/					B (c) C (ap)
324 †	M⁷													

¹ Cited as Tischendorf 23 p 687.   ² Cited at Rom 7.15 et passim (cf. card insert and Catalogus II (Paul Ca³)).

Gregory-Aland Number	Editions of the Greek New Testament									Synopses			Luke	Aland Categories
	Nestle-Aland²⁶	Bover-O'Callaghan	UBS³	MC	UBS¹ = UBS²	Merk⁹	Vogels⁴	BFBS²	Souter²	Synopsis¹⁰	Huck-Greeven¹³	Orchard	IGNTP	
325 †	M	/	/		/	/	/	/						
326 †	/ IV ap /c	/	/I		/I	/	/	/	/					C
327 †	/ M⁷		/		/	/	/	/	[/]					
328 †	M		[/]		[/]		/	/	/					
329 †	M									K				
330 †		/	/I		/I	/		/	/		S			C (p) E (eac)
331 †	M⁷		[/]	/	S¹						S			
332 †														
333 †														
334 †	M													
335 †	M²													
336³ †		[/]	/		/	/	/		/					
337 †	/ M⁷	/	[/]	/		/	/	/						
338 †														
C 339³ †			[/]	/										
340⁴ †											S			
341⁵ †														
342⁶ †	M⁷													

¹ Sundry at Jn 8.8.   ² Deleted in the 7th printing.   ³ Lost.   ⁴ Destroyed.   ⁵ Destroyed.
⁶ Burnt.

Gregory-Aland Number	Editions of the Greek New Testament									Synopses			Luke	Aland Categories
	Nestle-Aland[26]	Bover-O'Callaghan	UBS[3]	MC	UBS[1] = UBS[2]	Merk[9]	Vogels[4]	BFBS[2]	Souter[2]	Synopsis[10]	Huck-Greeven[13]	Orchard	IGNTP	
<u>343</u> †	M¹												/	
<u>344</u> †	M⁷													
<u>345</u> †											S			
<u>346</u> † F 13	[/]	/	/		/	/	/	/	/	/	/		/	C
<u>347</u> †	M													
<u>348</u> †	/	/	/		/	/	/	/		/	S		/	
<u>349</u> †		/	[/]	/	/						/		/	
<u>350</u> †	M¹													
<u>351</u> †	M													
<u>352</u> †	M⁷													
<u>353</u> †	M⁷													
<u>354</u> †	M⁷													
<u>355</u> †	M	S²												
<u>356</u> †	M		[/]	/			/		/					
<u>357</u> †	M⁷													
<u>358</u> †	M													
<u>359</u> †	M													
<u>360</u> †	M													

¹ Deleted in the 7th printing.   ² Sundry at Mt 7.28.

Gregory-Aland Number	Editions of the Greek New Testament									Synopses			Luke	Aland Categories
	Nestle-Aland26	Bover-O'Callaghan	UBS3	MC	UBS1 = UBS2	Merk9	Vogels4	BFBS2	Souter2	Synopsis10	Huck-Greeven13	Orchard	IGNTP	
361 †	M													
362 †	M7													
363 †		S¹												
364 †	M		[/]	/		S²	/			K				
365 †	/ IIp / eac		/	S³										C (p) E (eac)
366 †	M7													
C 367 †	M	S⁴	[/]	/		/			/					
368 †	M					/⁵								
369 †	M													
370 †														
371 †														
372 †		/	/		/	/				/	S	/	/	
373 †	M													
374 †	M													
375 †	M													
376 †	M													
377 †														
378 †		/	/		/	/	/	/						C (c) E (ap)

¹ Sundry at Eph 6.6.   ² Sundry at Jn 8.8.   ³ Sundry at pp 641, 669.   ⁴ Sundry cited frequently in Rev.   ⁵ Apparently taken as two separate mss. by the *Catalogus* p 31* of which e is bracketed (as unused ?) cf 70 above.

Gregory-Aland Number	Editions of the Greek New Testament									Synopses		Luke		
	Nestle-Aland[26]	Bover-O'Callaghan	UBS[3]	MC	UBS[1] = UBS[2]	Merk[9]	Vogels[4]	BFBS[2]	Souter[2]	Synopsis[10]	Huck-Greeven[13]	Orchard	IGNTP	Aland Categories
379 †	M													
380 †														
381 †	M[7]													
382 †											S			
383 †		/	/	/		/		/	/					
384 †	M						/							
385 †	[/] M[7]	/	[/]	/		/	/	/	/					
C 386 †	M					/								
387 †														
388 †	M													
389 †									/					
390 †	M[7]		[/]	/			/							
391 †														
392 †	M[7]													
393 †	M[7]													
394 †	M													
395 †	M[7]													
396 †	M													

Gregory-Aland Number	Editions of the Greek New Testament									Synopses			Luke	Aland Categories
	Nestle-Aland[26]	Bover-O'Callaghan	UBS[3]	MC	UBS[1] = UBS[2]	Merk[9]	Vogels[4]	BFBS[2]	Souter[2]	Synopsis[10]	Huck-Greeven[13]	Orchard	IGNTP	
397 †		/	/		/	/				/	S			
398 †	/		/	/	[/]	/			/					C (c) E (ap)
399 †	M	/	[/]	/		/				/K	S		/	
400 †														
401 †	M[7]													
402 †	M													
403 †														
404 †	M	S[1]	[/]	/										
405 †	M													
406 †		[/]									S			
407 †	M		/		/						S			
408 †	M													
409 †	M[7]						/	/		/	S			
410 †	M										S			
411 †	M									K				
412 †	M													
413 †	M													
414 †	M													

¹ Sundry at Rom 11.25.

Gregory-Aland Number	Editions of the Greek New Testament									Synopses			Luke	Aland Categories
	Nestle-Aland[26]	Bover-O'Callaghan	UBS³	MC	UBS¹ = UBS²	Merk⁹	Vogels⁴	BFBS²	Souter²	Synopsis[10]	Huck-Greeven[13]	Orchard	IGNTP	
415 †	M													
416 †														
417 †														
418 †	M⁷		[/]	/										
419 †	M													
420														
421 †					[/]	/	/	/						
422 †	M⁷													
423 †		/				/	/							
424 †	[/] cr / IVap	/	/			/	/	/	/					C E
425 †	M		/		/		/		/					
426 †	M⁷													
427 †														
428 †														
429 ap r †	[/]	/	[/]		[/]	[/]	/	/ /	/					C (ac) E (pr)
430 †		/				/								
431 †	/	/	/		/	/	/	/	/					C (ac) E (pr)
432 †	M	/				/	/		/					

Gregory-Aland Number	Editions of the Greek New Testament									Synopses			Luke	Aland Categories
	Nestle-Aland²⁶	Bover-O'Callaghan	UBS³	MC	UBS¹ = UBS²	Merk⁹	Vogels⁴	BFBS²	Souter²	Synopsis¹⁰	Huck-Greeven¹³	Orchard	IGNTP	
433¹ †							/				S			
434 †														
435 †	/		/		/		/	/	/	/	S			
436 †	/	/	/I		/I	/	/	/	/					C
437 †			[/]	[/]										
438 †	M⁷													
439 †	M⁷													
440 †	/	/	/		/	/	/	/	/		S			
441 †			[/]		[/]		/	/	/					C
442 †	/		/	/			/	/	/					C
443 †	M⁷	/				/					S		/	
444 †														
445 †														
446 †														
447 †														
448 †											S			
449 †											S			
450 †	M		[/]	/										

¹ Lost.

Gregory-Aland Number	Editions of the Greek New Testament									Synopses			Luke	Aland Categories
	Nestle-Aland[26]	Bover-O'Callaghan	UBS[3]	MC	UBS[1] = UBS[2]	Merk[9]	Vogels[4]	BFBS[2]	Souter[2]	Synopsis[10]	Huck-Greeven[13]	Orchard	IGNTP	
451 †	[/]		/I		/I									C (p) E (ac)
452 †	M					/			/					
453 †	/IVa [/]c	/	/	/		/	/		/					C
454 †	M													
455 †			[/]	/										
456 †		S[1]	[/]	/		/	/	/	/					
457 †	M													
458 †	M													
459 †		/	/	/		/								C (p) E (acr)
460 †	/	/	/		/	/	/	/	/					
461 †	M	[/]				/							/	E
462 †	/	/	/		/	/	/	/	/		S			
463[2]			[/]	/			/		/					
464 †			[/]	/			/		/					
465 †	M		/			/	/							
466 †	M		[/]	/										
467 †	/	/	/		/	/		/						C (p) E? (acr)
468 †		/	/		/			/	/					

[1] Sundry at Rev 3.17, 20; 21.4.   [2] This ms. ought to be deleted from the list according to ANTF III p 8.

Gregory-Aland Number	Editions of the Greek New Testament									Synopses		Luke		Aland Categories
	Nestle-Aland²⁶	Bover-O'Callaghan	UBS³	MC	UBS¹ = UBS²	Merk⁹	Vogels⁴	BFBS²	Souter²	Synopsis¹⁰	Huck-Greeven¹³	Orchard	IGNTP	
469 †	M	/	/		/	/		/	/					
470 †											S			
471 †			[/]	/			/			/	S			
472 †	/	/	/		/	/	/	/	/	/	S		/	
473 †	/	[/]				/				/	S			
474 †	/		/		/				/	/	S			
475 †							/				S		/	
476 †	M	/	/	/		/		/		/	S			
477 †		/				/	/				S		/	
478 †			/	/					/		S		/	
479 †		[/]												
480¹ †	M				[/]								/	
481 †		S²	/	/				/		/	S			
482 †	/	/	/		/	/	/	/	/	/	S			
483 †		/	/		/						S			
484 †		[/]	[/]								S			
485 †		/				/		/		/	S			
486 †														

¹ Part lost.　　² Sundry at Mt 12.4.

Gregory-Aland Number	Editions of the Greek New Testament									Synopses		Luke		Aland Categories
	Nestle-Aland[26]	Bover-O'Callaghan	UBS[3]	MC	UBS[1] = UBS[2]	Merk[9]	Vogels[4]	BFBS[2]	Souter[2]	Synopsis[10]	Huck-Greeven[13]	Orchard	IGNTP	
487[1] †										/	S			
488[1] †											S			
489 †	/	/	/		/	/		/	/		S		/	
490 †														
491 †	[/] M	/	/		/	S[2]								
492 †														
493 †														
494 †														
495 †		/	/		/	/	/			/	S			
496 †	M[7]													
497 †														
C 498 †	M						/		/					
499 †														
500 †														
501 †														
502 †									'					
503 †														
504 †														

[1] Lost.   [2] On Card Insert and Catalogus II (a D[2] p C b[2]).

	Gregory-Aland Number	Editions of the Greek New Testament									Synopses			Luke	Aland Categories
		Nestle-Aland[26]	Bover-O'Callaghan	UBS[3]	MC	UBS[1] = UBS[2]	Merk[9]	Vogels[4]	BFBS[2]	Souter[2]	Synopsis[10]	Huck-Greeven[13]	Orchard	IGNTP	
	505 †										K				
C	506 †	M	/	/	/		/	/		/		S			
	507 †	M[7]													
	508 †														
	509 †	M[7]													
	510 †	M[7]													
	511 †	M[7]													
	512 †	M[7]													
	513 †														
	514 †	M[7]				S[1]									
	515 †														
	516 †	M[7]													
C	517 †		/	/		/	/	/	/		/	/	/	/	
	518 †	M[7]													
	519 †	M[7]													
	520 †	M[7]													
	521 †	M[7]													
C	522 †	/	/	/		/	/	/							C (ac) E (epr)

[1] Sundry at Mt 8.17.

Gregory-Aland Number	Editions of the Greek New Testament									Synopses			Luke	Aland Categories
	Nestle-Aland[26]	Bover-O'Callaghan	UBS[3]	MC	UBS[1] = UBS[2]	Merk[9]	Vogels[4]	BFBS[2]	Souter[2]	Synopsis[10]	Huck-Greeven[13]	Orchard	IGNTP	
523 †	M[7]													
524 †	M[7]													
525 †	M[7]													
526 †	M[7]													
527 †														
528 †	M									K				
529 †	M													
530 †										K				
531 †	M													
532 †	M									K				
533 †	M	S[1]								K				
534 †	M[7]													
535 †	M													
536 †		/	[/]	/		/								
537 †														
538 †	M[7]													
539[2] †														
540 †	M													

[1] Sundry at Mt 5.39.　　　[2] Lost.

Gregory-Aland Number	Editions of the Greek New Testament									Synopses		Luke	Aland Categories
	Nestle-Aland[26]	Bover-O'Callaghan	UBS[3]	MC	UBS[1] = UBS[2]	Merk[9]	Vogels[4]	BFBS[2]	Souter[2]	Synopsis[10]	Huck-Greeven[13]	Orchard	IGNTP	
541 †	M													
542[1] †														
543 † F 13	[/]	/	/		/	/	/	/	[/]	/	/		/	C
544 †	/	/	/		/	/	/	/			/	/		/	
545 †					/									
546 †	M[7]													
547 †	M	/	/		/	/	/	/						
548 †	M[7]					/								
549 †	M													
550 †	M													
551 †	M[7]										S			
552 †														
553 †	M[7]													
554 †	M[7]													
555 †														
556 †	M[7]													
557 †														
558 †	M[7]													

[1] Lost.

| Gregory-Aland Number | Editions of the Greek New Testament | | | | | | | | | Synopses | | | Luke | Aland Categories |
	Nestle-Aland²⁶	Bover-O'Callaghan	UBS³	MC	UBS¹ = UBS²	Merk⁹	Vogels⁴	BFBS²	Souter²	Synopsis¹⁰	Huck-Greeven¹³	Orchard	IGNTP	
559 †	M⁷								/					
560 †	M⁷													
561 †														
562 †														
563 †														
564 †	M⁷													
565 † F I	/III	/	/I		/I	/	/	/	/	/	/	/	/	C
566 † (= 2149)		/	[/]	/	/¹					/	S			
567 †														
568 †	M													
569 †	/		[/]		[/]				/	S²	S			
570 †	M					S³								
571 †	M		[/]	[/]										
572 † (= 1231)														
573 †	M⁷		[/]	/										
574 †	M⁴									K				
575 †	M									K	S			
576 †														

¹ = Λ 039.   ² Sundry at Mk 6.35.   ³ Sundry at Jn 4.49.   ⁴ Deleted in the 7th printing.

Gregory-Aland Number	Editions of the Greek New Testament									Synopses		Luke	Aland Categories
	Nestle-Aland[26]	Bover-O'Callaghan	UBS[3]	MC	UBS[1] = UBS[2]	Merk[9]	Vogels[4]	BFBS[2]	Souter[2]	Synopsis[10]	Huck-Greeven[13]	Orchard	IGNTP	
577 †	M[7]												/	
578 †	M[7]													
579 †	/	/	/		/	/	/	/	/	/	/	/	/	C
580 †	M[7]													
581 †									c					
C 582 †		/	/	/		/			/					
583 †	M													
584 †	M													
585 †	M[7]													
586 †	M													
587 †	M[7]													
588 †	M[7]													
589 †														
590 †														
591 †														
592 †	M													
593 †	M[7]													
594 †	M													

Gregory-Aland Number	Editions of the Greek New Testament									Synopses			Luke	Aland Categories
	Nestle-Aland[26]	Bover-O'Callaghan	UBS[3]	MC	UBS[1] = UBS[2]	Merk[9]	Vogels[4]	BFBS[2]	Souter[2]	Synopsis[10]	Huck-Greeven[13]	Orchard	IGNTP	
595 †														
596 †	M[7]													
597 †	M[7]									[/]	S			C
598 †		/		[/]		/								
599[1] †														
600 †	M													
601 †	M													
602 †	M		[/]	/										
603 †	M		[/]	/			/							
604 †	M													
605 †	M[2]		/		/		/							
606 †			[/]	/										
607 †	M													
608 †														
609 †														
610 †	S[3]	[/]	[/]	/		/								C (a) E (c)
611 †			[/]	/				/						
612 †				S[4]										

[1] This number should be deleted according to the *Liste*.   [2] Deleted in the 7th printing.
[3] Sundry at Jas 1.27. Listed in the 7th printing.   [4] Cited as Tischendorf 134 on p 284.

Gregory-Aland Number	Editions of the Greek New Testament									Synopses			Luke	Aland Categories
	Nestle-Aland26	Bover-O'Callaghan	UBS3	MC	UBS1 = UBS2	Merk9	Vogels4	BFBS2	Souter2	Synopsis10	Huck-Greeven13	Orchard	IGNTP	
613¹ †		/												
614 †	/ IIac / IVp	/	/I		/I	/	/	/	/	/				C
615 †														
616 †	M	[/]	/	/		/			/					
617 †		[/]	[/]	/		/								
618 †	M		[/]		[/]		/		[/]					
619 †														
620 †	M		/	/		/								
621 †	/													C
622 †	M													
623 †	[/] ap / IV c	/	/		/	/								C
624 †	M													
625 †	M								/					
626 †	M													
627 †	M		[/]		[/]	/			S²					
628 †	M	/	[/]	/		/								
629 †	/ ac / IVp		/I		/I		/	/	S³					C
630 †	/ IIpc / IVa		/I		/I		/	/	/					C

¹ Burnt.   ² Cited as Tischendorf 24 at Rev 1.14.   ³ Sundry at 1 Jn 5.7 — like 61 a Greek witness to the longer text (see Kenyon: Text of the Greek Bible (ed. Adams)).

Gregory-Aland Number	Editions of the Greek New Testament									Synopses			Luke	Aland Categories
	Nestle-Aland²⁶	Bover-O'Callaghan	UBS³	MC	UBS¹ = UBS²	Merk⁹	Vogels⁴	BFBS²	Souter²	Synopsis¹⁰	Huck-Greeven¹³	Orchard	IGNTP	
631 †														
632 †	M													
633 †	M⁷													
634 †	M													
635 †		/	[/]		[/]	/	/							
636 †	/		/											
637 †	M													
638 †	M													
639 †	M	[/]				/	/							
640 †	M													
641 †														
642 †	/	/	[/]	/		/		/	/					C (c) E (ap)
643 †				S¹										
644 †	M													
645 †	M⁷													
646² †														
647² †														
648² †	M⁷													

¹ Sundry at p 710.   ² Lost.

Gregory-Aland Number	Editions of the Greek New Testament									Synopses			Luke	Aland Categories
	Nestle-Aland[26]	Bover-O'Callaghan	UBS[3]	MC	UBS[1] = UBS[2]	Merk[9]	Vogels[4]	BFBS[2]	Souter[2]	Synopsis[10]	Huck-Greeven[13]	Orchard	IGNTP	
649 †	M[7]													
650 †	M[7]													
651 †	M													
652 † F 1 ?														
653[1] †														
654[2] †														
655 †	M	/				/	/				S			
656 †	M													
657 †	M[7]													
658[2] †														
659[2] †		/	[/]	/		/	/			/	/			
660 †	M[3]	/	[/]	/		/	/			/	S			
661[2] †		/	/	/		/		/		/	S			
662[2] †	M[7 3]													
663 †	M[7]													
C 664 †	M	/	[/]	/		/								
665 †			/	/										
666 †	M[7]													

[1] Part lost.   [2] Lost.   [3] Possibly 662 in M[7] is a misprint for 660 (deleted in that edition).

| Gregory-Aland Number | Editions of the Greek New Testament | | | | | | | | | Synopses | | Luke | Aland Categories |
	Nestle-Aland²⁶	Bover-O'Callaghan	UBS³	MC	UBS¹ = UBS²	Merk⁹	Vogels⁴	BFBS²	Souter²	Synopsis¹⁰	Huck-Greeven¹³	Orchard	IGNTP	
667 †														
668 †	M⁷													
669 †	M⁷												/	
670¹ †														
671¹ †														
672 †	M									K				
673 †	M													
674 †	M⁷													
675 †														
676 †														
677 †	M⁷													
678 †														
679 †														
C 680 †	M		[/]	/		/			/					
681 †														
682 †														
683 †														
684 †	M⁷													

¹ Lost.

Gregory-Aland Number	Editions of the Greek New Testament									Synopses			Luke	Aland Categories
	Nestle-Aland[26]	Bover-O'Callaghan	UBS[3]	MC	UBS[1] = UBS[2]	Merk[9]	Vogels[4]	BFBS[2]	Souter[2]	Synopsis[10]	Huck-Greeven[13]	Orchard	IGNTP	
685 †	M[7]													
686 †	M[7]													
687 †														
688 †	M													
689 †	M[7]													
690 †	M[7]													
691 †	M[7]													
692 †	M	/	/		/	/					/			
693 †														
694 †	M[7]													
695 †														
696 †	M[7]													
697 †			[/]	/							S			
698 †	M[7]													
C 699 †	M				/									
700 †	/III	/	/I		/I	/	/	/	/	/	/	/	/	C
701¹ †														
702 †														

¹ Lost.

Gregory-Aland Number	Editions of the Greek New Testament									Synopses		Luke	Aland Categories
	Nestle-Aland[26]	Bover-O'Callaghan	UBS[3]	MC	UBS[1] = UBS[2]	Merk[9]	Vogels[4]	BFBS[2]	Souter[2]	Synopsis[10]	Huck-Greeven[13]	Orchard	IGNTP	
703 †														
704 (= 2284)														
705 †	M[7]													
706 †														
707 †	M									K				
708 †	M									K				
709 †														
710 †														
711 †	M[7]													
712 †														
713 †	[/]	/	/		/	/	/	/	/	/	S	/	/	
714 †	M[7]													
715 †	M[7]													
716 †		/				/		/			S		/	
717 †	M[7]													
718 †	M[7]													
719 †														
720 †	/													C (c) E (eap)

Gregory-Aland Number	Editions of the Greek New Testament									Synopses		Luke	Aland Categories
	Nestle-Aland[26]	Bover-O'Callaghan	UBS[3]	MC	UBS[1] = UBS[2]	Merk[9]	Vogels[4]	BFBS[2]	Souter[2]	Synopsis[10]	Huck-Greeven[13]	Orchard	IGNTP	
721 †	M[7]									K				
722 †														
723 †														
724 †	M[7]													
725 †	M[7]													
726 †		[/]	[/]	/		/					S		/	
727 †														
728 †														
729 †														
730 †														
731 †														
732 †														
733 †														
734 †	M[7]													
735 †														
736 †	M[7]													
737 †	M[7]													
738 †														

Gregory-Aland Number	Editions of the Greek New Testament									Synopses			Luke	Aland Categories
	Nestle-Aland[26]	Bover-O'Callaghan	UBS[3]	MC	UBS[1] = UBS[2]	Merk[9]	Vogels[4]	BFBS[2]	Souter[2]	Synopsis[10]	Huck-Greeven[13]	Orchard	IGNTP	
739 †	M[7]													
740 †														
741 †	M[7]													
742 †														
743 †		/	/	/		/								
744 †														
745 †	M[7]													
746 †	M									K				
747 †														
748 †	M									K				
749 †														
750 †	M									K				
751 †														
752 †														
753 a b														
754 †	M									K				
755 †	M[7]													
756 †	M									K				

Gregory-Aland Number	Editions of the Greek New Testament									Synopses			Luke	Aland Categories
	Nestle-Aland[26]	Bover-O'Callaghan	UBS[3]	MC	UBS[1] = UBS[2]	Merk[9]	Vogels[4]	BFBS[2]	Souter[2]	Synopsis[10]	Huck-Greeven[13]	Orchard	IGNTP	
C 757 †	M	[/]			[/]									
758 †														
759 †														
760 †														
761 †														
762 †														
763 †														
764 †														
765 †														
766 †														
767 (= 1281)														
768 †														
769 †														
770 †	M[7]													
771 †														
772 †														
773 †														
774 †														

Gregory-Aland Number	Editions of the Greek New Testament									Synopses		Luke		Aland Categories
	Nestle-Aland[26]	Bover-O'Callaghan	UBS[3]	MC	UBS[1] = UBS[2]	Merk[9]	Vogels[4]	BFBS[2]	Souter[2]	Synopsis[10]	Huck-Greeven[13]	Orchard	IGNTP	
775 †														
776 †														
777 †														
778 †														
779 †														
780 †														
781 †														
782 †			[/]	/										
783 †					[/]									
784 †														
785 †														
786 †														
787 †														
788 † F 13	[/]	/	/		/	/			[/]	/	/	/	/	C
789 †														
790 †														
791 †														
792 †		/	/		/	/		/	/					

| Gregory-Aland Number | Editions of the Greek New Testament | | | | | | | | | Synopses | | Luke | | Aland Categories |
	Nestle-Aland[26]	Bover-O'Callaghan	UBS[3]	MC	UBS[1] = UBS[2]	Merk[9]	Vogels[4]	BFBS[2]	Souter[2]	Synopsis[10]	Huck-Greeven[13]	Orchard	IGNTP	
793 †														
794 †	M	/	/	/		/								
795 †														
796 †														
797 †														
798 †	M[7]													
799 †														
800 †														
801 †	M													
802 †	M[7]													
803 †														
804 †														
805 †														
806 †														
807 †				[/]										
C 808 †		/	/		/	/		/			S			
809 †														
810[1]														

[1] Lost.

Gregory-Aland Number	Editions of the Greek New Testament									Synopses		Luke		Aland Categories
	Nestle-Aland²⁶	Bover-O'Callaghan	UBS³	MC	UBS¹ = UBS²	Merk⁹	Vogels⁴	BFBS²	Souter²	Synopsis¹⁰	Huck-Greeven¹³	Orchard	IGNTP	
<u>811</u> †														
812 (= 2278)														
<u>813</u>¹														
<u>814</u>¹														
815 (= 2276)														
816 (= 2277)														
<u>817</u> †														
<u>818</u> †														
<u>819</u> †														
<u>820</u> †														
<u>821</u> †		S²			/						S			
<u>822</u> †														
<u>823</u>¹ †		/	/	/	/									
C <u>824</u> †	M	[/]			[/]									
<u>825</u> †	M													
<u>826</u> † F 13	[/]	/	/		/	/	/	/	[/]		/		/	C
<u>827</u> †		[/]			/						/		/	
<u>828</u> † F 13	[/]	/	/		/	/	/	/	[/]	/	/		/	C

¹ Lost.   ² Sundry at Jn 14.20 (on card insert only).

Gregory-Aland Number	Editions of the Greek New Testament									Synopses		Luke	Aland Categories
	Nestle-Aland[26]	Bover-O'Callaghan	UBS[3]	MC	UBS[1] = UBS[2]	Merk[9]	Vogels[4]	BFBS[2]	Souter[2]	Synopsis[10]	Huck-Greeven[13]	Orchard	IGNTP	
829 †														
830 †														
831 †	M													
832 †														
833 †														
834 †														
835 †														
836 †	M[7]													
837 †		S[1]									S			
838 (= 657)														
839 †	M													
840 †	M[7]													
841 †	M[7]													
842 †														
843 †	M													
844 †	M					/		S[2]						
845 †	M													
846 †	M[7]													

[1] Sundry at Mk 1.10.   [2] Sundry at Lk 12.47.

Gregory-Aland Number	Editions of the Greek New Testament									Synopses			Luke	Aland Categories
	Nestle-Aland[26]	Bover-O'Callaghan	UBS[3]	MC	UBS[1] = UBS[2]	Merk[9]	Vogels[4]	BFBS[2]	Souter[2]	Synopsis[10]	Huck-Greeven[13]	Orchard	IGNTP	
847														
848 †	M[7]													
849 †		[/]												C
850[1] †		/	[/]	/		/		/		/	S			
851 †														
852 †	M													
853 †	M[7]													
854 †														
855 †														
856 †														
857 †	M													
858 †														
859 †														
860 †														
861 †														
862 †	M													
863 †														
864 †	M													

[1] This ms. should perhaps be deleted as it is not a continuous text.

Gregory-Aland Number	Editions of the Greek New Testament									Synopses			Luke	Aland Categories
	Nestle-Aland[26]	Bover-O'Callaghan	UBS[3]	MC	UBS[1] = UBS[2]	Merk[9]	Vogels[4]	BFBS[2]	Souter[2]	Synopsis[10]	Huck-Greeven[13]	Orchard	IGNTP	
865 †														
866a † b(= 1918) †	M[7]													
867 †	M													
868 †	M[7]													
869 †		/				/								
870 †	M[7]													
871 †														
872 † F1 ?		/				/					/			
873 †														
874 †														
875 †					S[1]									
876 †		/	/	/		/		/	[/]					
877 †	M													
878 †														
879 †														
880 †	M													
881 †														
882[2]														

[1] Sundry at Jn 8.11.   [2] This number should be deleted according to the *Liste*.

| Gregory-Aland Number | Editions of the Greek New Testament | | | | | | | | | Synopses | | | Luke | Aland Categories |
	Nestle-Aland[26]	Bover-O'Callaghan	UBS[3]	MC	UBS[1] = UBS[2]	Merk[9]	Vogels[4]	BFBS[2]	Souter[2]	Synopsis[10]	Huck-Greeven[13]	Orchard	IGNTP	
883 †														
884 †	M[7]													
885[1]														
C 886 †														C/?E
887 †	M													
888 †														
889 †														
890 †	M													
891 †														
892 †	/III	/	/I		/I	/	/	/		/	/	/	/	B
893 †	M[7]													
894 †	M[7]													
895 †														
896	M									K				
897 †														
898 †														
899 †		[/]								[/]				
900 †														

[1] This number should be deleted according to the *Liste*.

Gregory-Aland Number	Editions of the Greek New Testament									Synopses			Luke	Aland Categories
	Nestle-Aland[26]	Bover-O'Callaghan	UBS[3]	MC	UBS[1] = UBS[2]	Merk[9]	Vogels[4]	BFBS[2]	Souter[2]	Synopsis[10]	Huck-Greeven[13]	Orchard	IGNTP	
901 †	M									K				
902 †														
903 †													/	
904 †														
905 †														
906 †														
907 †														
908 †														
909 †				S¹										
910 †	M													
911 †	M		/	S²			/							E
912 †	M³													
913 †		/	[/]	/		/								
914 †	M		/											
915 †	/	/	/		/	/		/						C
916 †	M													
917 †		/	/		/	/		/						C (p) E (ac)
918 †	/		/											C (c) E (p)

¹ Cited as Tischendorf 225 on p 390.　² See 2040.　³ Deleted in the 7th printing.

| Gregory-Aland Number | Editions of the Greek New Testament | | | | | | | | | Synopses | | | Luke | Aland Categories |
	Nestle-Aland[26]	Bover-O'Callaghan	UBS[3]	MC	UBS[1] = UBS[2]	Merk[9]	Vogels[4]	BFBS[2]	Souter[2]	Synopsis[10]	Huck-Greeven[13]	Orchard	IGNTP	
919 †	M	/	[/]	/		/		/						
920 †	M	/	[/]	/		/								
921 †	M													
C 922 †	M	/				/								
923 †														
924 †														
925 †														
926 †														
927 †		/	/		/	/		/		K				
928 †	M									K				
929 †														
930 †														
931 †														
932 †														
933 †														
934 †														
C 935 †						/								
936 †	M													

Gregory-Aland Number	Editions of the Greek New Testament									Synopses			Luke	Aland Categories
	Nestle-Aland[26]	Bover-O'Callaghan	UBS[3]	MC	UBS[1] = UBS[2]	Merk[9]	Vogels[4]	BFBS[2]	Souter[2]	Synopsis[10]	Huck-Greeven[13]	Orchard	IGNTP	
937 †	M									K				
938 †	M									K				
939 †														
940 †														
941 †		[/]	[/]	/		/								
942 †	M									K				
943 †	M									K				
944 †	M									K				
945 †	/e /IIa / IV pc	/	/I		/I	/				K/	/			C (ac) E (ep)
946 †														
947 †														
948 †														
949 †														
950 †	M													
951 †	M									K				
952 †														
953 †														
954 †	/	/	/		/	/		/		/	/		/	

Gregory-Aland Number	Editions of the Greek New Testament									Synopses			Luke	Aland Categories
	Nestle-Aland[26]	Bover-O'Callaghan	UBS[3]	MC	UBS[1] = UBS[2]	Merk[9]	Vogels[4]	BFBS[2]	Souter[2]	Synopsis[10]	Huck-Greeven[13]	Orchard	IGNTP	
955 †														
956 †														
957 †														
958 †														
959 †	M						/	/		K				
960 †														
961 †														
962 †	M									K				
963 †														
964 †														
965 †														
966 †														
967 †	M[7]													
968 †														
969 †														
970 †	M													
971 †														
972 †														

Gregory-Aland Number	Editions of the Greek New Testament									Synopses			Luke	Aland Categories
	Nestle-Aland[26]	Bover-O'Callaghan	UBS[3]	MC	UBS[1] = UBS[2]	Merk[9]	Vogels[4]	BFBS[2]	Souter[2]	Synopsis[10]	Huck-Greeven[13]	Orchard	IGNTP	
973 †														
974 †														
975 †														
976 †														
977 †	M[7]													
978 †														
979 †														
980 †	M													
981 †														
982 †														
983 † F 13	[/]	[/]	[/]		[/]	/	/	/	[/]	/	/		/	C
984 ¹														
985 †														
C 986 †		[/]				/								
987 †														
988 †														
989 †														
990 †		/	[/]	/		/		/		/	/			

¹ Lost.

Gregory-Aland Number	Editions of the Greek New Testament									Synopses			Luke	Aland Categories
	Nestle-Aland[26]	Bover-O'Callaghan	UBS[3]	MC	UBS[1] = UBS[2]	Merk[9]	Vogels[4]	BFBS[2]	Souter[2]	Synopsis[10]	Huck-Greeven[13]	Orchard	IGNTP	
991 †	M									K				
992 †														
993 †	M													
994 †	M[7]	/			/									
995 †														
996 †														
997 †														
998 †	[/]	/	/		/	/	/			/K	S			
999 †		/	[/]	/		/	/			K				
1000 †														
1001 †														
1002 †														
1003 †														
1004 †														
1005 †													/	
1006 †	/e /IIr	/	/I		/I	/		/	S[1]					B (r) C (e)
1007 †														
1008 †														

[1] Sundry at Rev 13.16.

| Gregory-Aland Number | Editions of the Greek New Testament | | | | | | | | | Synopses | | Luke | | Aland Categories |
	Nestle-Aland[26]	Bover-O'Callaghan	UBS[3]	MC	UBS[1] = UBS[2]	Merk[9]	Vogels[4]	BFBS[2]	Souter[2]	Synopsis[10]	Huck-Greeven[13]	Orchard	IGNTP	
1009 †			/I		/I						S	/	/	
1010 †	/III	/	/I		/I	/	/			/	/	/	/	C
1011 †														
1012 †	[/]	/	[/]		[/]	/	/	/		/	S		/	
1013 †	M													
1014 †														
1015 †														
1016 †	M[7]													
1017 †														
1018 †														
1019 †														
1020 †														
1021 †														
1022 †							/							
1023 †	M									K				
1024 †														
1025 †														
1026 †														

Gregory-Aland Number	Editions of the Greek New Testament									Synopses		Luke		Aland Categories
	Nestle-Aland[26]	Bover-O'Callaghan	UBS[3]	MC	UBS[1] = UBS[2]	Merk[9]	Vogels[4]	BFBS[2]	Souter[2]	Synopsis[10]	Huck-Greeven[13]	Orchard	IGNTP	
1027[1] †														
1028 †	M[7]										S			
1029 †														
1030 †	M									K				
1031 †	M[7]													
1032 †														
1033 †														
1034 †														
1035 †														
1036 †														
1037 †														
1038 †	/	/				/	/	/		/	S			
1039 †														
1040 †														
1041 †														
1042 †														
1043 †			[/]	/										
1044 †														

[1] To be deleted according to ANTF III p 9.

Gregory-Aland Number	Editions of the Greek New Testament									Synopses			Luke	Aland Categories
	Nestle-Aland[26]	Bover-O'Callaghan	UBS[3]	MC	UBS[1] = UBS[2]	Merk[9]	Vogels[4]	BFBS[2]	Souter[2]	Synopsis[10]	Huck-Greeven[13]	Orchard	IGNTP	
1045 †	M													
1046 †														
1047 †		/	/		/	/	/			/	S			
1048 †														
1049[1] †														
1050 †														
1051[1] †														
1052 †														
1053 †														
1054 †														
1055 †														
1056 †														
1057 †														
1058 †														
1059 †														
1060 †														
1061 †														
1062 †														

[1] Lost.

Gregory-Aland Number	Editions of the Greek New Testament									Synopses			Luke	Aland Categories
	Nestle-Aland²⁶	Bover-O'Callaghan	UBS³	MC	UBS¹ = UBS²	Merk⁹	Vogels⁴	BFBS²	Souter²	Synopsis¹⁰	Huck-Greeven¹³	Orchard	IGNTP	
1063 †														
1064											S			
1065 †														
1066 †														
1067 †	/													C
1068 †														
1069 †	M								/					
1070 †	M		[/]	/										
1071 †	/	/	/I		/I	/	/	/	/	/	/		/	C
C 1072 †	M	/												
1073 †	M										K			
1074 †	M										K			
C 1075 †	M				[/]						S			
1076 †	M		[/]	/					/		K			
1077 †	M		[/]		[/]				/		K		/	
1078 †	M								/		K			
1079 †		[/]	/I		/I				/		S		/	
1080 †	M								/		K		/	

Gregory-Aland Number	Editions of the Greek New Testament									Synopses		Luke		Aland Categories
	Nestle-Aland[26]	Bover-O'Callaghan	UBS[3]	MC	UBS[1] = UBS[2]	Merk[9]	Vogels[4]	BFBS[2]	Souter[2]	Synopsis[10]	Huck-Greeven[13]	Orchard	IGNTP	
1081 †														
1082 †		/				/	/			/	/			
1083 †														
1084 †														
1085 †														
1086 †														
1087 †														
1088 †														
1089 †														
1090 †														
1091 †														
1092 †											S			
1093 †	/	/	[/]		[/]	/	/	/		/	S			
C 1094 †	M	[/]				/								
1095 †														
1096†														
1097 †														
1098 †														

Gregory-Aland Number	Editions of the Greek New Testament									Synopses			Luke	Aland Categories
	Nestle-Aland[26]	Bover-O'Callaghan	UBS[3]	MC	UBS[1] = UBS[2]	Merk[9]	Vogels[4]	BFBS[2]	Souter[2]	Synopsis[10]	Huck-Greeven[13]	Orchard	IGNTP	
1099 †	M	[/]	[/][1]	/		/								
1100 †	M					S[1]								
1101 †	M													
1102 †														
1103 †	M													
1104 †	M													
1105 †	M													
1106 †														
1107 †	M													
1108 †		/	/	/		/								
1109[2]														
1110 †	M		/		/					K				
1111 †														
1112	M													
1113 †														
1114 †														
1115 †														
1116 †														

[1] Sundry at Acts 4.34.   [2] Lost.

Gregory-Aland Number	Editions of the Greek New Testament									Synopses			Luke	Aland Categories
	Nestle-Aland[26]	Bover-O'Callaghan	UBS[3]	MC	UBS[1] = UBS[2]	Merk[9]	Vogels[4]	BFBS[2]	Souter[2]	Synopsis[10]	Huck-Greeven[13]	Orchard	IGNTP	
1117 †														
1118 †														
1119 †	M[7]													
1120 †														
1121 †	M									K				
1122 †														
1123 †														
1124 †														
1125 †		·												
1126 †										·				
1127 †														
1128 †														
1129 †	M													
1130 †														
1131 †														
1132 †														
1133 †														
1134 †														

Gregory-Aland Number	Editions of the Greek New Testament									Synopses			Luke	Aland Categories
	Nestle-Aland[26]	Bover-O'Callaghan	UBS[3]	MC	UBS[1] = UBS[2]	Merk[9]	Vogels[4]	BFBS[2]	Souter[2]	Synopsis[10]	Huck-Greeven[13]	Orchard	IGNTP	
1135 †														
1136 †														
1137 †														
1138 †														
1139														
1140 †														
1141 †														
1142 †														
1143 †														
1144														
1145 †														
1146														
1147 †														
1148 †	M[7]						/							
1149 †	M	/	[/]	/		/								
1150[1] †	M[7]													
1151[1] †														
1152 †														

[1] Lost.

Gregory-Aland Number	Editions of the Greek New Testament									Synopses		Luke		Aland Categories
	Nestle-Aland[26]	Bover-O'Callaghan	UBS[3]	MC	UBS[1] = UBS[2]	Merk[9]	Vogels[4]	BFBS[2]	Souter[2]	Synopsis[10]	Huck-Greeven[13]	Orchard	IGNTP	
1153 (= 2381)														
1154[1] †											S			
1155[1] †														
1156 †														
1157 †														
1158 †														
1159 †														
1160 † 1160 abs														
1161 †	M													
1162 †														
1163 †														
1164 †														
1165 †														
1166 †														
1167 †														
1168 †														
1169 †														
1170[2] †		/	/		/	/	/	/		/	S			

[1] Lost.　　[2] According to ANTF III p 10 this ms. is not the one known to Gregory or von Soden by this number.

Gregory-Aland Number	Editions of the Greek New Testament									Synopses			Luke	Aland Categories
	Nestle-Aland[26]	Bover-O'Callaghan	UBS[3]	MC	UBS[1] = UBS[2]	Merk[9]	Vogels[4]	BFBS[2]	Souter[2]	Synopsis[10]	Huck-Greeven[13]	Orchard	IGNTP	
1171 †														
1172 †														
1173 †														
1174 †														
1175 †	/IIap /c	/	/		/	/	/	/						B
1176 †														
1177 †	M[7]													
1178 †			[/]	[/]										
1179 †														
1180 †														
1181 †														
1182[1] †														
1183[1]														
1184[1]														
1185	M									K				
1186 †	M													
1187 †		/				/	/			/	S		/	
1188 †		[/]	[/]	/		/					/			

[1] Lost.

Gregory-Aland Number	Editions of the Greek New Testament									Synopses			Luke	Aland Categories
	Nestle-Aland²⁶	Bover-O'Callaghan	UBS³	MC	UBS¹ = UBS²	Merk⁹	Vogels⁴	BFBS²	Souter²	Synopsis¹⁰	Huck-Greeven¹³	Orchard	IGNTP	
1189 †	M									K				
1190 †	M									K				
1191 †	M									K				
1192¹ †													/	
1193 †	M									K	S			
1194 †	[/]	/	[/]	/		/	/	/		/	/		/	
1195 †	/		/I		/I						S		/	
1196 †	M									K				
1197 †														
1198 †	M									K				
1199 †	M									K				
1200 †	M⁷	/	[/]	/		/					S		/	
1201 †	M²									K	S			
1202 †	M													
1203 †	M									K			/	
1204 †														
1205 †	M⁷									K				
1206 †	M									K				

¹ According to von Soden part of F1.   ² Deleted in the 7th printing.

Gregory-Aland Number	Editions of the Greek New Testament									Synopses			Luke	Aland Categories
	Nestle-Aland[26]	Bover-O'Callaghan	UBS[3]	MC	UBS[1]=UBS[2]	Merk[9]	Vogels[4]	BFBS[2]	Souter[2]	Synopsis[10]	Huck-Greeven[13]	Orchard	IGNTP	
1207 †	M	/				/				K	/			
1208 †	M									K				
1209 †	M									K				
1210[1] †			/		/								/	
1211 †	M									K				
1212 †	M									K				
1213 †	M													
1214 †	M[7]									K				
1215 †	M		[/]		[/]								/	
1216 †	/	[/]	/I		/I	/[2]		/		/	S		/	
1217 †	M[7]		[/]		[/]									
1218 †	M									K				
1219 †		/	[/]	/	/								/	
1220	M[7]												/	
1221 †	M		/		/					K				
1222 †	M									K				
1223 †	M[7]	[/]	[/]	/		/	/					/	/	
1224 †	M		/		/					K				

[1] According to von Soden part of F1.   [2] Misprinted as 1210 at Jn 21.25.

Gregory-Aland Number	Editions of the Greek New Testament									Synopses		Luke	Aland Categories
	Nestle-Aland[26]	Bover-O'Callaghan	UBS[3]	MC	UBS[1] = UBS[2]	Merk[9]	Vogels[4]	BFBS[2]	Souter[2]	Synopsis[10]	Huck-Greeven[13]	Orchard	IGNTP	
1225 †	M									K				
1226 †	M[7]													
1227 †	M									K				
1228 †														
1229 †	/	[/]				/	/			/K	S		/	
1230 †	/		/I		/I									
1231 †	M													
1232 †	M									K				
1233 †	M													
1234 †	M									K				
1235 †	M									K				
1236 †	M									K				
1237 †														
1238 †	M									K				
1239 †														
1240 †	M									K				
1241 †	/III	/	/I		/I	/	/	/		/	/	/	/	A (c) C (p) E (a)
1242 †	/	/	/I		/I	/					S		/	

Gregory-Aland Number	Editions of the Greek New Testament									Synopses			Luke	Aland Categories
	Nestle-Aland[26]	Bover-O'Callaghan	UBS[3]	MC	UBS[1] = UBS[2]	Merk[9]	Vogels[4]	BFBS[2]	Souter[2]	Synopsis[10]	Huck-Greeven[13]	Orchard	IGNTP	
1243 †	/IV c [/] eap		[/]	/								/		A (c) C (eap)
1244 †	M													
1245 †		/	[/]	/		/		/						
1246[1]														
1247 †	M									K			/	
1248 †	M									K				
1249 †	M													
1250 †	M													
1251 †					S[2]					K				E?
1252 †														
1253 †	/		/I		/I									
1254	M[7]													
1255	M[7]													
1256														
1257[3] †														
1258[3] †														
1259[3] †														
1260 †	M[7]													

[1] Lost.   [2] Sundry at Acts 13.45 (cited as Tischendorf 300).   [3] Burnt.

Gregory-Aland Number	Editions of the Greek New Testament									Synopses			Luke	Aland Categories
	Nestle-Aland[26]	Bover-O'Callaghan	UBS[3]	MC	UBS[1] = UBS[2]	Merk[9]	Vogels[4]	BFBS[2]	Souter[2]	Synopsis[10]	Huck-Greeven[13]	Orchard	IGNTP	
1261 †														
1262 †														
1263 †														
1264 †	M[7]													
1265 †														
1266 †														
1267 †														
1268 †														
1269 †														
1270 †			[/]	[/]										
1271[1] †														
1272 †														
1273 †														
1274 a † b †														
1275 †														
1276 †														
1277 †	M													
1278 † F 1?		[/]							/		/			

[1] Lost.

Gregory-Aland Number	Editions of the Greek New Testament									Synopses		Luke		Aland Categories
	Nestle-Aland[26]	Bover-O'Callaghan	UBS[3]	MC	UBS[1] = UBS[2]	Merk[9]	Vogels[4]	BFBS[2]	Souter[2]	Synopsis[10]	Huck-Greeven[13]	Orchard	IGNTP	
1279 †		/	/	/		/		/		/	S			
1280 †														
1281 †														
1282 †														
1283 †	M													
1284 †														
1285 †	M													
1286 †														
1287[1]														
1288 †			[/]	[/]										
1289 †														
1290 †														
1291 †														
1292 †														B (c) C (eap)
1293 †	/	/	/		/	/		/		/	/			
1294 †														
1295 †		/	[/]	[/]		/		/		/	S		/	
1296 †											S			

[1] Lost.

Gregory-Aland Number	Editions of the Greek New Testament									Synopses			Luke	Aland Categories
	Nestle-Aland²⁶	Bover-O'Callaghan	UBS³	MC	UBS¹ = UBS²	Merk⁹	Vogels⁴	BFBS²	Souter²	Synopsis¹⁰	Huck-Greeven¹³	Orchard	IGNTP	
1297 †														
1298 †														
1299 †														
1300 †	M									K				
1301 †										K				
(1302) †											S			
1303¹ †														
1304 †														
1305 †														
1306 †														
1307 †														
1308 †														
1309 †	M													
1310 †	M													
1311 †		/	/		/	/		/						
1312 †	M									K				
1313 †													/	
1314 †	M													

¹ To be deleted according to ANTF III p 10.

| Gregory-Aland Number | Editions of the Greek New Testament | | | | | | | | | Synopses | | Luke | Aland Categories |
	Nestle-Aland[26]	Bover-O'Callaghan	UBS[3]	MC	UBS[1] = UBS[2]	Merk[9]	Vogels[4]	BFBS[2]	Souter[2]	Synopsis[10]	Huck-Greeven[13]	Orchard	IGNTP	
1315 †										K				
1316 †	M									K				
1317 †														
1318 †										K				
1319 †		/	/		/	/							/	C (eap) E (c)
1320 †	M									K				
1321 †		/	[/]		[/]	/					S			
1322 †														
1323 †	M									K				
1324 †	M									K				
1325	/									S[1]				
1326 †														
1327														
1328 †	M					[/]				K				
1329 †	[/]													
1330 †	M									K				
1331 †	M									K				
1332														

[1] Sundry at Mk 4.28.

Gregory-Aland Number	Editions of the Greek New Testament									Synopses			Luke	Aland Categories
	Nestle-Aland[26]	Bover-O'Callaghan	UBS[3]	MC	UBS[1] = UBS[2]	Merk[9]	Vogels[4]	BFBS[2]	Souter[2]	Synopsis[10]	Huck-Greeven[13]	Orchard	IGNTP	
1333 †	/		/											
1334 †	M									K				
1335 †														
1336														
1337														
1338 †													/	
1339 †	M									K				
1340 †	M									K				
1341 †	M			[/]						K				
1342 †		/	/		/	/		/	/	/	/	/	/	B (Mk)
1343 †	M									K				
1344 †			/I		/I						S			
1345 †	M									K				
1346 †	/	/	[/]	[/]		/				[/]	S			
1347 †	M									K			/	
1348 †														
1349 †														
1350 a/b †	M M									K				

Gregory-Aland Number	Editions of the Greek New Testament									Synopses			Luke	Aland Categories
	Nestle-Aland26	Bover-O'Callaghan	UBS3	MC	UBS1 = UBS2	Merk9	Vogels4	BFBS2	Souter2	Synopsis10	Huck-Greeven13	Orchard	IGNTP	
1351 †	M									K			/	
1352 ᵃᵦ †	M									K	S		/	
1353 †														
1354 †		[/]	/	/		/					S			
1355 †	/	/	[/]	/		/	/			/	S		/	
1356 †	M	[/]												
1357 †														
1358 †										K				
1359 †														C
1360 †	M													
1361¹ †														
1362 †														
1363 †														
1364 †										K				
1365 †		S²	/I		/I	/				/	S		/	
1366 †														
1367 †														
1368 (= 807)														

¹ Lost.   ² Sundry at Mt 8.18; 15.39; 19.10.

| Gregory-Aland Number | Editions of the Greek New Testament | | | | | | | | | Synopses | | Luke | Aland Categories |
	Nestle-Aland[26]	Bover-O'Callaghan	UBS[3]	MC	UBS[1] = UBS[2]	Merk[9]	Vogels[4]	BFBS[2]	Souter[2]	Synopsis[10]	Huck-Greeven[13]	Orchard	IGNTP	
1369 (= 2097)														
1370 †	M													
1371[1]	M[2]													
1372[3] †														
1373 †														
1374 †	M													
1375 †		/	[/]	/		/					S			
1376[3]														
1377 †														
1378[3]														
1379 †														
1380[3] †														
1381[3] †														
1382 †														
1383 †														
C 1384 †														
1385 †														
1386 †														

[1] This number should be deleted according to the *Liste*.   [2] Deleted in the 7th printing.
[3] Lost.

Gregory-Aland Number	Editions of the Greek New Testament									Synopses		Luke		Aland Categories
	Nestle-Aland[26]	Bover-O'Callaghan	UBS[3]	MC	UBS[1] = UBS[2]	Merk[9]	Vogels[4]	BFBS[2]	Souter[2]	Synopsis[10]	Huck-Greeven[13]	Orchard	IGNTP	
1387 †														
1388 †														
1389 †														
1390 †														
1391 †		/				/					/			
1392 †	M									K			/	
1393 †														
1394 †														
1395 †	M													
1396 †		/	/		/	/				/	S			
1397 †														
1398 †														C (p) E (cac)
1399 †														
1400 †	M													
1401 †														
1402 †		/	[/]	/		/	/				/			
1403 †														
1404 †										K				

Gregory-Aland Number	Editions of the Greek New Testament									Synopses		Luke		Aland Categories
	Nestle-Aland[26]	Bover-O'Callaghan	UBS[3]	MC	UBS[1] = UBS[2]	Merk[9]	Vogels[4]	BFBS[2]	Souter[2]	Synopsis[10]	Huck-Greeven[13]	Orchard	IGNTP	
<u>1405</u> †		[/]		/										
1406 †														
1407 †														
1408 †														
1409														B (ac) ?E (ep)
1410 †														
1411														
1412														
1413 †														
1414 †														
1415 †														
1416 †														
1417 †	M													
1418 †														
1419[1]														
1420														
1421[2] †														
1422[2] †														

[1] Not a continuous text ms. Therefore should be deleted.   [2] Lost.

Gregory-Aland Number	Editions of the Greek New Testament									Synopses		Luke		Aland Categories
	Nestle-Aland²⁶	Bover-O'Callaghan	UBS³	MC	UBS¹ = UBS²	Merk⁹	Vogels⁴	BFBS²	Souter²	Synopsis¹⁰	Huck-Greeven¹³	Orchard	IGNTP	
1423¹ †														
C 1424 †	/II e / apcr	/	/		/	/	/	/		/	/	/	/	C (Mk) E (Mt Lk Jn acpr)
1425¹ †														
1426¹ †														
1427¹ †														
1428¹ †														
1429¹ †														
1430¹ †														
1431¹ †														
1432 †														
1433 †														
1434 †							/²							
1435														
1436 †														
1437 †	M⁷													
1438 †	M									K				
1439 †														
1440 †														

¹ Lost.   ² Incorrectly given as 1474 in *Rev Bib* 92 (1984) p. 546.

| Gregory-Aland Number | Editions of the Greek New Testament | | | | | | | | | Synopses | | | Luke | Aland Categories |
	Nestle-Aland[26]	Bover-O'Callaghan	UBS[3]	MC	UBS[1] = UBS[2]	Merk[9]	Vogels[4]	BFBS[2]	Souter[2]	Synopsis[10]	Huck-Greeven[13]	Orchard	IGNTP	
1441 †														
1442 †														
1443 †			/		/				/				/	
1444 †	M								/	K				
1445 †	M		/		/				/	K				
1446 †														
1447 †	M													
1448 †	[/]									K				C (c) E (ap) ?E (e)
1449 †	M								/	K				
1450 †														
1451 †														
1452 †	M									K			/	
1453 †														
1454 †														
1455 †														
1456 †														
1457 †														
1458 †													/	

Gregory-Aland Number	Editions of the Greek New Testament									Synopses		Luke		Aland Categories
	Nestle-Aland[26]	Bover-O'Callaghan	UBS[3]	MC	UBS[1] = UBS[2]	Merk[9]	Vogels[4]	BFBS[2]	Souter[2]	Synopsis[10]	Huck-Greeven[13]	Orchard	IGNTP	
1459 †														
1460 †														
1461 †														
1462 †														
1463 †														
1464 †														
1465 †														
1466 †														
1467 †														
1468 †														
1469 †														
1470 †	M									K				
1471 †														
1472 †														
1473 †														
1474 †														
1475 †														
1476 †	M									K				

Gregory-Aland Number	Editions of the Greek New Testament									Synopses			Luke	Aland Categories
	Nestle-Aland[26]	Bover-O'Callaghan	UBS[3]	MC	UBS[1] = UBS[2]	Merk[9]	Vogels[4]	BFBS[2]	Souter[2]	Synopsis[10]	Huck-Greeven[13]	Orchard	IGNTP	
1477 †														
1478 †														
1479 †														
1480 †														
1481 †														
1482 †	M													
1483 †	M									K				
1484 †														
1485 †								/						
1486 †														
1487 †														
1488 †														
1489 †														
1490 †														
1491 †														
1492 †	M									K				
1493 †														
1494 †														

Gregory-Aland Number	Editions of the Greek New Testament									Synopses			Luke	Aland Categories
	Nestle-Aland²⁶	Bover-O'Callaghan	UBS³	MC	UBS¹ = UBS²	Merk⁹	Vogels⁴	BFBS²	Souter²	Synopsis¹⁰	Huck-Greeven¹³	Orchard	IGNTP	
1495 †														
1496 †														
1497 †														
1498 †														
1499 †														
1500 †														
1501 †														
1502 †														
C 1503 †	M									K				
1504 †	M⁷													
1505 †	[/] (eap) /II or IV (c)¹		/I		/I					K				C
1506 †	/II p / c													B (p) C (e)
1507 ²														
1508 †	M													
1509 †														
1510 †									/				/	
1511 †														
1512 †														

¹ See N–A²⁶ pp 53*, 708.   ² Not a continuous text ms. Therefore to be deleted.

Gregory-Aland Number	Editions of the Greek New Testament									Synopses			Luke	Aland Categories
	Nestle-Aland²⁶	Bover-O'Callaghan	UBS³	MC	UBS¹ = UBS²	Merk⁹	Vogels⁴	BFBS²	Souter²	Synopsis¹⁰	Huck-Greeven¹³	Orchard	IGNTP	
1513 †	M													
1514 †	M									K				
1515 †		/			/						S			
1516 †	M⁷													
1517 †	M	S¹												
1518² †	/	/	/		/	/	/	/	/					
1519 †														
1520 †	M									K				
1521 †	M		[/]	/										
1522³ †		/	/		/	/								
1523 †														C
1524 †														C (c) E (ap)
1525³ †		/			/									
1526 †														
1527 †														
1528 †														
1529 †														
1530 †														

¹ Sundry at Mt 4.4.   ² Present location not known.   ³ Lost.

Gregory-Aland Number	Editions of the Greek New Testament									Synopses		Luke		Aland Categories
	Nestle-Aland[26]	Bover-O'Callaghan	UBS[3]	MC	UBS[1] = UBS[2]	Merk[9]	Vogels[4]	BFBS[2]	Souter[2]	Synopsis[10]	Huck-Greeven[13]	Orchard	IGNTP	
1531 †														
1532 †														
1533 †														
1534 †														
1535 †														
1536 †														
1537 †											S			
1538 †														
1539 †	M									K				
1540 †	M									K				
1541 †														
1542 ᵃ/ᵇ †		/			/						S		/ /	b CMk E? Lk
1543 †	M									K				
1544 †														
1545 †	M													
1546 †			/I		/I						S			
1547 †	M									/	S			
1548 †	M									K				

Gregory-Aland Number	Editions of the Greek New Testament									Synopses			Luke	Aland Categories
	Nestle-Aland[26]	Bover-O'Callaghan	UBS[3]	MC	UBS[1] = UBS[2]	Merk[9]	Vogels[4]	BFBS[2]	Souter[2]	Synopsis[10]	Huck-Greeven[13]	Orchard	IGNTP	
1549 †														
1550 †														
1551 †														
1552 †														
1553 †														
1554 †										K				
1555 †		/	[/]	/		/	/	/		/	S			
1556 †	M									K				
1557 †										K				
1558 †														
1559 †														
1560 †														
1561 †														
1562 †														
1563 †														C
1564 †										K				
1565 †														
1566 †	M													

Gregory-Aland Number	Editions of the Greek New Testament									Synopses			Luke	Aland Categories
	Nestle-Aland[26]	Bover-O'Callaghan	UBS[3]	MC	UBS[1] = UBS[2]	Merk[9]	Vogels[4]	BFBS[2]	Souter[2]	Synopsis[10]	Huck-Greeven[13]	Orchard	IGNTP	
1567 †														
1568 †														
1569 †														
1570 †	M		[/]	/						K				
1571 †														
1572 †	M									K				
1573 †	/	/	[/]	/		/	/	/		/	S			C (p) E (eac)
1574 †		/	/		/	/	/	/		/	S			
1575 †														
1576 †														
1577 †	M													
1578 †		S¹												
1579 †		[/]	[/]	/		/				/	S		/	
1580 †														
1581 †														
1582 † F1	[/]	/	/		/	/	/	/	/	/	/		/	C/B
1583 †	M									K				
1584 †														

¹ Sundry at Rev 6.4.

Gregory-Aland Number	Editions of the Greek New Testament									Synopses		Luke		Aland Categories
	Nestle-Aland[26]	Bover-O'Callaghan	UBS[3]	MC	UBS[1] = UBS[2]	Merk[9]	Vogels[4]	BFBS[2]	Souter[2]	Synopsis[10]	Huck-Greeven[13]	Orchard	IGNTP	
1585 †														
1586 †														
1587 †														
1588 †		[/]			/						S			
1589 †														
1590 †														
1591 †														
1592 †		[/]	/											
1593 †														
1594 †	M									K				
1595 †														
1596 †														
C 1597 †	M		/		/	/				K				
1598 †														
1599 †														
1600 †														
1601 †														
1602 †														

Gregory-Aland Number	Editions of the Greek New Testament									Synopses		Luke		Aland Categories
	Nestle-Aland[26]	Bover-O'Callaghan	UBS[3]	MC	UBS[1] = UBS[2]	Merk[9]	Vogels[4]	BFBS[2]	Souter[2]	Synopsis[10]	Huck-Greeven[13]	Orchard	IGNTP	
1603 †														
1604 †	M	/	/	/		/	/	/		/K	/	/	/	
1605 †	M													
1606 †		/				/					/			
1607 †	M									K				
1608 †														
1609 †														
1610 †		/	[/]	/		/		/			S			
1611 †	/ acp /IIr	/	/I		/I	/	/	/	/[1]					B (r) C (apc)
1612 †														
1613 †	M[7]													
1614 †	M													
1615 †														
1616 †														
C 1617 †	M													
1618 †	M													
1619 †	M													
1620 †														

[1] Cited as 105.

Gregory-Aland Number	Editions of the Greek New Testament									Synopses			Luke	Aland Categories
	Nestle-Aland[26]	Bover-O'Callaghan	UBS[3]	MC	UBS[1] = UBS[2]	Merk[9]	Vogels[4]	BFBS[2]	Souter[2]	Synopsis[10]	Huck-Greeven[13]	Orchard	IGNTP	
1621 †														
1622 †	M													
1623 †														
1624 †														
1625 †														
C 1626 †	M	S¹	/		/	[/]								
1627														
1628 †	M									K				
1629 †														
1630 †													/	
1631														
1632 †														
1633 †														
1634 †														
1635 †											S			
1636 †	M													
C 1637 †	M									K				
1638 †														

¹ Cited frequently in Rev.

Gregory-Aland Number	Editions of the Greek New Testament									Synopses			Luke	Aland Categories
	Nestle-Aland²⁶	Bover-O'Callaghan	UBS³	MC	UBS¹ = UBS²	Merk⁹	Vogels⁴	BFBS²	Souter²	Synopsis¹⁰	Huck-Greeven¹³	Orchard	IGNTP	
1639 †														
1640														
1641 †														
1642 †		[/]	/							K	S			C (a) E (epc)
1643 †														
1644 †														
1645 †										K				
1646 †			/I		/I						S			
1647 †														
1648 †														
1649 †	M													
1650 †														
1651 †														
C 1652 †														
1653 †														
1654 †		[/]		/		/	/				S		/	
1655 †														
1656 †	M													

| Gregory-Aland Number | Editions of the Greek New Testament | | | | | | | | | Synopses | | Luke | Aland Categories |
	Nestle-Aland[26]	Bover-O'Callaghan	UBS[3]	MC	UBS[1] = UBS[2]	Merk[9]	Vogels[4]	BFBS[2]	Souter[2]	Synopsis[10]	Huck-Greeven[13]	Orchard	IGNTP	
1657 †														
1658 †														
1659 †														
1660 †														
1661 †											S			
1662 †	M													
1663 †														
1664 †														
1665 †														
1666 †														
1667 †														
C 1668 †	M													
1669 †														
1670 †														
1671 †														
1672 †	M													
1673 †	M													
1674 a b c d														

Gregory-Aland Number	Editions of the Greek New Testament									Synopses			Luke	Aland Categories
	Nestle-Aland²⁶	Bover-O'Callaghan	UBS³	MC	UBS¹ = UBS²	Merk⁹	Vogels⁴	BFBS²	Souter²	Synopsis¹⁰	Huck-Greeven¹³	Orchard	IGNTP	
1675 †		/	/		/	/	/	/			/		/	
1676 †														
1677 †														
C 1678 †	/	/	[/]	/		/		/						C
1679 †														
1680 †														
1681 a/b †¹														
1682 †														
1683 †	M⁷													
1684¹ †														
1685 †													/	
1686 †														
1687 †														
1688 †														
1689¹ † F 13		/	[/]		[/]	/	/		[/]	/	/			
1690 †														
1691 †													/	
1692 †														

¹ Lost.

Gregory-Aland Number	Editions of the Greek New Testament									Synopses		Luke	Aland Categories
	Nestle-Aland[26]	Bover-O'Callaghan	UBS[3]	MC	UBS[1] = UBS[2]	Merk[9]	Vogels[4]	BFBS[2]	Souter[2]	Synopsis[10]	Huck-Greeven[13]	Orchard	IGNTP	
1693 †	M									K				
1694 †														
1695 †														
1696[1] †														
1697 †														
1698 †														
1699 †														
1700 †														
1701 †	M[7]													
1702														
1703 †														
C 1704	/IV a [/] epcr		[/]	/	˘	S[2]								C (a) E (epcr)
1705 †														
1706														
1707 †														
1708														
1709 † F 13								[/]						
1710														

[1] Part lost.   [2] At Rev 1.6 as Tischendorf 214.

Gregory-Aland Number	Editions of the Greek New Testament									Synopses			Luke	Aland Categories
	Nestle-Aland²⁶	Bover-O'Callaghan	UBS³	MC	UBS¹ = UBS²	Merk⁹	Vogels⁴	BFBS²	Souter²	Synopsis¹⁰	Huck-Greeven¹³	Orchard	IGNTP	
1711														
1712 †														
1713 †														
1714 †	M													
1715 †														
1716 †														
1717 †	M													
1718 †														C
1719 †									/					
1720 †	M													
1721 †														
1722 †														
1723 †	M													
1724 †														
1725 †	M													
1726 †	M													
1727 †	M													
1728 †	M				/									

Gregory-Aland Number	Editions of the Greek New Testament									Synopses		Luke	Aland Categories
	Nestle-Aland[26]	Bover-O'Callaghan	UBS[3]	MC	UBS[1] = UBS[2]	Merk[9]	Vogels[4]	BFBS[2]	Souter[2]	Synopsis[10]	Huck-Greeven[13]	Orchard	IGNTP	
1729 †	[/]													
1730 †	M													
1731 †	M													
1732 †	M	[/]				/								
1733 †	M													
1734 †	M					/		/						
1735 †	[/]													B (c) C (ap)
1736 †	M													
1737 †	M													
1738 †	M	/	[/]	/		/								
1739 †	/III	/	/I		/I	/	/	/	/	/	S	/		A (pc) B (a)
1740 †	M				[/]									
1741 †	M													
1742 †	M													
1743 †	M[7]													
1744 †														
1745 †	M													
1746 †	M													

Gregory-Aland Number	Editions of the Greek New Testament									Synopses		Luke		Aland Categories
	Nestle-Aland[26]	Bover-O'Callaghan	UBS[3]	MC	UBS[1] = UBS[2]	Merk[9]	Vogels[4]	BFBS[2]	Souter[2]	Synopsis[10]	Huck-Greeven[13]	Orchard	IGNTP	
1747 †	M													
1748 †	M													
1749 †	M													
1750 †	M													
1751 †														C
1752 †	M													
1753 †		[/]	/											
1754 †	M[7]													
1755 a b c	M M													
1756	M													
1757 †	M													
1758 †	[/]	/	/		/	/		/						
1759 †	M[7]													
1760[1] †														
1761 †	M[7]													
1762 †	M[7]													
1763 †	M													
1764 †														

[1] Lost.

Gregory-Aland Number	Editions of the Greek New Testament									Synopses			Luke	Aland Categories
	Nestle-Aland[26]	Bover-O'Callaghan	UBS[3]	MC	UBS[1] = UBS[2]	Merk[9]	Vogels[4]	BFBS[2]	Souter[2]	Synopsis[10]	Huck-Greeven[13]	Orchard	IGNTP	
1765 †		/	[/]	/		/			/					
1766[1] †														
1767 †	M													
1768 †	M													
1769 †														
1770 †	M													
1771 †	M													
1772 †	M													
1773 †			/	/										
1774 †														
1775		/												
1776														
1777		S[2]												
1778 †		/	/		/	/		/						
1779[1] †														
C 1780 †														
1781[1] †														
1782[1] †														

[1] Lost.   [2] Sundry at Rev 1.3.

Gregory-Aland Number	Editions of the Greek New Testament									Synopses		Orchard	Luke	Aland Categories
	Nestle-Aland[26]	Bover-O'Callaghan	UBS[3]	MC	UBS[1] = UBS[2]	Merk[9]	Vogels[4]	BFBS[2]	Souter[2]	Synopsis[10]	Huck-Greeven[13]		IGNTP	
1783[1]†														
1784[1]†														
C 1785[1]†														
1786[1]†														
1787[1]†														
1788[1]†														
1789[1]†														
1790[1]†											S			
1791[1]†														
1792[1]†														
1793[1]†														
1794[1]†														
1795[2]†														
1796[1]														
1797†														
1798†														
1799 (†)			[/]	/				/						
1800†	M									K				

[1] Lost.   [2] Part lost.

Gregory-Aland Number	Editions of the Greek New Testament									Synopses			Luke	Aland Categories
	Nestle-Aland[26]	Bover-O'Callaghan	UBS[3]	MC	UBS[1] = UBS[2]	Merk[9]	Vogels[4]	BFBS[2]	Souter[2]	Synopsis[10]	Huck-Greeven[13]	Orchard	IGNTP	
1801[1] †														
1802														
1803 †														
1804 †														
1805[1] †														
1806[1] †														
1807[1] †														
1808 †														
1809[1] †														
1810[1] †														
1811[1] †														
1812 †														
1813[1] †														
1814[2] †														
1815 (= 2127)														
1816 †														
1817 †														
1818 †														

[1] Lost.   [2] Not a continuous text ms. Therefore to be deleted.

Gregory-Aland Number	Editions of the Greek New Testament									Synopses			Luke	Aland Categories
	Nestle-Aland[26]	Bover-O'Callaghan	UBS[3]	MC	UBS[1] = UBS[2]	Merk[9]	Vogels[4]	BFBS[2]	Souter[2]	Synopsis[10]	Huck-Greeven[13]	Orchard	IGNTP	
1819 †		S[1]	[/]	/										
1820 †		/	[/]	/		/								
1821 †	M[7]													
1822 †														
1823 †														
1824 †														
1825[2]														
1826 †	M									K				
1827 †	/	/	/	/		/	/	/						
1828 †	M	/	/I		/I	[/]			/					
1829 †	M	[/]	[/]	[/]		/								
1830 †														
1831 †	[/]	/	/	/		/		/			S			
1832 †	/													
1833[3] †														
1834 †		[/]					/							
1835 †	M	/	[/]		[/]	/								
1836 †	/	/	/		/	/	/	/						C

[1] Sundry cited frequently in Jn.   [2] Unassigned.   [3] Lost.

Gregory-Aland Number	Editions of the Greek New Testament									Synopses			Luke	Aland Categories
	Nestle-Aland26	Bover-O'Callaghan	UBS3	MC	UBS1 = UBS2	Merk9	Vogels4	BFBS2	Souter2	Synopsis10	Huck-Greeven13	Orchard	IGNTP	
1837 †		/	/		/	/								
1838 †	/	/	/		/	/	/	/			S			C
1839 †														
1840 †														
1841 †	/ acp /II r	/	/	/		/			S¹					B (r) E (apc)
1842 †														C
1843 †														
1844 †														C
1845 †	[/]	/	/	/		/		/		'				C?
1846 †	/IV c [/] ap						/							C (pc) E (a)
1847 †	M													
1848 †														
1849 †	M		[/]	[/]	[/]									
1850 †														
1851 †	M													
1852 †	/IV c / ap [/] r	/	/	/		/	/	/						B (c) C (ap) E (r)
1853 †														
1854 †	/ acp /IIr	/	/I		/I	/		/	/					B (r) E (apc)

¹ Sundry at Rev 13.16.

Gregory-Aland Number	Nestle-Aland[26]	Bover-O'Callaghan	UBS[3]	MC	UBS[1] = UBS[2]	Merk[9]	Vogels[4]	BFBS[2]	Souter[2]	Synopsis[10]	Huck-Greeven[13]	Orchard	IGNTP	Aland Categories
1855 †	M													
1856 †	M													
1857 †														
1858 †	M													
1859 †	M	[/]	/I		/I	/								
1860 †	M[7]													
1861 †	M[7]													
1862 †	M	/	/	/		/								
1863 †														
1864 †														
1865 †														
1866 (= l 1591)														
1867 †		/				/	/							
1868 †														
1869	M													
1870 †	M													
1871 †														
1872 †	M	/	[/]	/		/								

Gregory-Aland Number	Editions of the Greek New Testament									Synopses			Luke	Aland Categories
	Nestle-Aland²⁶	Bover-O'Callaghan	UBS³	MC	UBS¹ = UBS²	Merk⁹	Vogels⁴	BFBS²	Souter²	Synopsis¹⁰	Huck-Greeven¹³	Orchard	IGNTP	
1873 †		/	/		/	/								
1874 †		/	/	/		/								C (p) E (ac)
1875	[/]		/	/										C
1876 †	M	/	[/]	/		/	/							
1877 †	/		/I		/I									C (p) E (ac)
1878 †	M													
1879 †	M													
1880 †	M													
1881 †	/II p /IV c [/] a		/I		/I									B
1882 †	M													
1883 †	M⁷													
1884 †	/IV			/										C
1885 †														
1886 †														
1887 †														
1888 †	M		/	/		/								
1889 †	M													
1890 †														

Gregory-Aland Number	Editions of the Greek New Testament									Synopses		Luke		Aland Categories
	Nestle-Aland^26	Bover-O'Callaghan	UBS^3	MC	UBS^1 = UBS^2	Merk^9	Vogels^4	BFBS^2	Souter^2	Synopsis^10	Huck-Greeven^13	Orchard	IGNTP	
1891 †	/IVᶜa l/ p	/	/	/		/		/			S			C (a) E (cp)
1892 †														
1893 †			[/]	[/]		/								
1894 †		/					/	/						
1895 †			[/]	/										
1896 †			[/]	/										
1897 †	M													
1898 † (= 1875)		/	[/]		[/]	/		/			S			
1899 †	M													
1900 †														
1901														
1902 †	M													
1903														
1904 †														
1905 †	M			S^1										
1906 †	/M		/		/		/	/						
1907 †	M		/	S^2			/							
1908 †	/	[/]	/		/	/	/	/	/					C

[1] Cited as a Sundry on p 667.   [2] Cited as a Sundry on p 634.

Gregory-Aland Number	Editions of the Greek New Testament									Synopses		Luke		Aland Categories
	Nestle-Aland[26]	Bover-O'Callaghan	UBS[3]	MC	UBS[1] = UBS[2]	Merk[9]	Vogels[4]	BFBS[2]	Souter[2]	Synopsis[10]	Huck-Greeven[13]	Orchard	IGNTP	
1909 † / 1909 abs †							/		/					
1910 †														C
1911 †	M		[/]	/			/							
1912 †	/	/	/	/		/	/	/	/					C
1913 †					[/]	/			/					
1914 †	M													
1915 †	M			S[1]										
1916 †	M													
1917 †	M													
1918 †	M		/	/		/			/					
1919 †	M													
1920 †	M													
1921 †	M													
1922 †	M													
1923 †	M		[/]		[/]		/							
1924 †	M		[/]	/										
1925 †	M[7]		/		/		/							
1926 †	M													

[1] Cited as a Sundry on p 505.

Gregory-Aland Number	Editions of the Greek New Testament									Synopses			Luke	Aland Categories
	Nestle-Aland²⁶	Bover-O'Callaghan	UBS³	MC	UBS¹ = UBS²	Merk⁹	Vogels⁴	BFBS²	Souter²	Synopsis¹⁰	Huck-Greeven¹³	Orchard	IGNTP	
1927 †	M		[/]	/			/							
1928 †	M													
1929 † 1929 abs †	M													
1930 †	M		[/]	/										
1931 †	M													
1932 †	M			/										
1933 †	M													
1934 †	M	[/]			[/]									
1935 †														
1936 †	M													
1937 †	M													
1938 †	M													
1939 †														
1940¹ †														
1941 †	M													
1942 †														C
1943 †														
1944 (= 2288)			[/]	/			/		/					

¹ Destroyed.

Gregory-Aland Number	Editions of the Greek New Testament									Synopses			Luke	Aland Categories
	Nestle-Aland[26]	Bover-O'Callaghan	UBS[3]	MC	UBS[1] = UBS[2]	Merk[9]	Vogels[4]	BFBS[2]	Souter[2]	Synopsis[10]	Huck-Greeven[13]	Orchard	IGNTP	
1945 †														
1946 †	M													
1947 †														
1948 †	M													
1949 †														
1950 †														
1951 †	M													
1952 †	M		[/]	/			/		/					
1953 †														
1954 †	M													
1955 †	M					/								
1956 †	M													
1957 †	M	[/]				/	/							
1958 †	M													
1959 †														C
1960 †														
1961 †			[/]	/										
1962 †	/		/I		/I									C

Gregory-Aland Number	Editions of the Greek New Testament									Synopses		Luke		Aland Categories
	Nestle-Aland[26]	Bover-O'Callaghan	UBS[3]	MC	UBS[1] = UBS[2]	Merk[9]	Vogels[4]	BFBS[2]	Souter[2]	Synopsis[10]	Huck-Greeven[13]	Orchard	IGNTP	
1963 †														
1964 †	M[1]		[/]	/										
1965 †														
1966 †														
1967 †	M													
1968 †	M													
1969 †														
1970 †	M													
1971 †	M													
1972 †	M													
1973 †														
1974 †	M													
1975 †	M													
1976 †														
1977 †			[/]	/										
1978 †	M		[/]	/										
1979 †	M													
1980 †	M													

[1] Deleted in 7th printing.

Gregory-Aland Number	Editions of the Greek New Testament									Synopses			Luke	Aland Categories
	Nestle-Aland[26]	Bover-O'Callaghan	UBS[3]	MC	UBS[1] = UBS[2]	Merk[9]	Vogels[4]	BFBS[2]	Souter[2]	Synopsis[10]	Huck-Greeven[13]	Orchard	IGNTP	
1981 †	M													
1982 †	M													
1983 † 1983 abs †														
1984 †			/I		/I									
1985 †			/I		/I									
1986 †	M													
1987 †														
1988 †	M													
1989[1] †														
1990[1] †														
1991 †														
1992 †	M		[/]	/										
1993[2] †														
1994 †			[/]	/										
1995 †														
1996 †														
1997 †	M													
1998 †	M													

[1] Lost. [2] Not a continuous text ms. Therefore to be deleted.

Gregory-Aland Number	Editions of the Greek New Testament									Synopses			Luke	Aland Categories
	Nestle-Aland[26]	Bover-O'Callaghan	UBS[3]	MC	UBS[1] = UBS[2]	Merk[9]	Vogels[4]	BFBS[2]	Souter[2]	Synopsis[10]	Huck-Greeven[13]	Orchard	IGNTP	
1999 †														
2000 †			[/]	/										
2001 †	M													
2002 †														
2003 †	M													
2004 (= 1835) †		/	/	/										
2005 †		/	/	/		/		/						C
2006 †														
2007 †	M													
2008 †														
2009 †	M													
2010 †														
2011 †														
2012 †														
2013 †	M													
2014 †	[/]	/	[/]	/		/								
2015 †	/	/	[/]	/		/	/		/					
2016 †	/	/				/	/	/	/					

Gregory-Aland Number	Editions of the Greek New Testament									Synopses			Luke	Aland Categories
	Nestle-Aland²⁶	Bover-O'Callaghan	UBS³	MC	UBS¹ = UBS²	Merk⁹	Vogels⁴	BFBS²	Souter²	Synopsis¹⁰	Huck-Greeven¹³	Orchard	IGNTP	
2017 †		/	/	/		/	/		/					
2018 †		[/]	/	/		/	/		/					
2019 †		/	/	/		/	/	/	/					
2020 †	/	/	/I		/I	/	/	/	/					
2021 †						/	/		[/]					
2022 †						/								
2023 †		/	[/]	/		/	/	/	[/]					
2024 †														
2025 †														
2026 †		/				/		/	/					
2027 †	[/]					/	/							
2028 †	/	/	/		/	/		/						
2029 †		/	/		/	/		/						
2030 †	/III	/	/		/									C
2031 †		/	/	/		/		/						
2032 †														
2033 †		/	/		/	/								
2034 †		S¹				/			/					

¹ Sundry at Rev 3.14, 11.10.

Gregory-Aland Number	Editions of the Greek New Testament									Synopses			Luke	Aland Categories
	Nestle-Aland²⁶	Bover-O'Callaghan	UBS³	MC	UBS¹ = UBS²	Merk⁹	Vogels⁴	BFBS²	Souter²	Synopsis¹⁰	Huck-Greeven¹³	Orchard	IGNTP	
2035 †														
2036 † 2036 abs †	/	/	[/]	/		/	/	/	/					
2037 †		[/]	[/]	/		/		/	/					
2038 †		[/]	[/]		[/]				/					
2039¹ †			[/]	/		/	/		[/]					
2040 (= 911)		/		S²		/			/					
2041 †		[/]							/					
2042 †	/	/	/I		/I	/		/						
2043 †		/		S³		/								
2044 †		[/]	/			/	/							
2045 †		[/]	[/]	/		/		/						
2046 †			[/]	/										
2047 †		/	[/]	/		/								
2048 †			[/]		[/]	/								
2049 †			/		/			/	/					
2050 †	/III	/	[/]		[/]	/		/	/					B
2051 †		[/]	/	/		/		/	S⁴					
2052 †														

¹ Burnt.   ² Cited as Sundry pp 752–6, 760–4.   ³ Cited as Sundry p 755.   ⁴ Cited at Rev 1.15, by Tischendorf number 144.

Gregory-Aland Number	Editions of the Greek New Testament									Synopses			Luke	Aland Categories
	Nestle-Aland[26]	Bover-O'Callaghan	UBS[3]	MC	UBS[1] = UBS[2]	Merk[9]	Vogels[4]	BFBS[2]	Souter[2]	Synopsis[10]	Huck-Greeven[13]	Orchard	IGNTP	
2053 †	/III	/	/I		/I	/		/	/¹					A
2054 †		/	/		/	[/]								
2055 †		/	/	/		/								
2056 †		/	[/]	/		/			/					
2057 †		/	[/]	/		/			/					
2058 †		/	[/]		[/]	/								
2059 † 2059s		/	/	/		/		/ /	[/]					
2060 †	S²	/	[/]	/		/	/							
2061 †		/				/								
2062 †	/III	/	/	/		/			S³					A
2063⁴ †			/	/										
2064 †		/	/	/		/								
2065 †		/	/I		/I	/								
2066 †		S⁵	/	/										
2067 †	[/]	/	/		/	/		/						
2068 †			/		/									
2069 †	/	/	[/]		[/]	S⁶								
2070		/	[/]	/					/					

¹ Cited at Rev 1.10 by Tischendorf number 146.   ² Sundry at Rev 18.2 but listed in the 7th printing.   ³ Cited as Sundry at Rev 1.10 by Tischendorf number 155 (see Hoskier II p 39). ⁴ Should be deleted according to ANTF III p 12).   ⁵ Cited as a Sundry at Rev 1.19, 2.13. ⁶ Sundry at Rev 2.13.

Gregory-Aland Number	Editions of the Greek New Testament									Synopses			Luke	Aland Categories
	Nestle-Aland²⁶	Bover-O'Callaghan	UBS³	MC	UBS¹ = UBS²	Merk⁹	Vogels⁴	BFBS²	Souter²	Synopsis¹⁰	Huck-Greeven¹³	Orchard	IGNTP	
2071 †		/	/		/				/					
2072 †														
2073 †	/	/	/I		/I	/		/						
2074 †		[/]	[/]		[/]	/								
2075 †		[/]				/								
2076 †			/	/										
2077 †														
2078 †		/	/	/										
2079 †														
2080 †	/	/	[/]	/		/		/						
2081 †		/	/I		/I	/								
2082 †		/	[/]	/		/								
2083 †			/		/	/								
2084¹ †			[/]	/		/								
2085 †	M⁷													
2086 †														
2087² †							/							
2088¹ †														

¹ Lost.   ² This number should be deleted according to the *Liste*.

Gregory-Aland Number	Editions of the Greek New Testament									Synopses			Luke	Aland Categories
	Nestle-Aland[26]	Bover-O'Callaghan	UBS[3]	MC	UBS[1] = UBS[2]	Merk[9]	Vogels[4]	BFBS[2]	Souter[2]	Synopsis[10]	Huck-Greeven[13]	Orchard	IGNTP	
2089														
2090[1]	M													
2091 †		/	/		/				/					
2092 †														
2093[2] †		[/]												
2094[3]														
2095 †														
2096 †	M												/	
2097 †														
2098 †	M													
2099 †														
2100 †														
2101 †														
2102 †														
2103 †														
2104 †			[/]	/										
2105 †														
2106 †														

[1] This number should be deleted according to the *Liste*.   [2] Burnt.   [3] This number should be deleted according to the *Liste*.

Gregory-Aland Number	Editions of the Greek New Testament									Synopses		Luke	Aland Categories
	Nestle-Aland²⁶	Bover-O'Callaghan	UBS³	MC	UBS¹ = UBS²	Merk⁹	Vogels⁴	BFBS²	Souter²	Synopsis¹⁰	Huck-Greeven¹³	Orchard	IGNTP	
2107 †														
2108 †														
2109 †														
2110¹ †														C
2111 †	M⁷													
2112 †														
2113 †														
2114² †														
2115³ †														
2116³ †														
2117³ †														
2118³ †														
2119 †	M													
2120 †														
2121 †														
2122 †														
2123 †														
2124 †														

¹ This number should be deleted according to the *Liste*.   ² This ms. is modern Greek and should be deleted (see ANTF III p 12).   ³ Lost.

Gregory-Aland Number	Editions of the Greek New Testament									Synopses		Luke	Aland Categories
	Nestle-Aland[26]	Bover-O'Callaghan	UBS[3]	MC	UBS[1] = UBS[2]	Merk[9]	Vogels[4]	BFBS[2]	Souter[2]	Synopsis[10]	Huck-Greeven[13]	Orchard	IGNTP	
2125 †	M		[/]	/					(S)[1]					
2126 †	M													
2127 †	/	/	/I		/I	/								B (p) E (eac)
2128[2] †														
2129 †														
2130 †														
2131 †			/	/										
2132 †	M													
2133 †	M													
2134 †														
2135 †	M									K				
C 2136 †														
2137 †														
2138 †	/	/	/I		/I	/	/	/	/					C (acp) E (r)
2139 †	M									K				
2140 †	M									K				
2141 †	M													
2142 †	M									K				

[1] Cited at 1 Tim 1.17 (Introduction incorrectly lists this ms as extant only for Acts). Not found in the apparatus to Acts. [2] This number should be deleted according to the *Liste*.

Gregory-Aland Number	Editions of the Greek New Testament									Synopses		Luke	Aland Categories
	Nestle-Aland[26]	Bover-O'Callaghan	UBS[3]	MC	UBS[1] = UBS[2]	Merk[9]	Vogels[4]	BFBS[2]	Souter[2]	Synopsis[10]	Huck-Greeven[13]	Orchard	IGNTP	
2143 †	[/]	/	/	/		/								
2144 †	M													
2145 †	/	/	[/]	/		/	/	/		/	S			
2146 †														
2147 †	/	/	[/]	/		/	/	/	/	K				C (c) E (eap)
2148 †	[/]		/I		/I						S			
2149 (= 566)														
2150 (= 1346)														
2151 (= l1019)														
2152 (= 609)														
2153 (= 1209)														
2154 (= 1338)														
2155 (= 1334)														
2156 (= 925)														
2157 (= 1329)														
2158 (= 1206)														
2159 (? = l1101)														
2160	M													

Gregory-Aland Number	Editions of the Greek New Testament									Synopses		Luke		Aland Categories
	Nestle-Aland[26]	Bover-O'Callaghan	UBS[3]	MC	UBS[1] = UBS[2]	Merk[9]	Vogels[4]	BFBS[2]	Souter[2]	Synopsis[10]	Huck-Greeven[13]	Orchard	IGNTP	
2161 (= 938)														
2162 (= 1891)														
2163 (= 1352)														
2164 (= 712)														
2165 (= 928)														
2166 (= 951)														
2167 (= 1238)														
2168 (= 903)														
2169 (= 1348)														
2170 (= 1336)														
2171[1]														
2172 †	M													
2173 †	M													
2174 †			/I		/I									
2175 †	M									K				
2176 †	M									K				
2177 †	M									K				
2178 †	M									K				

[1] Number unassigned.

Gregory-Aland Number	Editions of the Greek New Testament									Synopses			Luke	Aland Categories
	Nestle-Aland²⁶	Bover-O'Callaghan	UBS³	MC	UBS¹ = UBS²	Merk⁹	Vogels⁴	BFBS²	Souter²	Synopsis¹⁰	Huck-Greeven¹³	Orchard	IGNTP	
2179 †														
2180 †		/	[/]	/		[/]								
2181 †	M									K				
2182 †										K				
2183 †	M		[/]	/										
2184 †														
2185¹ †														
2186 †		[/]	[/]	/			/		/					
2187 †	M⁷													
2188 †														
2189 †	M													
2190 †														
2191 †	M										[/]			
2192 †														
2193² † F1?		/	[/]		[/]	/						/		C
2194 †														
2195														
2196 †			[/]	/					/					

¹ Not a continuous text ms. Therefore to be deleted according to ANTF III p 12.   ² Lost.

Gregory-Aland Number	Editions of the Greek New Testament									Synopses		Luke		Aland Categories
	Nestle-Aland[26]	Bover-O'Callaghan	UBS[3]	MC	UBS[1] = UBS[2]	Merk[9]	Vogels[4]	BFBS[2]	Souter[2]	Synopsis[10]	Huck-Greeven[13]	Orchard	IGNTP	
2197 †														C
2198[1] †														
2199 †	M													
C 2200 †					[/]									C (ea pc) E (r)
C 2201 †														
2202[2] †														
2203 †														
2204 †														
2205 †														
2206† (——)														
2207 †														
2208[3]														
2209[1] †														
2210 † (= l1908)														
2211 †														
2212 † (= l2049)														
2213[1] †														
2214[1] †														

[1] Lost.　　[2] Not a continuous text ms. Therefore to be deleted.　　[3] Illegible.

Gregory-Aland Number	Editions of the Greek New Testament									Synopses			Luke	Aland Categories
	Nestle-Aland[26]	Bover-O'Callaghan	UBS[3]	MC	UBS[1] = UBS[2]	Merk[9]	Vogels[4]	BFBS[2]	Souter[2]	Synopsis[10]	Huck-Greeven[13]	Orchard	IGNTP	
2215[1] †														
2216[1] †														
2217 †														
2218 †	M													
2219 (= 1715)														
2220 †														
2221 †	M													
2222[2]														
2223[1] †														
2224 †														
2225[1]														
2226[1] †														
2227[1] †														
2228[1] †														
2229 †														
2230[1] †														
2231[1] †														
2232[1] †														

[1] Lost.   [2] Part lost.

Gregory-Aland Number	Editions of the Greek New Testament									Synopses			Luke	Aland Categories
	Nestle-Aland[26]	Bover-O'Callaghan	UBS[3]	MC	UBS[1] = UBS[2]	Merk[9]	Vogels[4]	BFBS[2]	Souter[2]	Synopsis[10]	Huck-Greeven[13]	Orchard	IGNTP	
2233[1] †														
2234[1] †														
2235[1] †														
2236 †	M													
2237 †														
2238 †														
2239[1] †														
2240 †														
2241 (= l1390)														
2242														
2243 †														
2244 †														
2245 †														
2246 †														
2247 †														
2248 †			[/]	/										
2249[1] †														
2250[1] †														

[1] Lost.

Gregory-Aland Number	Editions of the Greek New Testament									Synopses			Luke	Aland Categories
	Nestle-Aland[26]	Bover-O'Callaghan	UBS[3]	MC	UBS[1] = UBS[2]	Merk[9]	Vogels[4]	BFBS[2]	Souter[2]	Synopsis[10]	Huck-Greeven[13]	Orchard	IGNTP	
2251 †														
2252 †														
2253 †														
2254 †		S^1	/	/										
2255 †														
2256 †			[/]	[/]										
2257^2 †														
2258 †			[/]	/		S^3			/					
2259 †		[/]				/								
2260 †														
2261 †	M													
2262^2 †														
2263 †														
2264^2														
2265 †														
2266 †	M									K				
2267	M^7													
2268 †														

¹ Sundry in Rev *passim* (see Card Insert).   ² Lost.   ³ Probably a Sundry at Rev 6.1, cited by Tischendorf number 217.

Gregory-Aland Number	Editions of the Greek New Testament									Synopses			Luke	Aland Categories
	Nestle-Aland[26]	Bover-O'Callaghan	UBS[3]	MC	UBS[1] = UBS[2]	Merk[9]	Vogels[4]	BFBS[2]	Souter[2]	Synopsis[10]	Huck-Greeven[13]	Orchard	IGNTP	
2269														
2270 (= 2311)														
2271[1] †														
2272 (= 1826)														
2273 †	M													
2274														
2275 †	M													
2276														
2277 †	M													
2278 †														
2279 †														
2280 †														
2281 †	M									K				
2282 †														
2283 †														
2284 †														
2285 †														
2286 †		/	/	/		/								

[1] Lost.

Gregory-Aland Number	Editions of the Greek New Testament									Synopses			Luke	Aland Categories
	Nestle-Aland[26]	Bover-O'Callaghan	UBS[3]	MC	UBS[1] = UBS[2]	Merk[9]	Vogels[4]	BFBS[2]	Souter[2]	Synopsis[10]	Huck-Greeven[13]	Orchard	IGNTP	
2287 †														
<u>2288</u> †														
2289 †	M													
2290 †														
2291 †														
2292 †														
2293 (= 1282)														
2294 (= 2466)														
2295 †	M													
2296 †														
<u>2297</u> †														
<u>2298</u> †	/IV c [/] ap	/	/	/		/	/	/	/					C
2299[1] †														
2300[1] †	M[7]													
2301[1]														
2302 †		/	/		/	/			/					
2303 †	M													
2304 †														

[1] Present whereabouts unknown.

Gregory-Aland Number	Editions of the Greek New Testament									Synopses			Luke	Aland Categories
	Nestle-Aland[26]	Bover-O'Callaghan	UBS[3]	MC	UBS[1] = UBS[2]	Merk[9]	Vogels[4]	BFBS[2]	Souter[2]	Synopsis[10]	Huck-Greeven[13]	Orchard	IGNTP	
2305		/				S[1]		/	/					
2306 a b c d	M													
2307	M													
2308[2]														
2309	M[7]													
2310	M													
2311	M													
2312 (= 1435)														
2313														
2314 †														
2315 †														
2316 †														
2317														
2318	/	[/]												
2319[2]														
2320[2]														
2321			[/]						/					
2322			[/]					[/]					/	

[1] Sundry at Rev 2.8.   [2] Lost.

Gregory-Aland Number	Editions of the Greek New Testament									Synopses			Luke	Aland Categories
	Nestle-Aland[26]	Bover-O'Callaghan	UBS[3]	MC	UBS[1] = UBS[2]	Merk[9]	Vogels[4]	BFBS[2]	Souter[2]	Synopsis[10]	Huck-Greeven[13]	Orchard	IGNTP	
2323														
2324		S[1]								/				
2325[2]														
2326		S[3]												
2327 (= 1359)														
2328														
2329 †	/III	/	/		/	/		/	S[4]					B
2330[2]														
2331[2]														
2332[2]														
2333 (= 1810)														
2334 (= 1811)														
2335 (= 1802)														
2336 (= 1803)														
2337[2]														
2338[2]														
2339[2]														
2340[2]														

[1] Sundry cited frequently in Mt, Mk and Lk.   [2] Lost.   [3] Sundry at Lk 8.28.   [4] Sundry at Rev 1.14, 15 as Hoskier number 200.

Gregory-Aland Number	Editions of the Greek New Testament									Synopses			Luke	Aland Categories
	Nestle-Aland[26]	Bover-O'Callaghan	UBS[3]	MC	UBS[1] = UBS[2]	Merk[9]	Vogels[4]	BFBS[2]	Souter[2]	Synopsis[10]	Huck-Greeven[13]	Orchard	IGNTP	
2341[1]														
2342[1]														
2343[1]														
2344	/IV r / [a] c [p]	[/]	/I		/I	/		/						A (r) B (c) C (ap)
2345														
2346		S[2]												
2347 (= 1701)														
2348 (= 2098)														
2349 (= 1795)		[/]				/								
2350														
2351 †	/III	/	/		/	/								C
C 2352	M	/			[/]									
2353	M													
2354														
2355	M										K	S		
2356	M										K			
2357														
2358														

[1] Lost.   [2] Sundry at Mt 19.3, 20.23, 27.11.

Gregory-Aland Number	Editions of the Greek New Testament									Synopses		Luke		Aland Categories
	Nestle-Aland[26]	Bover-O'Callaghan	UBS[3]	MC	UBS[1] = UBS[2]	Merk[9]	Vogels[4]	BFBS[2]	Souter[2]	Synopsis[10]	Huck-Greeven[13]	Orchard	IGNTP	
2359[1]														
2360														
2361														
2362														
2363														
2364														
2365														
2366 (= 895)														
2367														
2368														
2369														
2370														
2371														
2372													/	
2373	M									K				
2374														C (c) E (eap)
2375														
2376	M													

[1] This number should be deleted according to the *Liste*.

Gregory-Aland Number	Editions of the Greek New Testament									Synopses			Luke	Aland Categories
	Nestle-Aland[26]	Bover-O'Callaghan	UBS[3]	MC	UBS[1] = UBS[2]	Merk[9]	Vogels[4]	BFBS[2]	Souter[2]	Synopsis[10]	Huck-Greeven[13]	Orchard	IGNTP	
2377	/IV													C
2378	M													
2379 (= l2004)														
2380	M													
2381 †	M									K				
2382	M													
2383														
2384														
2385														
2386	M		[/]	/	[/]					[/]				
2387														
2388														
2389	M[7]													
2390	M													
2391														
2392														
2393 (= l826)														
2394														

Gregory-Aland Number	Editions of the Greek New Testament									Synopses			Luke	Aland Categories
	Nestle-Aland[26]	Bover-O'Callaghan	UBS[3]	MC	UBS[1] = UBS[2]	Merk[9]	Vogels[4]	BFBS[2]	Souter[2]	Synopsis[10]	Huck-Greeven[13]	Orchard	IGNTP	
2395														
2396														
2397														
2398														
2399													/	
2400														C (ep) E (ac)
2401			[/]	/				/						
2402[1]														
2403														
2404														
2405														
2406														
2407														
2408														
2409	M²													
2410 (= 2266)														
2411														
2412			/I		/I			/						C (c) E? (ap)

[1] To be deleted according to the *Liste*.   ² Deleted in the 7th printing.

Gregory-Aland Number	Editions of the Greek New Testament									Synopses			Luke	Aland Categories
	Nestle-Aland[26]	Bover-O'Callaghan	UBS[3]	MC	UBS[1] = UBS[2]	Merk[9]	Vogels[4]	BFBS[2]	Souter[2]	Synopsis[10]	Huck-Greeven[13]	Orchard	IGNTP	
2413 (= 2268)														
2414														
2415														
2416[1]														
2417 (= 2460)														
2418														
2419														
2420														
2421														
2422														
2423	M						/							
2424	M													
2425	M													
2426														
2427														A
2428														
2429														
2430		[/]	[/]	/		/								

[1] Not a continuous text ms. Therefore to be deleted.

| Gregory-Aland Number | Editions of the Greek New Testament | | | | | | | | | Synopses | | Luke | Aland Categories |
	Nestle-Aland[26]	Bover-O'Callaghan	UBS[3]	MC	UBS[1] = UBS[2]	Merk[9]	Vogels[4]	BFBS[2]	Souter[2]	Synopsis[10]	Huck-Greeven[13]	Orchard	IGNTP	
2431	M													
2432			/I		/I									
2433[1]														
2434														
2435														
2436														
2437														
2438														
2439														
2440														
2441	M													
2442														
2443 (= 2121)														
2444														
2445														
2446														
2447	M[7]													
2448														

[1] To be deleted (ANTF III p 13).

Gregory-Aland Number	Editions of the Greek New Testament									Synopses			Luke	Aland Categories
	Nestle-Aland[26]	Bover-O'Callaghan	UBS[3]	MC	UBS[1] = UBS[2]	Merk[9]	Vogels[4]	BFBS[2]	Souter[2]	Synopsis[10]	Huck-Greeven[13]	Orchard	IGNTP	
2449[1]														
2450[1]	M[7]													
2451														
2452														
2453[2]														
2454														
2455														
2456														
2457														
2458														
2459														
2460														
2461[3]														
2462[3]														
2463[3]														
2464	/II p /IV ac		/	/										B
2465														
2466 †	M													

[1] To be deleted — modern Greek ms. (see ANTF III p 12).   [2] Not a continuous text ms. Therefore to be deleted.   [3] Lost. Possibly 2461 was a lectionary text.

Gregory-Aland Number	Editions of the Greek New Testament									Synopses		Luke	Aland Categories
	Nestle-Aland[26]	Bover-O'Callaghan	UBS[3]	MC	UBS[1] = UBS[2]	Merk[9]	Vogels[4]	BFBS[2]	Souter[2]	Synopsis[10]	Huck-Greeven[13]	Orchard	IGNTP	
2467														
2468	M													
2469														
2470														
2471														
2472														
2473[1]														
2474														
2475	M													
2476														
2477														
2478														
2479	M													
2480														
2481[2]														
2482 †														
2483	M[3]													
2484	M													

[1] Lost.   [2] Not a continuous text ms. Therefore to be deleted.   [3] Deleted in the 7th printing.

	Gregory-Aland Number	Editions of the Greek New Testament									Synopses			Luke	Aland Categories
		Nestle-Aland²⁶	Bover-O'Callaghan	UBS³	MC	UBS¹ = UBS²	Merk⁹	Vogels⁴	BFBS²	Souter²	Synopsis¹⁰	Huck-Greeven¹³	Orchard	IGNTP	
	2485														
	2486														
	2487													/	
	2488														
	2489														
	2490	M													
	2491	M													
	2492	/		/I		/I									C (cp) / E? (ea)
	2493														
C	2494										K				
C	2495	/II acp / er		/I		/I									C
	2496	M									K				
	2497										K				
	2498														
	2499	M									K				
	2500	M													
	2501	M													
	2502	M									K				

Gregory-Aland Number	Editions of the Greek New Testament									Synopses			Luke	Aland Categories
	Nestle-Aland²⁶	Bover-O'Callaghan	UBS³	MC	UBS¹ = UBS²	Merk⁹	Vogels⁴	BFBS²	Souter²	Synopsis¹⁰	Huck-Greeven¹³	Orchard	IGNTP	
2503	M									K				
2504 (= 1176)														
2505														
2506														
2507	M⁷													
2508¹														
2509¹														
2510¹														
2511														
2512														
2513														
2514														
2515														
2516														C (ep) E (ac)
2517														
2518														
2519														
2520														

¹ Lost.

Gregory-Aland Number	Editions of the Greek New Testament									Synopses			Luke	Aland Categories
	Nestle-Aland[26]	Bover-O'Callaghan	UBS[3]	MC	UBS[1] = UBS[2]	Merk[9]	Vogels[4]	BFBS[2]	Souter[2]	Synopsis[10]	Huck-Greeven[13]	Orchard	IGNTP	
2521														
2522														
2523														C
2524														
2525														
2526														
2527														
2528	.													
2529														
2530														
2531[1]														
2532	M													
2533											S			
2534	M													
2535														
2536	M													
2537														
2538 (= 2285)														

[1] Lost.

Gregory-Aland Number	Editions of the Greek New Testament									Synopses			Luke	Aland Categories
	Nestle-Aland[26]	Bover-O'Callaghan	UBS[3]	MC	UBS[1] = UBS[2]	Merk[9]	Vogels[4]	BFBS[2]	Souter[2]	Synopsis[10]	Huck-Greeven[13]	Orchard	IGNTP	
2539														
2540	M													
2541														C (c) E? (ap)
2542													/	C
2543														
2544														C (p) E (c)
2545	M													
2546														
2547	M													
2548														
2549	M													
2550														
2551														
2552	M													
2553														
C 2554[1]	M													
2555[1]														
2556 (= 1873)														

[1] Lost.

| Gregory-Aland Number | Editions of the Greek New Testament | | | | | | | | | Synopses | | Luke | Aland Categories |
	Nestle-Aland[26]	Bover-O'Callaghan	UBS[3]	MC	UBS[1] = UBS[2]	Merk[9]	Vogels[4]	BFBS[2]	Souter[2]	Synopsis[10]	Huck-Greeven[13]	Orchard	IGNTP	
2557														
2558	M													
2559														
2560 (= l2016)														
2561														
2562														
2563														
2564 (= l2022)														
2565 (= l2023)														
2566 (= l2024)														
2567														
2568	M													
2569														
2570														
2571														
2572	M													
2573 †	M													
2574														

| Gregory-Aland Number | Editions of the Greek New Testament | | | | | | | | | Synopses | | | Luke | Aland Categories |
	Nestle-Aland[26]	Bover-O'Callaghan	UBS[3]	MC	UBS[1] = UBS[2]	Merk[9]	Vogels[4]	BFBS[2]	Souter[2]	Synopsis[10]	Huck-Greeven[13]	Orchard	IGNTP	
2575														
2576			[/]	/										
2577														
2578	M[7]													
2579	M													
2580 (= 837)														
2581	M[7]													
2582														
2583														
2584	M													
2585[1] †														
2586														
2587	M													
2588														
2589														
2590														
2591														
2592														

[1] Illegible.

Gregory-Aland Number	Editions of the Greek New Testament									Synopses			Luke	Aland Categories
	Nestle-Aland[26]	Bover-O'Callaghan	UBS[3]	MC	UBS[1] = UBS[2]	Merk[9]	Vogels[4]	BFBS[2]	Souter[2]	Synopsis[10]	Huck-Greeven[13]	Orchard	IGNTP	
2593	M[7]													
2594														
2595 †			[/]		[/]									
2596														C
2597														
2598														
2599														
2600	M[7]													
2601														
2602 (= 851)														
2603														
2604														
2605														
2606[1]														
2607														
2608														
2609 (= 2474)														
2610														

[1] This number should be deleted according to the Liste.

| Gregory-Aland Number | Editions of the Greek New Testament | | | | | | | | | Synopses | | Luke | Aland Categories |
	Nestle-Aland[26]	Bover-O'Callaghan	UBS[3]	MC	UBS[1] = UBS[2]	Merk[9]	Vogels[4]	BFBS[2]	Souter[2]	Synopsis[10]	Huck-Greeven[13]	Orchard	IGNTP	
2611 (= 677)														
2612														
2613													/	
2614														
2615														
2616														
2617 (= 2491)														
2618 (= 927)														
2619	M													
2620														
2621														
2622[1] †														
2623														
2624														
2625														
2626	M													
2627	M													
2628 (= l2127)														

[1] Lost.

Gregory-Aland Number	Editions of the Greek New Testament									Synopses			Luke	Aland Categories
	Nestle-Aland[26]	Bover-O'Callaghan	UBS[3]	MC	UBS[1] = UBS[2]	Merk[9]	Vogels[4]	BFBS[2]	Souter[2]	Synopsis[10]	Huck-Greeven[13]	Orchard	IGNTP	
2629	M													
2630														
2631	M[7]													
2632														
2633	.													
2634														
2635														
2636	M[7]													
2637														
2638														
2639	M													
2640 (= 2108)														
2641														
2642														
2643													/	
2644														
2645														
2646[1] †														

[1] Mis-numbered as 2246 on *Liste* p 371.

Gregory-Aland Number	Editions of the Greek New Testament									Synopses		Luke		Aland Categories
	Nestle-Aland[26]	Bover-O'Callaghan	UBS[3]	MC	UBS[1] = UBS[2]	Merk[9]	Vogels[4]	BFBS[2]	Souter[2]	Synopsis[10]	Huck-Greeven[13]	Orchard	IGNTP	
2647														
2648														
2649														
2650														
2651														
2652														C (c) E (p)
2653														
2654														
2655														
2656														
2657	M													
2658														
2659														
2660														
2661														
2662														
2663														
2664														

| Gregory-Aland Number | Editions of the Greek New Testament | | | | | | | | | Synopses | | Luke | Aland Categories |
	Nestle-Aland[26]	Bover-O'Callaghan	UBS[3]	MC	UBS[1] = UBS[2]	Merk[9]	Vogels[4]	BFBS[2]	Souter[2]	Synopsis[10]	Huck-Greeven[13]	Orchard	IGNTP	
2665[1]														
2666[1]	M													
2667														
2668	M													
2669														
2670														
2671	M													
2672														
2673														
2674														
2675	M													
2676														
2677														
2678														
2679														
2680														
2681														
2682														

[1] See p 215.

Gregory-Aland Number	Editions of the Greek New Testament									Synopses			Luke	Aland Categories
	Nestle-Aland[26]	Bover-O'Callaghan	UBS[3]	MC	UBS[1] = UBS[2]	Merk[9]	Vogels[4]	BFBS[2]	Souter[2]	Synopsis[10]	Huck-Greeven[13]	Orchard	IGNTP	
2683														
2684														
2685			[/]	/										
2686														
2687														
2688														
2689														
2690	M		[/]	/										
2691	M													
2692														
2693														
2694														
2695														
2696	M													
2697														
2698	M													
2699	M													
2700	M													

Gregory-Aland Number	Editions of the Greek New Testament									Synopses		Luke	Aland Categories
	Nestle-Aland[26]	Bover-O'Callaghan	UBS[3]	MC	UBS[1] = UBS[2]	Merk[9]	Vogels[4]	BFBS[2]	Souter[2]	Synopsis[10]	Huck-Greeven[13]	Orchard	IGNTP	
2701														
2702														
2703														
2704	M													
2705														
2706														
2707														
2708														
2709														
2710														
2711	M[7]													
2712	M													
2713														
2714														
2715														
2716	M													
2717														
2718														C

Gregory-Aland Number	Editions of the Greek New Testament									Synopses		Luke		
	Nestle-Aland[26]	Bover-O'Callaghan	UBS[3]	MC	UBS[1] = UBS[2]	Merk[9]	Vogels[4]	BFBS[2]	Souter[2]	Synopsis[10]	Huck-Greeven[13]	Orchard	IGNTP	Aland Categories
2719														
2720														
2721														
2722														
2723	M													
2724														
2725														
2726														
2727														
2728														
2729														
2730														
2731														
2732														
2733														
2734														
2735														
2736														

Gregory-Aland Number	Editions of the Greek New Testament									Synopses			Luke	Aland Categories
	Nestle-Aland[26]	Bover-O'Callaghan	UBS[3]	MC	UBS[1] = UBS[2]	Merk[9]	Vogels[4]	BFBS[2]	Souter[2]	Synopsis[10]	Huck-Greeven[13]	Orchard	IGNTP	
2737														
2738														
2739			[/]	/										
2740														
2741														
2742														
2743														
2744														C
2745														
2746	M													
2747														
2748														
2749														
2750														
2751														
2752														
2753														
2754														

Gregory-Aland Number	Editions of the Greek New Testament									Synopses			Luke	Aland Categories
	Nestle-Aland[26]	Bover-O'Callaghan	UBS[3]	MC	UBS[1] = UBS[2]	Merk[9]	Vogels[4]	BFBS[2]	Souter[2]	Synopsis[10]	Huck-Greeven[13]	Orchard	IGNTP	
2755														
2756														
2757													/	
2758														
2759														
2760														
2761	M[7]													
2762														
2763														
2764														
2765														
2766													/	
2767														
2768	/	S[1]	[/]			/[2]					/			
2769														
2770														
2771														
2772														

[1] Cited frequently in Jn — as 053 in Apparatus but as X[b] on Card Insert.   [2] Cited as X[b].

Gregory-Aland Number	Editions of the Greek New Testament									Synopses		Luke	Aland Categories
	Nestle-Aland[26]	Bover-O'Callaghan	UBS[3]	MC	UBS[1] = UBS[2]	Merk[9]	Vogels[4]	BFBS[2]	Souter[2]	Synopsis[10]	Huck-Greeven[13]	Orchard	IGNTP	
2773														
2774														
2775														
2776														
2777														
2778														
2779														
2780														
2781														
2782														
2783														
2784	M													
2785	M													
2786														
2787														
2788														
2789														
2790														

SECTION V

LECTIONARIES

Gregory-Aland Number	Editions of the Greek New Testament									Synopses		Luke		Aland Categories
	Nestle-Aland26	Bover-O'Callaghan	UBS3	MC	UBS1 = UBS2	Merk9	Vogels4	BFBS2	Souter2	Synopsis10	Huck-Greeven13	Orchard	IGNTP	
l 1		[/]			I						S			
l 2											S			
l 3											S			
l 4			/								S			
l 5			/								S			
l 6			/				/2				S			
l 7			/								S			
l 8											S			
l 9											S			
l 10			/I								S	/		
l 11			/								S			
l 12			/I								S	/		
l 13			/								S			
l 14			/								S			
l 15			/								S			
l 16											S			
l 17			/								S			
l·18			/								S			

[1] Throughout this section, UBS1 = UBS2 = UBS3, which accounts for the blank entries in this column.   [2] Cited at I Pet 2.23.

Gregory-Aland Number	Editions of the Greek New Testament									Synopses			Luke	Aland Categories
	Nestle-Aland[26]	Bover-O'Callaghan	UBS[3]	MC	UBS[1] = UBS[2]	Merk[9]	Vogels[4]	BFBS[2]	Souter[2]	Synopsis[10]	Huck-Greeven[13]	Orchard	IGNTP	
l 19			/								S			
l 20			/								S			
l 21			/								S			
l 22											S			
l 24			/								S			
l 26			/								S			
l 27											S			
l 28											S			
l 29											S			
l 30											S			
l 31			/								S			
l 32	[/]		/I								S		/	
l 33[1] (= l 563)			/								S			
l 34		[/]	/								S			
l 36		[/]	/								S			
l 37			/								S			
l 38			/								S			
l 39											S			

[1] See K. Junack, 'Zu den griechischen Lektionaren und ihrer Überlieferung der katholischen Briefe' in K. Aland, *Die Alten Übersetzungen des Neuen Testaments, die Kirchenväterzitate und Lektionare* (Berlin, New York 1972) = ANTF V pp 488–590 esp. pp 500 f.

Gregory-Aland Number	Editions of the Greek New Testament									Synopses			Luke	Aland Categories
	Nestle-Aland[26]	Bover-O'Callaghan	UBS[3]	MC	UBS[1] = UBS[2]	Merk[9]	Vogels[4]	BFBS[2]	Souter[2]	Synopsis[10]	Huck-Greeven[13]	Orchard	IGNTP	
l 40											S			
l 42											S			
l 44	/		/								S			
l 46											S			
l 47			/							/	S			
l 48		/	/								S		/	
l 49			/								S			
l 50											S			
l 51			/								S			
l 52											S			
l 53			/								S			
l 54			/								S			
l 55			/								S			
l 57			/											
l 59			/I											
l 60			/I								S			
l 62			/											
l 63			/								S			

Gregory-Aland Number	Editions of the Greek New Testament									Synopses			Luke	Aland Categories
	Nestle-Aland[26]	Bover-O'Callaghan	UBS[3]	MC	UBS[1] = UBS[2]	Merk[9]	Vogels[4]	BFBS[2]	Souter[2]	Synopsis[10]	Huck-Greeven[13]	Orchard	IGNTP	
l 64			/								S			
l 67											S			
l 68			/								S			
l 69			/I								S		/I	
l 70			/I								S		/	
l 72											S			
l 76			/I								S		/	
l 77											S			
l 80			/I								S		/	
l 88											S			
l 108											S			
l 118										[/]				
l 124											S			
l 130											S			
l 134											S			
l 135											S			
l 147			/I											
l 148											S			

Gregory-Aland Number	Editions of the Greek New Testament									Synopses			Luke	Aland Categories
	Nestle-Aland²⁶	Bover-O'Callaghan	UBS³	MC	UBS¹ = UBS²	Merk⁹	Vogels⁴	BFBS²	Souter²	Synopsis¹⁰	Huck-Greeven¹³	Orchard	IGNTP	
l 150			/I								S		/	
l 158											S			
l 159			/											
l 164			[/]											
l 174			/											
l 181			/							[/]	S			
l 182										/				
l 183			/							/	S			
l 184		/	/I					/¹			S		/	
l 185	[/]		/I							/	S			
l 187			/								S			
l 191			/											
l 195											S			
l 196											S			
l 210			/											
l 211			/I								S		/	
l 219²			/								S			
l 223			/											

¹ Cited at Jn 4.49.   ² Lost.

Gregory-Aland Number	Editions of the Greek New Testament									Synopses		Orchard	Luke	Aland Categories
	Nestle-Aland26	Bover-O'Callaghan	UBS3	MC	UBS1 = UBS2	Merk9	Vogels4	BFBS2	Souter2	Synopsis10	Huck-Greeven13		IGNTP	
l 224			/											
l 225			/											
l 226			/											
l 227			/											
l 230			[/]											
l 238											S			
l 241			[/]								S			
l 243		[/]												
l 246											S			
l 251											S			
l 253			/								S		/	
l 258											S			
l 259											S			
l 260[1]			/								S			
l 276			[/]											
l 292			/I										/	
l 299			/I								S		/	
l 302			/								S			

[1] Lost.

Gregory-Aland Number	Editions of the Greek New Testament									Synopses			Luke	Aland Categories
	Nestle-Aland[26]	Bover-O'Callaghan	UBS[3]	MC	UBS[1] = UBS[2]	Merk[9]	Vogels[4]	BFBS[2]	Souter[2]	Synopsis[10]	Huck-Greeven[13]	Orchard	IGNTP	
l 303			/I								S			
l 305			/								S			
l 309			/I								S			
l 313			/I								S			
l 331			[/]								S			
l 333			/I								S		/I	
l 351 †														
l 360											S			
l 368			/											
l 372			/											
l 374			/I								S			
l 381			/I											
l 382											S			
l 490			/I								S			
l 513													/I	
l 524													/	
l 543											S			
l 547			/I								/		/	

Gregory-Aland Number	Editions of the Greek New Testament									Synopses			Luke	Aland Categories
	Nestle-Aland[26]	Bover-O'Callaghan	UBS[3]	MC	UBS[1] = UBS[2]	Merk[9]	Vogels[4]	BFBS[2]	Souter[2]	Synopsis[10]	Huck-Greeven[13]	Orchard	IGNTP	
l 574			[/]											
l 597			/I											
l 598			/I											
l 599			/I											
l 603			/I											
l 611			/											
l 668 †														
l 680			/I											
l 689		[/]												
l 720		[/]												
l 749		[/]												
l 805		[/]	/											
l 806		[/]												
l 807		[/]												
l 808		[/]												
l 809			/I											
l 823			/								S			
l 844		[/]												

| Gregory-Aland Number | Editions of the Greek New Testament | | | | | | | | | Synopses | | Luke | Aland Categories |
	Nestle-Aland²⁶	Bover-O'Callaghan	UBS³	MC	UBS¹ = UBS²	Merk⁹	Vogels⁴	BFBS²	Souter²	Synopsis¹⁰	Huck-Greeven¹³	Orchard	IGNTP	
l 845		[/]	/								S			
l 847			/I											
l 848		[/]												
l 850			/								S			
l 852													/I	
l 853													/I	
l 854			/								S		/	
l 855			/											
l 859													/	
l 861			/								S			
l 867													/I	
l 871			/								S			
l 883					I¹						S¹			
l 890													/	
l 932											S			
l 950			/I								S		/	
l 952			[/]								S			
l 956			/								S			

¹ This ms. is now known as *l* 1761 q.v.

Gregory-Aland Number	Editions of the Greek New Testament									Synopses			Luke	Aland Categories
	Nestle-Aland²⁶	Bover-O'Callaghan	UBS³	MC	UBS¹ = UBS²	Merk⁹	Vogels⁴	BFBS²	Souter²	Synopsis¹⁰	Huck-Greeven¹³	Orchard	IGNTP	
l 961		[/]	[/]			/								
l 963¹	/I		/							/	[/]			
l 965											[/]			
l 983			[/]											
l 991													/I	
l 995													/I	
l 997			/								S			
l 1014			[/]											
l 1016													/	
l 1021			/I											
l 1043		/	/		/²						S			
l 1056 (= 0114)													/	
l 1074													/	
l 1084			/								S		/I	
l 1127			/I								S		/	
l 1141			/											
l 1153a			/I											
l 1231			/I								S		/	

¹ In these editions cited as 0100, which number subsumes 0195. This is not noted by H Bachmann, Münster *Bericht* (1982), but by K and B Aland, *Der Text Des Neuen Testaments*, p 127, cf p 132.
² Merk uses the obsolete number l 1596 (cf. Bover-O'Callaghan p LVII).

Gregory-Aland Number	Editions of the Greek New Testament									Synopses		Luke	Aland Categories
	Nestle-Aland[26]	Bover-O'Callaghan	UBS[3]	MC	UBS[1] = UBS[2]	Merk[9]	Vogels[4]	BFBS[2]	Souter[2]	Synopsis[10]	Huck-Greeven[13]	Orchard	IGNTP	
l 1276		[/]												
l 1291			[/]											
l 1294			/											
l 1298			/I											
l 1300			[/]											
l 1311			[/]											
l 1345		[/]	/								S			
l 1346			/								S			
l 1347		[/]									S			
l 1348		[/]	/								S			
l 1349		/	/								S			
l 1350			/								S			
l 1353		[/]	/								S			
l 1354		[/]									S			
l 1355 †											S			
l 1356			/I											
l 1357			/											
l 1364			/I											

Gregory-Aland Number	Editions of the Greek New Testament									Synopses			Luke	Aland Categories
	Nestle-Aland[26]	Bover-O'Callaghan	UBS[3]	MC	UBS[1] = UBS[2]	Merk[9]	Vogels[4]	BFBS[2]	Souter[2]	Synopsis[10]	Huck-Greeven[13]	Orchard	IGNTP	
l 1365			/I											
l 1384 †														
l 1385 †														
l 1386 †														
l 1417 †														
l 1439			/I											
l 1440			/											
l 1441			/I											
l 1443			/I											
l 1485 †		[/]												
l 1504¹			/											
l 1536											S			
l 1564			/								S			
l 1566 (= l 1602)		[/]			/									
l 1575	/		/²											
l 1578			/								S			
l 1579			/I								S		/	
l 1590			/I											

¹ Lost.   ² Cited as 0129 at I Cor 1.28. This number subsumes 0203. See H Bachmann, Münster *Bericht* (1982) p 70; K and B Aland, *Der Text Des Neuen Testaments*, p 130, cf p 132.

Gregory-Aland Number	Editions of the Greek New Testament									Synopses			Luke	Aland Categories
	Nestle-Aland[26]	Bover-O'Callaghan	UBS[3]	MC	UBS[1] = UBS[2]	Merk[9]	Vogels[4]	BFBS[2]	Souter[2]	Synopsis[10]	Huck-Greeven[13]	Orchard	IGNTP	
l 1599			/I								S		/	
l 1602	/		/							S¹	S			
l 1604				S²							S			
l 1610			[/]I											
l 1613			/											
l 1623											S			
l 1627			/I								S		/	
l 1629											S			
l 1632			/								S			
l 1634			/I								S		/	
l 1635			[/]											
l 1642			/I								S		/	
l 1663			/I								S		/	
l 1693											S			
l 1749											S			
l 1750													/I	
l 1761			/I³										/	
l 1837											S			

¹ Cited at the conclusion to Mark.   ² Sundry at Mk 15.34 as 0192 q.v.   ³ In UBS¹·² = *l* 883 q.v.

Gregory-Aland Number	Editions of the Greek New Testament									Synopses		Luke	Aland Categories
	Nestle-Aland[26]	Bover-O'Callaghan	UBS[3]	MC	UBS[1] = UBS[2]	Merk[9]	Vogels[4]	BFBS[2]	Souter[2]	Synopsis[10]	Huck-Greeven[13]	Orchard	IGNTP	
l 1963											S			
l 2071		[/]												
l 2072		[/]												
l 2073		[/]												

Lectionaries in Tischendorf[8]

Manuscripts in the above list are, where indicated by underlining, known to Tischendorf[8] or rather to the *Prolegomena* to that text by Gregory. Now follows a complete list of the lectionaries found in that *Prolegomena* with the numbers translated where necessary to the current Gregory-Aland system.[1] Where the Tischendorf number differs this is given in parentheses. It is uncertain how many of the mss. included by Gregory in his *Prolegomena* were known to Tischendorf, but what is certain is that he made very little use of them in his 8th edition. Their inclusion here is intended to underline how few lectionaries have been included in printed editions of the Greek New Testament even though large numbers have been classified for one hundred years or longer.

(a) The following are listed by Gregory *Prolegomena* and have been abstracted from Sigelkonkordanz I in Aland, *Kurzgefasste Liste* with corrections. Those entries marked in the *Liste* with a query (pp. 321–333) are itemized separately under (b) below. Those marked in the *Liste* with a dash (pp. 321–333) have been ignored.

A query in the following columns indicates *either* a discrepancy between Gregory *Prolegomena* and the *Liste* regarding the contents of a lectionary[2] *or* my doubts in interpreting the conversion table.

Gregory gospel lectionary numbers correspond to Tischendorf's evl numbers unless otherwise stated.

[1] In the list e (or evl) refers to a lectionary containing the gospels, a (or apl) = apostolos, to a lectionary containing readings from the Acts or epistles.
[2] An attempted solution appears under (c) below.

---

l 1	e	
l 2	e	
l 3	e	
l 4	e	
l 5	e	
l 6	ea	(a = apl 1)
l 7	e	
l 8	e	
l 9	e	
l 10	e	
l 11	e	
l 12	e	
l 13	e	
l 14	e	(also = e 322)
l 15	e	
l 16	e	
l 17	e	
l 18	e	
l 19	e	
l 20	e	

l 21	e	
l 22	e	
l 23	a	(= apl 2)
l 24	e	
l 25	e	
l 26	ea	? (a = apl 28)
l 27	e	
l 28	e	
l 29	e	
l 30	ea	(a = apl 265)
l 31	e	
l 32	e	
l 34	e	
l 35	e	
l 36	e	
l 37	ea	(a = apl 7)
l 38	a	(= apl 5)
l 39	a	(= apl 11)
l 40	e	
l 41	e	

l 42 e

l 43 e

l 44 ea (a = apl 8)

l 45 e

l 46 e

l 47 e

l 48 e

l 49 e

l 50 e

l 51 e

l 52 ea (a = apl 16)

l 53 ea (a = apl 17)

l 54 ea (a = apl 18)

l 55 ea (a = apl 19)

l 56 ea (a = apl 20)

l 57 ea (a = ?)

l 58 e

l 59 a   (= apl 13)

l 60 ea (a = apl 12)

l 61 e

l 62 a   (= apl 14)

l 63 e

l 64 e

l 65 e

l 66 e

l 67 e

l 68 e

l 69 e

l 70 c

l 71 e

l 72 e

l 73 e

l 74 e

l 75 e

l 76 e

l 77 e

l 78 e

l 79 e

l 80 e

l 81 e

l 82 ea (a = apl 31)

l 83 ea (a = apl 21)

l 84 ea (a = apl 9)

l 85 ea (a = apl 10)

l 86 e

l 87 e

l 88 e

l 89 e

l 90 e

l 91 e

l 92 ea (a = apl 35)

l 93 ea (a = apl 36)

l 94 ea (a = apl 29)

l 95 e

l 96 ea (a = apl 262)

l 97 ea (a = apl 32)

l 98 e (also = e 325)

l 99 e (also = e 327)

l 100 e (also = e 328)

l 101 e (also = e 321)

l 102 e

l 103 e

l 104 ea (a = apl 47)

l 105 e

l 106 e

l 107 e

l 108 e

l 109 e

l 110 e

l 111 e

l 112 ea (a = apl 48 + apl 4)

l 113 e

l 114 e

l 115 e

l 116 e

l 117 e (also = evl 38)

l 118 e (also = evl 39)

l 119 e

l 120 e

l 121 e

l 122 e

l 123 e

l 124 e

l 125 e

l 126 e

l 127 e

l 128 e

l 129 e

l 130 e

l 131 e

l 132 e   *l* 174 ea (e = evl 259 and evl 257
l 133 ea (a = apl 39)   a = apl 72 and apl 74)
l 134 e   *l* 175 a   (= apl 76)
l 135 e   *l* 176 a   (= apl 77)
l 136 e   *l* 177 a   (= apl 79)
l 137 e   *l* 178 a   (= apl 80)
l 138 e   *l* 179 ea (a = apl 55)
l 139 e   *l* 180 e
l 140 e¹   *l* 181 e
l 141 e   *l* 182 e
l 142 e   *l* 183 e
l 144 a   (= apl 22)   *l* 184 e
l 145 a   (= apl 23)   *l* 185 ea (?a = apl 59)
l 146 e   *l* 186 e
l 147 a   (= apl 25)   *l* 187 e
l 148 a   (= apl 26)   *l* 188 e
l 149 a   (= apl 27)   *l* 189 ea (?a = apl 175)
l 150 e   *l* 190 e
l 151 e   *l* 191 e
l 152 e   *l* 192 e
l 153 a   (= apl 30)   *l* 193 e
l 154 e   *l* 194 e
l 155 e   *l* 195 e
l 156 a   (= apl 33)   *l* 196 e
l 157 e   *l* 197 ea (a = ?)
l 158 a   (= apl 34)   *l* 198 e
l 159 e   *l* 199 e
l 160 a   (= apl 38)   *l* 200 e
l 161 a   (= apl 42)   *l* 201 e
l 162 a   (= apl 45)   *l* 202 e
l 163 a   (= apl 46)   *l* 203 e
l 164 a   (= apl 58)   *l* 204 e
l 165 a   (= apl 60)   *l* 205 e
l 166 a   (= apl 61)   *l* 206 e
l 167 a   (= apl 63)   *l* 207 e
l 168 a   (= apl 64)   *l* 208 e
l 169 a   (= apl 65)   *l* 209 e
l 170 a   (= apl 68)   *l* 210 e
l 171 a   (= apl 70 a)   *l* 211 e
l 172 a   (= apl 75)   *l* 212 e
l 173 a   (= apl 73)   *l* 213 e

---

¹ Lost according to *Liste*.

l 214 e[1]   *l* 255 e
l 215 ea (? a = apl 176)   *l* 256 ea (a = apl 180)
l 216 ea (a = apl 66)   *l* 257 a   (= apl 81)
l 217 e[1]   *l* 258 e
l 218 e[1]   *l* 259 a   (= apl 83)
l 219 e[1]   *l* 260 e[1]
l 220 e   *l* 261 e
l 221 e[1]   *l* 262 e
l 222 e[1]   *l* 263 e
l 223 ea (a = apl 67)   *l* 264 e
l 224 e   *l* 265 e
l 225 e   *l* 266 e
l 226 e   *l* 267 e
l 227 e   *l* 268 e
l 228 ea (a = apl 263)   *l* 269 e
l 229 e   *l* 270 e
l 230 e   *l* 271 e
l 231 e   *l* 272 e
l 232 e   *l* 273 e
l 233 e   *l* 274 ea (a = ?)
l 234 e   *l* 275 e
l 235 e   *l* 276 e
l 236 e   *l* 277 e
l 237 e   *l* 278 e
l 238 e   *l* 279 e
l 239 e   *l* 280 e
l 240 e   *l* 281 e
l 241 ea (a = apl 44 + apl 177)   *l* 282 e
[*l* 242 e   = *l* 1386]   *l* 283 e
l 243 e   *l* 284 e
l 244 e   *l* 285 e[2]
l 245 e   *l* 286 e
l 246 e   *l* 287 ea (a = apl 181)
l 247 e   *l* 288 e
l 248 e   *l* 289 e
l 249 ea (a = apl 69 + apl 178)   *l* 290 ea (a = apl 182)
l 250 ea (a = apl 179)   *l* 291 e
l 251 e   (also = e 567)   *l* 292 e
l 252 e   *l* 293 e
l 253 e   *l* 294 e
l 254 e   *l* 295 e[1]

---

[1] Lost according to *Liste*.
[2] 285[a]: formerly known as *l* 1919. 285[b] = *l* 1920.

l 296 e		*l* 337 e	
l 297 e		*l* 338 e	
l 298 e		*l* 339 e	
l 299 e		*l* 340 ea	(a = apl 186)
l 300 e		*l* 341 e	
l 301 e		*l* 342 e	
l 302 e		*l* 343 e	
l 303 e		*l* 344 e	
l 304 e		*l* 345 e	
l 305 e		*l* 346 e	
l 306 e		*l* 347 e	
l 307 e		*l* 350 e	
l 308 e		*l* 351 e	
l 309 e		*l* 352 e	
l 310 e		*l* 353 e	
l 311 e		*l* 354 e	
l 312 e[1]		*l* 355 e	
l 313 e		*l* 356 e	
l 314 e[1]		*l* 357 e	(also = evl 368)
l 315 ea	(a = apl 184)[1]	*l* 358 e	
l 316 e		*l* 359 e	
l 317 e		*l* 360 e	
l 318 e		*l* 361 e	
l 319 e		*l* 362 e	
l 320 e		*l* 363 e	
l 321 e		*l* 364 e	
l 322 e		*l* 365 e	
l 323 e		*l* 366 e	
l 324 ea	(? a = apl 258)	*l* 367 e	
l 325 e		*l* 368 a	(= apl 84)
l 326 e		*l* 369 e	
l 327 e		*l* 370 ea	(? a = apl 187)
l 328 e		*l* 371 e	
l 329 e		*l* 372 e	
l 330 e		*l* 373 e	
l 331 e		*l* 374 e	
l 332 e		*l* 375 e[1]	
l 333 e		*l* 376 e[1]	
l 334 e		*l* 377 e[1]	
l 335 e		*l* 378 e[1]	
l 336 e		*l* 379 e	

---

[1] Lost according to *Liste*.

l 380 e¹   *l* 421 ea (a = apl 188)

l 381 e   *l* 422 ea (a = apl 189)

l 382 e   *l* 423 ea (a = apl 190)

l 383 ea (?a = apl 259)   *l* 424 e

l 384 e   *l* 425 e

l 385 e   *l* 426 ea (a = apl 191)²

l 386 e   *l* 427 ea (a= apl 192)

l 387 e   *l* 428 e

l 388 e   *l* 429 e

l 389 e   *l* 430 e

l 390 e   *l* 431 e

l 391 e   *l* 432 e

l 392 e   *l* 433 e

l 393 e   *l* 434 e

l 394 e   *l* 435 e

l 395 e   *l* 436 e

l 396 e   *l* 437 e

l 397 e (= evl 398b)   *l* 438 e

l 398 e   *l* 439 ea (a = apl 193)

l 399 e   *l* 440 ea (a = apl 194)

l 400 e (= evl 399b)   *l* 441 e

l 401 e   *l* 442 e

l 402 e   *l* 443 ea (a = apl 195)

l 403 e   *l* 444 e

l 404 e   *l* 445 e

l 405 e   *l* 446 ea (a = apl 196)

l 406 e   *l* 447 e

l 407 e   *l* 448 e

l 408 e   *l* 449 c

l 409 e   *l* 450 e

l 410 e   *l* 451 e

l 411 e   *l* 452 e (also = evl 452b)¹

l 412 e   *l* 453 e¹

l 413 e   *l* 454 e

l 415 e   *l* 455 e

l 416 e   *l* 456 e¹

l 417 e   *l* 457 e¹

l 418 e   *l* 458 e¹

l 419 e   *l* 462 e

l 420 e   *l* 463 e

                                    l 464 e

---

¹ Lost according to *Liste*.
² Formerly known as *l* 1508.

l 465 e

l 466 e

l 467 e

l 468 e

l 469 e

l 470 e

l 471 e

l 472 e

l 473 ea (a = apl 197)

l 474 e

l 475 ea (a = apl 198)

l 476 ea (a = apl 78 + apl 199)

l 477 ea (a = apl 62)

l 478 ea (a = apl 102)

l 479 a   (= apl 85)

l 480 e

l 481 e

l 482 e

l 483 e

l 484 e

l 485 e

l 486ab ea (? a = apl 200)

l 486c e (= evl 486d)

l 487 e

l 488 ea (a = apl 201)

l 489 ea (a = apl 202)

l 490 e

l 491 e

l 492 ea (a = apl 203)

l 493 e

l 494 ea (a = apl 204)

l 495 ea (a = apl 205)

l 496 e

l 497 ea (a = apl 206)

l 498 ea (a = apl 207)

l 499 e

l 500 ea (a = apl 208)

l 501 ea (a = apl 209)

l 502 ea (a = apl 210)

l 503 e

l 504 ea (? a = apl 211)

l 505 ea (a = apl 212)

l 506 ea (a = apl 213)

l 507 e

l 508 e

l 509 e

l 510 e

l 511 e

l 512 e

l 513 e

l 514 e

l 515 e

l 516 e

l 517 e

l 518 e

l 519 e

l 520 e

l 521 e

l 522 e

l 523 ea (a = apl 214)

l 524 e

l 525 e

l 526 e

l 527 e

l 528 ea (a = apl 215)

l 529 ea (a = apl 216)

l 530 ea (a = apl 217)

l 531 e

l 532 ea (a = apl 218)

l 533 ea (a = apl 219)

l 534 e

l 535 e

l 536 e

l 537 e

l 538 e

l 539 e

l 540 e

l 541 e

l 542 e

l 543 e

l 544 e

l 545 e

l 546 e

l 547 e

l 548 ea (a = apl 220)

l 549 e

l 550 e

l 551 e

l 552 e

l 553 e

l 554 ea (a = apl 221)			*l* 595 a	(= apl 100)
l 555 ea (a = apl 222)			*l* 596 a	(= apl 101)
l 556 ea (a = apl 223)			*l* 597 a	(= apl 103)
l 557 ea (a = apl 224)			*l* 598 a	(= apl 104)
l 558 ea (a = apl 225)			*l* 599 a	(= apl 105)
l 559 e			*l* 600 a	(= apl 106)
l 560 e			*l* 601 a	(= apl 107)
l 561 e			*l* 602 a	(= apl 108)
l 562 e			*l* 603 a	(= apl 109)
l 563 e[1]			*l* 604 a	(= apl 111)
l 564 e			*l* 605 a	(= apl 112)
l 565 e			*l* 606 a	(= apl 113)
l 566 e			*l* 607 a	(= apl 114)
l 567 e			*l* 608 a	(= apl 115)
l 568 e			*l* 609 a	(= apl 116)
l 569 e			*l* 610 a	(= apl 117)
l 570 e			*l* 611 a	(= apl 118)
l 571 e			*l* 612 a	(= apl 119)
l 572 ea (a = apl 226)			*l* 613 a	(= apl 120)
l 573 ea (a = apl 227)			*l* 614 a	(= apl 121)
l 574 e			*l* 615 a	(= apl 122)
l 575 ea (a = apl 228)			*l* 616 a	(= apl 123)
l 576 e			*l* 617 a	(= apl 124)
l 577 e			*l* 618 a	(= apl 125)
l 578 e			*l* 619 a	(= apl 127a)
l 579 e			*l* 620 a	(= apl 127b)
l 580 e			*l* 621 a	(= apl 128)
l 581 e			*l* 622 a	(= apl 129)
l 582 e			*l* 623 a	(= apl 130)
l 583 a	(= apl 86)		*l* 624 a	(= apl 131)
l 584 a	(= apl 88)		*l* 625 a	(= apl 132)
l 585 a	(= apl 89)		*l* 626 a	(= apl 133)
l 586 a	(= apl 90)		*l* 627 e	
l 587 a	(= apl 91)		*l* 628 e	
l 588 a	(= apl 92)		*l* 629 e	
l 589 a	(= apl 93)		*l* 630 e	
l 590 a	(= apl 94)		*l* 631 e	
l 591 a	(= apl 95)		*l* 632 e	
l 592 a	(= apl 96)		*l* 633 e	
l 593 a	(= apl 98)		*l* 634 e	
l 594 a	(= apl 99)		*l* 635 e	

---

[1] Formerly known as *l* 33.

l 636 e	*l* 677 e	
l 637 e	*l* 678 e	
l 638 e	*l* 679 e	
l 639 e	*l* 680 ea (a = apl 229)	
l 640 e	*l* 682 e	
l 641 e	*l* 683 e	
l 642 ea (a = apl 170)	*l* 684 ea (a = apl 322)	
l 643 e	*l* 685 e	
l 644 e	*l* 686 ea (a = apl 230)	
l 645 e	*l* 687 ea (a = apl 231)	
l 646 e	*l* 688 e	
l 647 e	*l* 689 e	
l 648 e	*l* 690 e	
l 649 e	*l* 691 e	
l 650 e	*l* 692 e	
l 651 e	*l* 694 e	
l 652 e¹a (a=?)	*l* 695 e	
l 653 e	*l* 696 e	
l 654 e	*l* 697 e	
l 655 e	*l* 698 e	
l 656 e	*l* 699 e	
l 657 e	*l* 700 e	
l 658 e	*l* 701 e	
l 659 e	*l* 702 e	
l 660 e²	*l* 703 e	
l 661 e	*l* 704 e	
l 662 e	*l* 706 e	
l 663 e	*l* 707 ea (a = apl 233)	
l 664 e	*l* 708 e	
l 665 e	*l* 710 e	
l 666 e	*l* 711 e	
l 667 e	*l* 712 ea (a = apl 235)	
l 668 e	*l* 713 e	
l 669 e	*l* 714 e	
l 670 e	*l* 715 e	
l 671 e	*l* 716 e	
l 672 e	*l* 717 e	
l 673 e	*l* 718 e	
l 674 e	*l* 719 e	
l 675 e	*l* 720 e	
l 676 e	*l* 721 ea (a = apl 231)	

¹ = 2665.
² = 2666.

l 722 e   *l* 767 e
l 723 e   *l* 768 e
l 724 e   *l* 769 e
l 725 e   *l* 770 e
l 726 e   *l* 771 e[1]
l 727 e   *l* 772 e[1]
l 728 e   *l* 773 e
l 729 e   *l* 774 e
l 731 e   *l* 775 e
l 732 e   *l* 776 e
l 733 e   (= evl 713 b)   *l* 777 e
l 734 e   (= evl 730)   *l* 778 e
l 736 ea (e = evl 755; a = 240)   *l* 779 e
l 737 ea (e = evl 757; a = 241)   *l* 780 e
l 738 a   (= apl 134)   *l* 781 e
l 739 a   (= apl 135)   *l* 782 e
l 740 a   (= apl 136)   *l* 783 e
l 741 a   (= apl 137)   *l* 784 e
l 742 a   (= apl 138)   *l* 785 e
l 743 a   (= apl 139)   *l* 786 e
l 744 e   *l* 787 e
l 745 e   *l* 788 e
l 746 e   *l* 789 e
l 747 e   *l* 790 e
l 748 e   *l* 791 e
l 749 e   *l* 792 e[1]
l 750 e   *l* 793 e[1]
l 751 ea (= apl 239)   *l* 794 e[1]
l 752 e   *l* 795 e[1]
l 753 ea (a = apl 267)   *l* 796 e
l 754 e   *l* 798 e
l 756 e   *l* 799 e
l 757 e   (= evl 938 + e 1140)   *l* 800 e
l 758 e   *l* 801 e
l 759 ea (a = apl 242)   *l* 802 e
l 760 e   *l* 803 e
l 761 e   *l* 805 e
l 762 e   *l* 806 e
l 763 e   *l* 807 e
l 764 e   *l* 808 e
l 765 e   *l* 810 e
l 766 e

---

[1] Lost according to *Liste*.

l 811 e	*l* 855 e	
l 812 e	*l* 856 e	
l 813 e	*l* 857 e	
l 814 e	*l* 858 e	
l 815 e	*l* 859 e	
l 816 e	*l* 860 e³	
l 817 e	*l* 861 e	
l 819 e	*l* 862 e	
l 820 e	*l* 863 e	
l 821 e	*l* 864 e	
l 822 e	*l* 865 e	
l 823 e	*l* 866 e	
l 824 e	*l* 867 e	
l 825 e	*l* 868 e	
l 826 e	*l* 869 e	
l 827 e	*l* 870 e	
l 830 e¹	*l* 871 e	
l 831 e	*l* 872 a	(= apl 144)
l 832 e	*l* 873 a	(= apl 151)
l 833 e	*l* 874 e	
l 834 e	*l* 875 e	
l 835 e	*l* 876 e	
l 836 e	*l* 877 e	
l 837 ea (a = apl 245)	*l* 878 e	(= evl 879)
l 838 e²	*l* 880 e	(see *l* 1758)
l 839 a (= apl 140a)	*l* 881 a	(= apl 152)
l 840 a (= apl 140b)	*l* 882 a	(= apl 153)
l 841 a (= apl 141)	*l* 883 a	(= apl 154)
l 842 a (= apl 142)	*l* 884 a	(= apl 155)
l 843 a (= apl 143)	*l* 885 e	
l 844 e	*l* 886 e	
l 845 e	*l* 887 e	
l 846 e	*l* 888 e	
l 847 e	*l* 889 e	
l 848 e (= evl 946)	*l* 890 e	
l 849 e	*l* 891 e	
l 850 e	*l* 892 ea (a = ?)	
l 851 e	*l* 893 ea (a = apl 246)	
l 852 e	*l* 894 ea (a = apl 260)	
l 853 e	*l* 895 a (= apl 156)	
l 854 e	*l* 896 e	
	l 897 e	

---

¹ Formerly known as *l* 1654.
² Lost according to *Liste*.
³ apl 264 said by Gregory to = evl 860 should read e 860.

l 898	ea	(a = ?)	*l* 941	e
l 899	ea	(a =?)	*l* 942	e
l 900	ea	(a = apl 247)	*l* 944	e
l 901	e		*l* 945	ea (a = apl 268)[1]
l 902	e		*l* 947	e[1]
l 903	e		*l* 948	e[1]
l 904	e		*l* 949	e
l 906	ea	(a = ?)	*l* 950	e
l 907	e		*l* 951	e
l 908	e		*l* 952	e
l 909	ea	(a = ?)	*l* 953	e
l 910	ea	(a = ?)	*l* 1053	e (= evl 190[a])
l 911	ea	(a = apl 249)	*l* 1054	e (e = 1115)
l 912	ea	(a = ?)	*l* 1146	a (= p 409)
l 913	ea	(a = ?)	*l* 1147	e (e = 1066)
l 914	ea	(a = ?)	*l* 1148	e (e = 1067)
l 915	ea	(a = apl 250)	*l* 1149	e (e = 1069)
l 916	ea	(a = apl 251)	*l* 1150	e (e = 1070)
l 917	ea	(a = apl 252)	*l* 1164	a (= apl 159)
l 918	ea	(a = ?)	*l* 1178	a (= apl 160)
l 919	ea	(a = ?)	*l* 1202	a (= p 468 + a 379)
l 920	ea	(a =?)	*l* 1278	a (= apl 162)
l 921	a	(= apl 157)	*l* 1279	a (= apl 163)
l 922	e		*l* 1280	a (= apl 164)
l 923	e[1]		*l* 1281	a (= apl 165)
l 924	ea	(a = apl 253)	*l* 1282	a (= apl 166)
l 925	e		*l* 1283	a (= apl 167)
l 926	e		*l* 1284	a (= apl 168)
l 927	ea	(a = apl 185)	*l* 1285	a (= apl 169)
l 928	e		*l* 1286	a (= apl 171)
l 929	ea	(a = apl 254)	*l* 1287	a (= apl 172)
l 930	e		*l* 1288	a (= apl 173)
l 931	ea	(a = apl 126)	*l* 1289	a (= apl 255)
l 932	e		*l* 1311	a (= apl 15)
l 933	e		*l* 1312	a (= apl 24)
l 934	e		*l* 1313	a (= apl 87[a])
l 935	ea	(a = apl 256)	*l* 1314	a (= apl 87[b])
l 936	ea	(a = apl 257)	*l* 1315	a (= apl 97)
l 937	ea	(a = apl 266)[1]	*l* 1316	a (= apl 110)
l 938	a	(= apl 158)	*l* 1317	a (= evl 237)
l 939	e		*l* 1319	e (= evl 328)
l 940	e		*l* 1320	e (= evl 400)

---

[1] Lost according to *Liste*.

l 1321 e (= evl 444^{b})

l 1322 e (= evl 944^{a})

l 1323 e (= evl 946^{a})^{1}

l 1345 e (= o^{a} e)

l 1346 e (= o^{b} e)

l 1347 e (= o^{c} e)

l 1348 e (= o^{d} e)

l 1349 e (= o^{e} e)

l 1350 e (= o^{f} e)

l 1351 e (= o^{g} e)

l 1352 e (= o^{h} e)

l 1356 a (= a 404)

l 1357 a (= apl 6)

l 1358 e (= evl 72^{a})

l 1364 a (= a 405)

l 1365 a (= a 407)

l 1371 ea (e = 1175, a = ?)

l 1372 e (= evl 302^{a})

l 1373 e (= evl 302^{b})

l 1375 e (= evl 452^{a})

l 1386 e (= evl 242)

l 1436 ea (e = e1249,
      p = p346, a = a298)

l 1439 a (= a 408)

l 1440 a (= a 409)

l 1441 a (= a 410)

l 1442 a (= a 411)

l 1443 a (= a 412)

l 1470 ea (e = e1244, p = p341,
      a = a293)

l 1471 ea (e = e1245, p = p342,
      a = a294)

l 1494 e (= evl 460)

l 1495 e (= evl 459)

l 1496 e (= evl 461)

l 1504 a (= apl 40)^{1}

l 1505 a (= apl 41)

l 1551 a (= apl 82)^{1}

l 1590 a (= a 406)

l 1591 a [= 1866] (= apl 174)

l 1592 a (= a 414)

l 1750 e (= evl 839)

l 1752 e (= evl 840)

l 1753 e (= evl 841)

l 1754 e (= evl 842)

l 1755 e (= evl 843)

l 1756 e (= evl 872)

l 1757 e (= evl 873)

l 1758 e (= evl 880)^{2}

l 1759 e (= evl 881)

l 1760 e (= evl 882)

l 1761 e (= evl 883)

l 1762 e (= evl 884)

l 1824 e (= evl 397)

l 1911 e (= evl 144)

l 1912 e (= evl 145)

l 1920   (= evl 285b)

---

[1] Lost according to *Liste*.

[2] See *Liste* p 333 (fn 2) 2 mss = Sinai 246. One = *l* 880, other = *l* 1758.

(b) The following mss. known to Gregory *Prolegomena* are not now identifiable:

apl 243 + evl 797, apl 244 + evl 829.

evl 158, 160, 161, 162, 163, 164, 165, 166, 167, 168, 169, 170, 171, 172, 173, 174, 175, 176, 177, 178, 583, 584, 585, 586, 587, 588, 589, 590, 591, 592, 593, 594, 595, 596, 597, 598, 599, 600, 601, 602, 603, 604, 605, 606, 607, 608, 609, 610, 611, 612, 613, 614, 615, 616, 617, 618, 619, 620, 621, 622, 623, 624, 625, 626, 828.

apl 49, 50, 51, 52, 53, 54.

(c) Several discrepancies between Gregory's *Prolegomena* and the *Liste* can be resolved because investigation of mss. later than 1894, the publication date of the *Prolegomena*, by Gregory himself and others has revealed that the description of the ms. in 1894 was inadequate or inaccurate. Those that can be resolved are:

*l*26: the portion previously known as apl 28 is too small to justify the lectionary being classified as ea.

*l*185, *l*189, *l*324, *l*370, *l*383, *l*486ab. The editor of the *Liste* has decided that as the non-gospel readings in these mss. amount to only a few isolated readings the mss. cannot truly be classified as ea as Gregory did.

Later investigation by Gregory corrects the information in *Prolegomena* either in his *Textkritik* (1900–1909) or his *Griechische Handschriften* (1908) and brings it into line with what we find in the *Liste*. This is so for *l*57, *l*215, *l*652, *l*892, *l*898, *l*899, *l*909, *l*910, *l*912, *l*914, *l*918, *l*919, *l*920, *l*1371. The discovery by Gregory that a ms. previously thought to contain (and therefore classified as) only evl is in fact evl + apl did not require by 1908 an apl number as this system of classification had by then been abandoned.

In the case of *l*197, *l*274 Gregory seems to have been in error.

In the case of *l*504 the *Liste* should read ea.

APPENDIX I

Huck-Greeven's Sundries

(a) Cursives

ms.	Ref.		Pericope	Page	ms.	Ref.		Pericope	Page
2e	Mk	5.35	120	103		Lk	4.11	20	21
	Mk	9.38	144	143		Lk	8.50	120	103
	Lk	5.14	57	45		Lk	9.43b	141	140
3	Mk	4.12	104	88	17	Mk	14.70	256	254
	Mk	13.35	236	227		Jn	6.69	/ /	129
4e	Mt	5.29	35	33	18	Mk	9.22	140	139
	Mt	20.5	204	183		Lk	20.14	218	203
	Mt	21.31	217	201					
	Mt	26.36	254	245	19	Mk	12.29	222	210
	Mt	26.74	256	254		Lk	5.12	57	44
	Mk	3.4	82	67					
	Mk	5.19	119	101	20	Mk	6.44	125	117
	Mk	9.47	145	145		Mk	16.9-20[sch]	275	282
	Mk	14.7	244	234		Lk	8.26	119	98
	Lk	3.23	19	18					
	Lk	8.35	119	100	21	Mt	18.31	150	147
	Lk	9.17	125	116		Mt	19.30	203	183
	Lk	12.9	169	158		Mk	4.7	103	87
	Lk	14.34	185	168		Mk	6.40	125	115
	Lk	19.7	208	189		Mk	6.41	125	116
	Lk	19.45	214	196		Mk	8.33	136	133
	Lk	20.2	216	199		Lk	12.8	169	158
	Lk	20.13	218	203		Lk	12.11	169	158
	Lk	20.14	218	203		Lk	13.27	179	164
	Lk	24.39	273	280		Lk	20.15	218	204
	Jn	19.19	/ /	266		Lk	23.21	261	261
6	Mt	21.41	218	204	25	Lk	23.50	266	272
	Mt	24.48	238	228					
	Mk	6.3	121	105	29	Lk	18.1	199	175
	Mk	6.13	122	109		Lk	23.55	266	273
	Mk	6.21	124	111					
					34	Lk	10.39	159	152
11	Mk	10.21	203	180					
	Mk	13.28	233	225	37	Jn	19.30	/ /	270
	Mk	14.46	255	248					
					38	Mk	9.28	140	140
15	Mk	10.21	203	180		Mk	13.11	229	220
						Mk	13.29	233	225
16	Mt	9.35	70	56		Mk	14.61	256	252
	Mt	10.17	71	58		Lk	10.42	159	152
	Mt	12.4	81	65		Lk	20.10	218	202
	Mt	16.24	137	131					
	Mt	21.2	210	192	39	Lk	8.4	103	86
	Mt	21.37	218	203					
	Mt	25.40	241	230	40	Mk	9.21	140	139
	Mk	3.29	99	83					
	Mk	8.12	132	126	44	Mk	8.25	134	128
	Mk	15.40	265	270		Mk	14.67	256	253

ms.	Ref.		Pericope	Page	ms.	Ref.		Pericope	Page
	Lk	8.18	107	92		Lk	8.2	97	80
	Lk	19.20	209	190		Lk	8.32	119	99
45	Mk	5.40	120	104		Lk	9.12	125	113
						Lk	13.18	178	163
46	Lk	5.13	57	45		Lk	20.21	220	206
						Lk	22.47	255	247
47	Mk	6.17	124	110	61	Mt	6.33	47	39
	Lk	20.19	218	204		Mt	9.24	67	56
						Mt	14.2	123	109
49	Mk	4.22	107	92		Mt	14.3	124	110
	Lk	8.32	119	99		Mt	22.43	223	212
	Lk	18.25	203	181		Mk	6.15	123	110
50	Mk	9.7	138	136		Mk	8.26^{semel} sic	134	128
	Lk	11.4	160	152		Mk	10.4	201	176
	Lk	22.47	255	247		Mk	10.52	207	188
51	Mk	10.28	203	182		Mk	11.22	215	198
	Lk	12.56	174	162		Mk	11.24	215	198
52	Mk	9.2	138	135		Mk	11.29	216	200
						Lk	13.20	178	163
53	Mt	23.26	224	215		Lk	22.67	256	252
						Ac	1.13	/ /	71
54	Mk	6.39	125	115	63	Mk	9.27	140	139
						Mk	10.46	207	187
56	Mk	7.12	128	121					
	Mk	15.2	259	257	64	Mk	2.8	64	50
	Lk	9.24	137	131		Lk	16.18	190	171
						Lk	22.69	256	252
57	Lk	10.11	153	149					
					66	Mt	19.13	202	178
59	Mt	10.7	70	57		Mk	6.32^{mg}	125	112
	Mt	10.42	75	60					
	Mt	11.8	77	61	67	Mk	10.49	207	188
	Mt	14.22	126	117		Lk	6.17	84	69
	Mt	21.45	218	204		Lk	12.12	169	158
	Mt	25.17	240	229					
	Mt	27.47	265	269	68	Lk	4.34	24	25
	Mt	27.56^c	265	271		Lk	10.13	153	149
	Mk	6.37	125	114		Lk	12.39	172	160
	Mk	13.35	236	227		Lk	13.30	179	164
	Mk	14.37	254	246	70	Mk	9.18	140	138
	Mk	15.29	264	267					
	Lk	4.4	20	19	72	Mk	10.37	206	185
	Lk	5.20	64	50		Lk	5.31	65	53
	Lk	8.18	107	92					
	Lk	9.26	134	137	73	Mk	1.4	13	13
	Lk	10.8	153	149					
	Lk	11.7	161	152	74	Mk	15.36^c	265	269
	Lk	12.22	171	159		Lk	6.32	88	73
	Jn	6.11	/ /	115		Lk	8.5	103	87
						Lk	19.30	210	192
60	Mk	8.33	136	133	76	Mk	3.19	85	71
	Mk	15.2	259	257		Mk	15.26	264	266
						Mk	15.28	264	266

ms.	Ref.	Pericope	Page
77	Jn 20.2	//	276
80	Mt 5.32	36	33
	Mt 27.55	265	271
	Lk 6.45	90	76
81	1 Cor 11.25	//	240
86	Lk 13.15	177	163
90	Mk 5.21	120	101
	Mk 7.27	129	123
	Mk 9.38	144	143
	Mk 9.45	145	144
	Mk 10.27	203	182
	Mk 14.40	254	246
	Mk 15.32	264	267
	Lk 19.21	209	190
96	Lk 18.25	203	181
98	Lk 4.8	20	20
106	Mk 5.7	119	99
	Mk 6.39	125	115
	Mk 11.32	216	200
	Mk 12.23	221	209
	Mk 15.5	259	257
	Lk 6.29	88	73
	Lk 11.13	162	153
107	Lk 4.1	20	19
108	Mk 4.7	103	87
	Mk 10.48	207	188
	Mk 14.65	256	253
	Lk 10.13	153	149
111	Lk 6.3	81	65
114	Mk 10.21	203	180
116	Lk 17.34	198	174
	Lk 20.23	220	206
122	Mt 4.22	23	24
	Mt 10.3	70	57
	Mt 21.41	218	204
	Mk 13.33	236	227
	Mk 14.64	256	253
	Lk 7.27	95	79
	Lk 13.27	179	164
	Lk 21.7	227	218
125	Mk 8.30^{mg}	135	130
	Mk 9.43	145	144

ms.	Ref.	Pericope	Page
126	Mt 4.21	23	24
	Lk 5.13	57	45
	Lk 10.13	153	149
127	Mk 12.8	218	203
	Mk 15.16	262	263
	Lk 24.22	272	279
	Jn 20.23	//	281
130	Lk 5.20	64	49
	Lk 6.45	90	76
	Lk 7.22	94	78
	Lk 7.34	95	79
	Lk 20.3	216	200
	Lk 21.11	228	219
	Lk 23.23	261	261
137	Mk 16.9^{+}–20	275	282
138	Mk 16.9^{+}–20	275	282
	Jn 20.1	//	275
	Jn 20.20	//	280
139	Lk 4.2	20	19
142	Lk 9.8	123	110
	Lk 22.23	249	241
145	Lk 20.43	223	212
156	Lk 8.26	119	98
	Lk 8.32	119	99
158	Lk 22.22	249	241
161	Mk 14.50	255	249
	Lk 4.23	22	22
	Lk 5.20	64	49
	Lk 6.15	83	68
	Lk 6.39	89	74
	Lk 6.41 ^{bis}	89	75
	Lk 7.4	92	77
	Lk 7.32	95	79
	Lk 9.7	123	109
	Lk 12.42	172	160
	Lk 14.34	185	168
162	Lk 11.2	160	152
185	Jn 1.27	//	15
	Jn 4.51	//	46
205	Mk 7.12	128	121
213	Mt 4.14	21	21
	Mt 5.37	37	33
	Mt 5.44	39	34

ms.	Ref.	Pericope	Page
	Mt 10.39	74	60
	Mt 12.2	81	64
	Mt 12.44	101	84
	Mt 23.6	224	213
	Mt 24.24	231	223
	Mt 25.11	239	228
	Mt 27.23	261	261
	Mt 28.2	268	276
	Mt 28.15	270	278
	Mk 1.28	24	25
	Mk 2.21	66	54
	Mk 4.25	107	92
	Mk 5.20	119	101
	Mk 5.33	120	103
	Mk 6.35	125	113
	Mk 6.36	125	114
	Mk 7.32	130	124
	Mk 10.39[bis]	206	186
	Mk 11.15	214	197
	Mk 12.13	218	205
	Mk 13.29	233	225
	Mk 14.22	248	239
	Mk 15.23	264	265
	Mk 15.26	264	266
	Mk 15.35[bis]	265	269
	Mk 15.42	266	271
	Lk 1.60	9	7
	Lk 2.13	9	8
	Lk 2.42	12	10
	Lk 3.23	19	18
	Lk 5.29	65	52
	Lk 5.30	65	52
	Lk 5.37	66	55
	Lk 6.15	83	68
	Lk 6.21	86	72
	Lk 6.25	87	73
	Lk 6.33	88	74
	Lk 6.47	91	76
	Lk 7.28	95	79
	Lk 7.50	96	80
	Lk 8.20[bis]	117	96
	Lk 8.32	119	99
	Lk 9.5[bis]	122	108
	Lk 9.13	125	115
	Lk 9.20	135	129
	Lk 9.22	136	133
	Lk 9.27[bis]	137	134
	Lk 9.39	140	138
	Lk 9.50	144	153
	Lk 11.51	168	156
	Lk 11.52	168	157
	Lk 11.54	168	157
	Lk 12.9	169	158
	Lk 12.38	172	160
	Lk 13.24	179	164
	Lk 13.29	179	164

ms.	Ref.	Pericope	Page
	Lk 14.5	182	165
	Lk 14.24[c]	184	167
	Lk 17.6	194	172
	Lk 17.16	196	173
	Lk 17.26	198	174
	Lk 18.10	200	175
	Lk 18.23	203	180
	Lk 18.30	203	183
	Lk 19.30	210	192
	Lk 19.46	214	197
	Lk 20.6	216	200
	Lk 20.7	216	201
	Lk 20.8	216	201
	Lk 20.9	218	202
	Lk 20.11	218	202
	Lk 20.24	220	207
	Lk 20.37	221	210
	Lk 22.10	246	236
	Lk 22.12	246	236
	Lk 22.34	251	242
	Lk 23.26	263	263
	Lk 23.52	266	272
	Jn 2.15	//	196
	Jn 6.7	//	114
	Jn 11.52	//	231
	Jn 12.3	//	233
	Jn 12.5	//	233
	Jn 13.19	//	223
	Jn 19.4	//	260
217	Mk 4.3	103	87
220	Mk 4.22	107	92
	Lk 17.24	198	174
225	Mk 6.33	125	112
	Lk 5.39	66	55
	Lk 12.10	169	158
	Lk 22.18	248	239
	Jn 18.13	//	249
226	Lk 12.30	171	159
229	Mt 27.24	261	262
	Mt 27.37	264	266
	Mk 10.43	206	186
	Mk 12.29	222	210
	Lk 9.1	122	106
	Lk 21.25[c]	232	224
234	Lk 22.56	256	250
235	Mk 4.20	106	91
	Mk 4.24	107	92
	Mk 9.33	143	141

ms.	Ref.	Pericope	Page	ms.	Ref.	Pericope	Page
	Mk 12.27	221	210		Lk 20.26	220	207
	Mk 12.28	222	210		Jn 15.20	/ /	75
	Mk 13.18	230	222	239	Mk 16.9–20[sch]	275	282
	Mk 14.22	248	239		Lk 11.53	168	157
	Lk 9.10	125	112		Lk 11.54	168	157
	Lk 20.45	224	213		Lk 22.47	255	247
	Lk 22.56	256	250		Lk 23.38	264	267
237	Mt 3.11	16	15				
	Mt 5.37	37	33	240	Mt 28.1	268	275
	Mt 25.39	241	230		Mk 13.2	227	217
	Mt 27.58	266	272		Lk 8.42	120	102
	Mk 1.1[sch]	13	12				
	Mk 10.6	201	176	241	Mt 27.1	257	255
	Mk 14.52	255	249		Mk 7.21	128	122
	Mk 16.9–20[sch]	275	282		Lk 22.71	256	253
	Lk 3.9	14	14				
	Lk 6.21	86	72	242	Mt 14.19	125	116
	Lk 9.40	140	138		Mt 27.60	266	273
	Lk 24.46	273	281		Lk 12.40	172	160
	Lk 24.50	274	281		Lk 18.25	203	181
238	Mt 9.2	64	49	243	Mt 5.44	20	19
	Mt 10.13	70	57		Mt 9.10	65	52
	Mt 21.1	81	64		Mt 10.11	70	57
	Mt 15.10	128	121		Mt 10.13	70	57
	Mt 19.26	203	182		Mt 12.4	81	65
	Mt 21.10	215	197		Mt 26.26	248	239
	Mt 22.45	223	212		Mt 27.60[bis]	266	272f
	Mt 26.29	248	240		Mt 28.1	268	275
	Mt 27.35	264	266		Lk 2.25	11	9
	Mk 1.1	13	12		Lk 4.2	20	19
	Mk 1.40	57	44		Lk 4.10	20	21
	Mk 3.13	85	70		Lk 4.12	20	21
	Mk 4.8	103	83		Lk 5.23	64	50
	Mk 5.14	119	100		Lk 5.25	64	51
	Mk 5.39	120	104		Lk 7.33	95	79
	Mk 5.40	120	104		Lk 10.38	159	151
	Mk 5.42	120	104		Lk 16.15	189	170
	Mk 6.8	122	107		Lk 23.22	261	261
	Mk 6.17	124	110		Lk 23.26	263	264
	Mk 7.14	128	121				
	Mk 7.23	128	122	244	Mt 6.18	84	70
	Mk 9.11	139	137		Mk 13.2	227	217
	Mk 10.5	201	176		Lk 18.30	203	183
	Mk 10.17	203	179		Lk 19.2	208	189
	Mk 10.44	206	186				
	Mk 12.17	220	207	245	Mt 11.25	79	63
	Mk 13.14	230	221		Mt 12.14	82	68
	Mk 14.6	244	233		Mt 14.23	126	117
	Mk 14.13	246	236		Mt 17.5	138	136
	Mk 14.19	247	237		Mt 20.3	204	183
	Lk 5.2	29	29		Mt 21.1	210	192
	Lk 6.32	88	73		Mt 21.21	215	198
	Lk 13.11	177	163		Mt 26.60	256	252
	Lk 16.19	191	171		Mt 27.45	265	268

ms.	Ref.	Pericope	Page
	Mk 1.6	13	13
	Mk 1.7	13	15
	Mk 2.11	64	51
	Mk 10.17	203	179
	Mk 13.7	228	219
	Mk 15.42	266	271
	Lk 5.14	57	45
	Lk 8.16	107	92
	Lk 9.46	143	141
	Lk 12.10	169	158
	Lk 12.22	171	159
	Lk 12.47	173	161
	Lk 17.26	198	174
	Lk 17.33	198	174
	Lk 18.18	203	179
	Lk 18.20	203	179
	Lk 18.39	207	188
	Lk 19.2	208	189
	Lk 19.30	210	192
	Lk 20.33	221	209
	Lk 23.8	260	258
	Jn 19.4	/ /	260
	Jn 20.5	/ /	276
247	Mt 4.10	20	20
	Mt 12.27	99	82
	Mt 15.37	131	125
	Mt 26.18	246	236
	Mk 14.23	248	240
248	Mt 9.20	67	56
	Mt 10.20	71	57
	Mt 12.48	102	85
	Mt 26.42	254	246
	Mk 14.3	244	232
	Lk 6.31	88	73
	Lk 17.24	198	174
	Lk 18.26	203	181
	Lk 18.27	203	182
249	Jn 1.49	/ /	130
	Jn 14.14	/ /	198
	Jn 19.18	/ /	265
251	Mt 10.7	70	57
	Mt 10.14	70	57
	Mt 14.4	124	111
	Mt 18.35	150	147
	Mt 22.45	223	212
	Mk 12.14	220	206
	Mk 14.71	256	255
	Lk 4.9	20	21
	Lk 4.34	24	25
	Lk 6.4	81	65
	Lk 6.28	88	73
	Lk 8.25	119	98
	Lk 8.30	119	99
	Lk 8.40	120	101
	Lk 9.3	122	107
	Lk 9.57	152	148
	Lk 12.9	169	158
	Lk 13.29	179	164
	Lk 13.35	181	165
	Lk 17.27	198	174
	Lk 18.29	203	182
	Lk 18.39	207	188
	Lk 18.41	207	188
	Lk 19.36[bis]	210	193
	Lk 21.5	227	217
	Jn 15.7	/ /	198
252	Mt 6.16	43	37
	Mt 12.26	99	82
	Mt 17.4	138	136
	Mt 27.33[c]	264	265
	Mk 3.11	84	70
	Mk 14.64	256	253
	Lk 21.7[mg]	227	218
253	Mt 6.45	126	117
	Mk 8.9	131	125
	Mk 9.5	138	135
	Mk 15.19	262	263
	Lk 12.24	171	159
258	Mt 12.48	102	85
	Mt 22.13	219	205
	Mk 2.15	65	52
	Mk 5.23[bis]	120	102
	Mk 9.31	141	140
	Mk 9.42	145	144
	Mk 11.3	210	192
	Mk 15.47	266	273
	Lk 23.52	266	272
259	Mt 4.18	23	23
	Mt 25.39	241	230
	Mt 27.3	258	256
	Mk 1.1[sch]	13	12
	Mk 9.43	145	144
	Mk 10.33	205	184
	Mk 13.9	229	220
	Mk 13.28	233	225
	Mk 16.9–20[sch]	275	282
	Lk 12.8	169	158
262	Mt 24.23	231	223
	Lk 19.45	214	196
	Lk 19.46	214	197
270	Lk 2.43	12	10
	Lk 6.25	87	73

ms.	Ref.	Pericope	Page	ms.	Ref.	Pericope	Page
	Lk 14.27	185	168		Mk 11.14	213	196
	Jn 6.12	//	116		Mk 12.21	221	208
					Mk 12.24	221	209
271	Mk 2.26	81	65		Mk 13.2	227	217
	Mk 4.31	110	94		Mk 13.5	228	218
					Mk 13.8	228	219
272	Jn 8.1	//	231		Mk 13.9	229	220
273	Mt 5.29bis	35	33	300	Mk 15.46	266	273
	Mt 6.21	44	38		Lk 17.37	198	175
	Mt 20.5	204	183		Lk 24.12	268	277
	Mt 21.31	217	201		Lk 24.39bis	273	280
	Mt 24.24	231	223				
	Mt 26.55	255	249	301	Mt 6.33	47	39
	Mt 26.74	256	254		Mt 9.20	67	56
	Mt 27.40	264	267		Mt 13.12	104	88
	Mk 3.4	82	67		Mt 16.5	133	126
	Mk 5.19	119	101		Mt 26.60	256	251
	Mk 6.4	121	106		Lk 5.38	66	55
	Mk 6.6b	122	106				
	Mk 9.1	137	134	330	Mk 6.35	125	113
	Mk 9.47	145	145		Mk 9.19	140	139
	Mk 10.35	206	185		Mk 12.14	220	206
	Mk 11.26	215	199		Mk 14.1	243	232
	Mk 11.33	216	201		Mk 14.6	244	234
	Mk 13.21	231	223		Mk 14.11	245	235
	Mk 14.7	244	234		Mk 15.14	261	261
	Mk 14.15	246	236				
	Lk 1.13	6	5	331	Mt 9.25	67	56
	Lk 3.23	19	18				
	Lk 8.13	106	90	340	Mk 16.9–20	275	282
274	Mk 16.9mg/quater	275	282	345	Mt 16.9	133	127
280	Mt 1.20	2	2	348	Mt 7.18	53	42
	Mt 10.17	71	58		Mt 15.10	128	121
	Mt 13.3	103	87		Mt 20.25	206	186
	Mk 13.28	233	225		Mt 22.23	221	208
	Mk 14.29	253	243		Mt 22.26	221	208
	Lk 12.43	172	161		Mt 22.35	222	210
	Lk 22.46	254	246		Mt 23.28	224	215
	Jn 20.1	//	275		Mt 24.25	231	223
					Mt 26.39	254	245
281	Mk 14.45	255	247		Mt 27.1	257	255
					Mt 27.8	258	256
282	Mk 15.20a	262	263		Mt 27.28bis	262	263
	Mk 15.43	266	272		Mt 27.30	262	263
					Mt 27.33	264	265
291	Mt 12.45	101	84		Mk 6.6b	122	106
	Mt 16.4	132	126		Mk 9.2	138	135
	Mk 4.21	107	91		Mk 10.47	207	187
	Mk 6.15	123	110		Mk 14.3	244	232
					Mk 14.45	255	247
299	Mt 13.32	110	94		Mk 14.46	255	248
	Mt 14.11	124	112		Mk 15.32	264	267
	Mk 9.24	140	139		Lk 5.34	66	54

ms.	Ref.	Pericope	Page	ms.	Ref.	Pericope	Page
	Lk 6.41	89	75		Mt 8.34	63	49
	Lk 10.7	152	149		Mt 10.26	72	58
	Lk 11.34	167	155		Mt 11.16	77	62
	Lk 12.58	175	162		Mt 16.13	135	129
	Lk 15.4	186	168	406	Mk 10.27	203	181
	Lk 21.9	228	219				
	Lk 21.13	229	220	407	Lk 9.2	122	107
	Lk 22.5	245	235				
	Lk 22.22	249	241	409	Mk 10.51	207	188
	Lk 22.48	255	247		Lk 9.49	144	143
	Lk 23.13	261	258				
	Lk 23.19^c	261	261	410	Mk 10.16	202	178
	Jn 6.2	//	113				
	Jn 19.18	//	266	433	Mk 4.24	107	92
	Jn 20.6	//	276		Mk 12.1	218	202
372	Mt 2.13^{bis}	4	4		Mk 13.8	228	219
	Mt 3.16	18	17		Lk 20.26	220	207
	Mt 4.4^{semel} sic	20	19		Lk 23.4	259	258
	Mt 4.8	20	20				
	Mt 5.30	35	33	435	Mk 4.16	106	90
	Mt 6.22	45	38		Mk 9.34	143	141
	Mt 9.2	64	50		Mk 9.43	145	144
	Mt 9.5	64	50		Mk 14.41	254	246
	Mt 9.6	64	51		Lk 9.2	122	107
	Mt 11.23	78	63		Lk 22.52	256	249
	Mt 12.10	82	66				
	Mt 12.15	84	69	440	Mt 6.33	47	39
	Mt 17.2	138	135		Mt 10.42	75	60
	Mt 21.6	210	193		Mt 19.9	201	177
	Mt 21.30	217	201		Mt 20.7	204	183
	Mt 22.16	220	206		Mt 21.23	216	199
	Mt 22.35	222	210		Mt 21.27	216	201
	Mt 26.22	247	237		Mt 23.37	225	216
	Mk 3.3^{ter}	82	67		Mt 24.39	235	226
	Mk 3.19	85	71		Mk 6.22	124	111
	Mk 3.27	99	82		Mk 7.4	128	120
	Mk 4.6	103	87		Mk 9.43	145	144
	Mk 4.18^{bis}	106	90		Mk 14.61	256	252
	Mk 7.6^{ter}	128	120		Lk 8.34	119	100
	Mk 11.3^{bis}	210	192		Lk 8.46	120	103
	Mk 15.27	264	266		Lk 11.11	162	153
	Lk 2.14^{bis}	10	9		Lk 11.42	168	156
	Lk 8.17	107	92		Lk 22.1	243	231
	Lk 9.5	122	108		Lk 23.14	261	258
	Lk 24.19	272	279		Jn 1.23	//	13
382	Lk 18.22	203	180		Jn 18.15	//	250
	Lk 24.28	272	280	443	Mt 18.7	145	144
					Mt 21.25	216	200
397	Jn 6.10	//	115		Mt 27.16	261	259
	Jn 15.6	//	14		Mk 4.12	104	89
	Jn 20.5	//	276		Mk 14.50	255	249
399	Mt 1.24	2	3		Lk 11.2	160	152
	Mt 2.9	3	3	448	Mk 5.23	120	101

ms.	Ref.	Pericope	Page
449	Mk 5.18	119	101
462	Ac 1.13	//	71
470	Lk 11.2	160	152
471	Mt 4.4	20	19
	Mt 6.16	43	37
	Mt 8.32	63	48
	Mk 11.7	210	193
	Lk 22.4[bis]	245	235
472	Mt 2.23	4	4
	Mt 3.10	14	14
	Mt 8.34	63	49
	Mt 12.40	100	84
	Mt 15.30	130	123
	Mt 15.37	131	125
	Mt 21.25	216	200
	Mt 26.6	244	232
	Mt 27.50	265	270
	Mk 1.20	24	24
	Mk 2.21	66	54
	Mk 3.29	99	83
	Mk 3.32	102	85
	Mk 4.21	107	91
	Mk 4.38	118	97
	Mk 6.2	121	105
	Mk 6.7	122	106
	Mk 6.11	122	109
	Mk 6.43	125	116
	Mk 8.7[bis]	131	125
	Mk 8.17	133	127
	Mk 8.28[bis]	135	129
	Mk 9.2	138	135
	Mk 9.19	140	139
	Mk 9.43	145	144
	Mk 10.30	203	183
	Mk 10.46	207	187
	Mk 10.49	207	188
	Mk 11.2	210	192
	Mk 11.7	210	193
	Mk 11.29	216	200
	Mk 12.9	218	204
	Mk 12.10	218	204
	Mk 12.14	220	206
	Mk 12.36	223	212
	Mk 13.28	233	255
	Mk 14.29	253	243
	Mk 14.32	254	244
	Mk 15.19	262	263
	Mk 15.20a	262	263
	Mk 15.42	266	271
	Mk 15.47	266	273
	Lk 3.16	16	15
	Lk 4.2	20	19

ms.	Ref.	Pericope	Page
	Lk 4.14	21	21
	Lk 6.7	82	66
	Lk 6.42	89	75
	Lk 7.9	92	77
	Lk 7.50	96	80
	Lk 8.5	103	87
	Lk 8.7	103	87
	Lk 8.14	106	91
	Lk 8.16	107	91
	Lk 8.26	119	98
	Lk 8.27	119	98
	Lk 8.34	119	100
	Lk 8.40	120	101
	Lk 9.25	137	134
	Lk 10.9	153	149
	Lk 10.25	157	151
	Lk 10.26	157	151
	Lk 11.49	168	156
	Lk 12.45	172	161
	Lk 14.2	182	165
	Lk 14.17	184	167
	Lk 16.17	190	170
	Lk 18.7	199	175
	Lk 19.31	210	192
	Lk 20.3	216	200
	Lk 20.6	216	200
	Lk 20.44	223	212
	Lk 21.38	242	231
	Lk 22.19	248	239
	Lk 22.22	249	241
	Lk 22.52	255	248
	Lk 22.59	256	250
	Lk 22.61	256	250
	Lk 22.64	256	251
	Lk 22.67	256	252
	Lk 23.16	261	258
	Lk 23.52	266	272
	Lk 24.32	272	280
	Lk 24.49	273	281
	Jn 1.34	//	18
	Jn 4.1	//	21
	Jn 6.4	//	113
473	Mt 17.12	139	137
	Mt 20.25	206	186
	Mk 4.41	118	98
	Mk 5.35	120	103
	Mk 6.56	127	119
	Mk 10.49	207	188
	Mk 13.15	230	221
	Lk 19.38	210	194
	Lk 21.12	229	220
474	Mt 21.21	215	198
	Mt 22.36	222	210
	Mt 27.41	264	267

ms.	Ref.	Pericope	Page
	Mk 5.43	120	104
	Mk 9.31	141	140
	Mk 14.18	248	240
	Mk 16.19	275	283
	Mk 11.19	163	154
475	Mk 6.3	121	105
	Lk 5.36	66	54
	Lk 18.27^{semel} sic	203	182
	Lk 19.2	208	189
	Lk 19.23	210	191
	Lk 20.14	218	203
	Lk 21.27	232	224
	Lk 22.23	249	241
	Lk 22.46	254	246
	Lk 23.45	265	268
	Lk 23.53	266	272
	Jn 8.1	/ /	231
476	Mt 16.11	133	127
	Mt 26.29	248	240
	Mt 27.33	264	265
	Mk 4.21	107	91
	Mk 14.12	246	236
	Lk 7.13	93	78
	Lk 9.49	144	143
	Lk 17.35	198	174
477	Mt 15.26	129	123
	Mt 18.6	145	144
	Mt 21.19	213	195
	Mk 5.9^{bis}	119	99
	Mk 6.29	124	112
	Mk 13.13	229	221
	Lk 9.26	137	134
	Lk 10.2	153	149
	Lk 11.19	163	154
	Lk 11.54	168	157
	Lk 12.5	169	157
	Lk 14.26	185	167
	Lk 19.15	209	190
	Lk 19.16	209	190
	Lk 19.48	214	197
	Lk 20.40^{bis}	221	210
	Lk 22.13	246	236
	Lk 22.13	253	243
	Lk 23.51	266	272
	Jn 19.20	/ /	266
478	Mt 9.14	66	54
	Mt 17.12	139	137
	Mt 22.21	220	207
	Mt 24.14	229	221
	Mk 1.2	13	13
	Mk 15.25^{c}	264	266
	Lk 16.31	191	171
481	Mt 12.4	81	65
	Mt 22.21	220	207
	Mt 28.10	269	278
	Mk 13.12	229	220
482	Mt 6.33	48	40
	Mt 21.2	210	192
	Mt 24.32	233	225
	Mk 5.35	120	103
	Mk 8.11	132	126
	Mk 8.17	133	127
	Mk 10.23	203	181
	Mk 12.26	221	210
	Mk 15.40	265	270
	Lk 3.16	16	15
	Lk 7.39	96	80
	Lk 8.45	120	102
	Jn 19.24	/ /	266
483	Mt 26.2	243	231
	Mk 5.13	119	100
	Mk 5.20	119	101
	Mk 5.34	120	103
	Mk 7.8	128	121
	Mk 10.27	203	182
	Mk 15.32	264	267
	Lk 8.5	103	87
	Lk 8.33	119	100
484	Lk 10.25^{c}	157	151
485	Mt 7.12	51	41
	Mt 10.18	71	58
	Mt 13.3	103	87
	Mt 13.4	103	87
	Mt 21.27	216	201
	Mt 28.2	268	276
	Mk 4.21	107	91
	Mk 6.56	127	119
	Lk 4.31	24	24
	Lk 21.8	228	218
487	Mt 26.52	255	248
488	Mk 1.16	23	23
	Mk 2.4	64	49
489	Mt 8.34	63	49
	Mk 2.22	66	55
495	Mk 1.28	24	25
	Mk 2.12	64	51
	Mk 3.34	102	85
	Mk 4.12	104	89
	Mk 6.48	126	118
	Mk 11.9	210	194

ms.	Ref.	Pericope	Page	ms.	Ref.	Pericope	Page
	Mk 14.53[bis]	256	249f		Lk 23.26	263	263
	Mk 14.65	256	253		Lk 23.53	266	273
	Mk 14.70	256	254		Jn 1.27	/ /	15
	Mk 15.5	259	257		Jn 13.27	/ /	243
	Mk 15.36	265	269		Jn 19.20	/ /	266
	Mk 15.46	266	273				
	Lk 7.28	95	79	661	Mt 10.2	70	57
	Lk 9.20	135	129		Lk 9.44	141	140
	Jn 7.46	/ /	24				
				697	Mt 4.14	21	21
506	Mk 15.40	265	270		Mt 25.26	240	229
	Lk 4.44	28	28		Mt 26.26	248	239
					Mk 12.5	218	202
551	Mk 10.46	207	187		Mk 15.5	259	257
					Lk 7.32	95	79
566	Mt 20.16	204	184		Lk 13.29	179	164
	Mt 21.21	215	198		Lk 18.37	207	187
	Mt 21.33	218	202				
	Mt 22.17	220	206	713	Mt 4.4	20	19
	Mt 27.42	264	267		Mt 5.13	32	31
	Mk 1.4	13	13		Mt 6.32	47	39
	Mk 1.31	26	26		Mt 8.29	63	48
	Mk 9.36	143	142		Mt 9.16	66	54
	Mk 12.16	220	207		Mt 9.23	67	56
	Mk 13.18	230	222		Mt 9.31	68	56
	Mk 14.61	256	252		Mt 13.14	110	94
	Mk 16.1	268	275		Mt 13.54	121	105
					Mt 14.13	125	112
569	Mt 23.23	224	214		Mt 19.14	202	178
	Mt 24.31	232	224f		Mt 19.15	202	178
	Mt 27.40	264	267		Mt 20.9	204	184
	Mt 28.15	270	278		Mt 23.29	225	216
	Mk 3.32	102	85		Mt 24.9	229	221
	Mk 6.6a	121	106		Mt 24.24	231	223
	Mk 11.17	214	197		Mt 25.1	239	228
	Mk 12.37	223	212		Mt 25.7	239	228
	Mk 15.46	266	273		Mt 25.11	239	228
					Mt 25.27	240	229
575	Mk 2.6	64	50		Mt 26.39	254	245
					Mt 27.33	264	265
597	Lk 23.39	264	268		Mk 2.16	65	53
					Mk 3.5	82	67
655	Mt 10.42	75	60		Mk 3.35	102	86
	Mt 17.19	140	139		Mk 4.24	107	92
	Lk 12.8	169	158		Mk 6.6b	122	106
	Lk 23.39	263	264		Mk 6.49	126	118
					Mk 9.21	140	139
660	Mt 5.32	36	33		Mk 11.1	210	191
	Mt 19.17	203	179		Mk 11.15	214	196
	Mt 22.45	223	212		Mk 11.27	216	199
	Lk 6.7	82	66		Mk 13.2	227	217
	Lk 10.41	159	152		Mk 14.19	247	237
	Lk 14.7	183	166		Mk 14.23	248	240
	Lk 18.15	202	178		Mk 15.32	264	268
	Lk 21.23	230	222		Mk 15.40	265	270
	Lk 22.42	254	245		Lk 2.25	11	9

ms.	Ref.	Pericope	Page	ms.	Ref.	Pericope	Page
	Lk 4.44	28	28		Mk 1.12	20	19
	Lk 6.10	82	68		Mk 1.20	24	24
	Lk 8.2	97	80		Mk 1.27	24	25
	Lk 8.12	106	90		Mk 1.31	26	26
	Lk 9.3	122	107				
	Lk 9.6	122	107	850	Jn 6.4	//	113
	Lk 10.10	153	149		Jn 9.4[bis]	//	128
	Lk 12.28	171	159				
	Lk 14.27	185	168	998	Mt 16.11	133	127
	Lk 19.32	210	193		Mt 21.25	216	200
	Lk 20.11	218	202		Mt 21.45	218	204
	Lk 20.23	220	206		Mt 23.23	224	214
	Lk 20.27	221	207		Mt 23.25	224	215
	Lk 20.34	221	209		Mt 26.46	254	246
	Lk 20.44	223	212		Mk 3.18	85	71
	Lk 21.21	230	221		Mk 3.35	102	86
	Lk 22.13	246	236		Mk 5.2	119	98
	Lk 22.34	251	242		Mk 8.5	131	124
	Lk 22.39	253	243		Mk 10.4	201	176
	Lk 23.55	266	273		Mk 11.32	216	200
	Lk 24.43	273	280		Mk 12.19	221	208
	Jn 2.12	//	24		Mk 14.2	243	232
	Jn 2.13	//	196		Lk 5.23	64	50
	Jn 3.3	//	178		Lk 5.30	65	52
	Jn 12.7	//	233		Lk 6.33[bis]	88	74
	Jn 16.23	//	198		Lk 7.32	95	79
	Jn 18.36	//	257		Lk 8.20	117	96
	Jn 19.18	//	265		Lk 9.36	138	137
					Lk 11.30	166	155
716	Mk 1.32	26	26		Lk 12.39	172	160
	Lk 8.35	119	100		Lk 13.34	181	165
	Lk 9.2	122	107		Lk 20.21	220	206
	Lk 9.17	125	116		Lk 20.23	220	206
	Lk 9.41	140	139		Jn 14.13	//	198
	Lk 9.44	141	140				
	Lk 9.54	151	148	1009	Mt 23.14	224	214
	Lk 9.57	152	148				
	Lk 12.33	171	159	1012	Mt 12.48	102	85
	Lk 14.27	185	168		Mt 13.4	103	87
	Lk 15.8	186	169		Mt 13.5	103	87
	Lk 15.14	187	169		Mt 21.2	210	192
	Lk 19.18	209	190		Mt 21.25	216	200
	Lk 20.5	216	200		Mt 22.45	223	212
	Lk 20.13	218	203		Mt 26.71	256	254
	Lk 20.19	218	204		Mk 1.11	18	17
	Lk 20.24	220	207		Mk 3.13	85	70
	Lk 21.11	228	219		Mk 7.28	129	123
					Mk 8.16	133	127
726	Mt 13.4	103	87		Mk 9.19	140	139
	Lk 22.17	248	239		Mk 13.19	230	222
					Mk 14.22	248	239
808	Ac 1.13	//	71		Lk 4.4	20	19
					Lk 4.38	25	26
821	Jn 19.10	//	261		Lk 7.11	93	78
					Lk 7.32	95	79
837	Mk 1.10	18	17		Lk 8.23	137	131

ms.	Ref.	Pericope	Page	ms.	Ref.	Pericope	Page
	Lk 9.14	125	115	1079	Mk 11.26	215	199
	Lk 9.23	137	131				
	Lk 10.37	158	151	1092	Mt 24.51	238	228
	Lk 12.28	171	159				
	Lk 17.7	195	172	1093	Mt 4.8	20	20
	Lk 18.18	203	179		Mt 8.12	58	46
	Lk 18.20	203	179		Mt 8.29	63	48
	Lk 19.2	208	189		Mt 12.27	99	82
	Lk 19.42^{bis}	211	194		Mt 12.35	99	83
	Lk 19.47	214	197		Mt 14.23	126	117
	Lk 20.25	220	207		Mt 14.24	126	117
	Lk 20.42	223	212		Mt 14.26	126	118
	Lk 21.6	227	218		Mt 16.8	133	127
	Lk 23.33	264	265		Mt 16.20	137	130
	Lk 23.34	264	265		Mt 17.4	137	136
	Lk 24.50	274	281		Mt 17.17	140	138
					Mt 18.8	145	144
1028	Lk 12.45	172	161		Mt 19.21	203	180
					Mt 21.13	212	195
1038	Mk 6.47	126	117		Mt 21.25	216	200
	Mk 8.11	132	126		Mt 21.27	216	201
	Mk 9.2	138	135		Mt 22.15	220	206
	Mk 11.27	216	199		Mt 22.17	220	206
	Mk 13.35	236	227		Mt 22.37	222	210
	Lk 5.37	66	55		Mt 22.43	223	212
	Lk 6.2	81	64		Mt 23.4	224	213
	Lk 6.45	90	76		Mt 23.25	224	215
	Lk 7.32	95	79		Mt 24.2	227	218
	Lk 8.33	119	100		Mt 24.28	231	223
	Lk 9.40	140	138		Mt 24.31	232	225
	Lk 12.56	174	162		Mt 24.32	233	225
	Lk 13.13	177	163		Mt 24.39	235	226
	Lk 19.37	210	194		Mt 26.71	256	254
	Lk 22.43	254	245		Mk 2.11	64	51
	Lk 24.7	268	277		Mk 8.1	131	124
	Lk 24.12	268	277		Mk 8.25	134	128
					Mk 8.33	136	133
1047	Mk 10.23	203	181		Mk 8.35	137	131 *sic*
	Mk 12.8	218	203		Mk 9.4^{bis}	138	135
	Mk 14.12	246	235		Mk 9.5	138	136
	Mk 14.66	256	253		Mk 9.7	138	136
	Lk 4.2	20	9		Mk 9.11	139	137
	Lk 6.13	83	68		Mk 9.12^{ter}	139	137
	Lk 6.32	88	73		Mk 10.7	201	176
	Lk 6.40	89	75		Mk 10.21	203	180
	Lk 6.49	91	77		Mk 11.4	210	193
	Lk 8.24	118	97		Mk 11.13	213	195
	Lk 8.33	119	100		Mk 12.8	218	203
	Lk 10.27	157	151		Mk 12.12	218	205
	Lk 11.52	168	157		Mk 12.13	220	206
	Lk 12.6	169	157		Mk 12.17^{bis}	220	207
	Lk 21.4	226	217		Mk 12.20^{semel} *sic*	221	208
					Mk 12.27	221	210
1064	Lk 23.25	261	262		Mk 13.19	230	222
					Mk 13.25	232	224
1075	Lk 20.2	216	199		Mk 14.17	247	237

ms.	Ref.	Pericope	Page
	Mk 15.32	264	267
	Lk 4.9	21	21
	Lk 4.34	24	25
	Lk 6.1	81	64
	Lk 6.15	83	68
	Lk 6.45	90	76
	Lk 7.9	92	77
	Lk 7.36	96	79
	Lk 7.40	96	80
	Lk 8.16	107	92
	Lk 8.25	119	98
	Lk 8.29	119	99
	Lk 9.21	135	130
	Lk 9.26	137	134
	Lk 9.28bis	138	135
	Lk 9.33	138	136
	Lk 10.37	158	151
	Lk 11.11	162	153
	Lk 11.32	166	155
	Lk 12.16	170	158
	Lk 12.24	171	159
	Lk 12.34	171	159
	Lk 12.51bis	174	161
	Lk 13.22	179	164
	Lk 14.7	183	166
	Lk 15.4	186	168
	Lk 17.37	198	175
	Lk 18.15	202	178
	Lk 18.22	203	180
	Lk 19.4	208	189
	Lk 19.5	208	189
	Lk 20.14	218	203
	Lk 20.41	223	212
	Lk 20.43	223	212
	Lk 20.44	223	212
	Lk 21.12	229	219
	Lk 22.18	248	239
	Lk 22.42	254	244
	Lk 24.30	272	280
	Jn 1.34	/ /	18
	Jn 3.5	/ /	178
	Jn 9.6	/ /	128
	Jn 12.31	/ /	150
	Jn 19.6	/ /	260
	Jn 19.17	/ /	264
1154	Lk 9.10	125	112
1170	Mt 9.5	64	50
	Mt 20.34	207	188
	Mt 27.51	265	270
	Mt 27.58	266	272
	Jn 1.21	/ /	110
	Jn 6.12	/ /	116
1187	Mt 22.17	220	206
	Lk 6.45	90	76
	Lk 8.29	119	99
	Jn 1.38	/ /	23
	Jn 18.10	/ /	248
	Jn 20.16	/ /	278
1193	Mt 12.22	99	81
1195	Mt 9.26	67	56
	Jn 18.13	/ /	249
1200	Mt 12.43	101	84
	Mt 15.37	131	125
	Mt 19.5	201	177
	Mt 26.22	247	237
	Mt 26.35	253	244
	Mt 26.36	254	244
	Mk 6.51	126	119
	Mk 13.27	232	225
	Mk 14.1	243	232
	Mk 15.16	262	263
	Lk 4.15	21	21
	Lk 5.33	66	53
	Lk 15.4	186	168
	Lk 23.35	264	267
	Lk 24.20	272	279
1201	Mk 7.28	129	123
1216	Mt 23.37	225	216
	Mt 26.42	254	246
	Mk 10.28	203	182
	Mk 13.27	232	224
	Lk 8.17	107	92
	Lk 21.31	233	225
	Lk 24.10	268	277
1229	Lk 5.33	66	53
1242	Jn 12.40	/ /	89
1279	Mt 11.26	79	63
	Mt 12.15	84	69
	Mt 23.28	224	215
	Mt 24.6	228	219
	Mt 26.10	244	233
	Mt 27.1	257	256
	Mt 27.30	262	263
	Mk 8.29	135	129
	Mk 12.13	220	205
	Lk 5.24	64	51
	Lk 6.41	89	75
	Lk 7.28	95	79
	Lk 17.37bis	198	175
	Jn 2.16	/ /	197

ms.	Ref.		Pericope	Page	ms.	Ref.		Pericope	Page
1295	Mt	14.3	124	110		Mt	26.51	255	248
	Mt	14.22	126	117		Mt	26.71	256	254
	Mt	19.7	201	117		Mk	13.22	231	223
	Mt	19.29	203	182f		Mk	14.61	256	252
	Mt	20.33	207	188		Lk	8.14	106	91
	Mt	21.1	210	191		Lk	8.54bis	120	104
	Mt	21.7	210	193		Lk	9.50	144	143
	Mt	21.18	213	195		Lk	11.42	168	156
	Mt	22.19	220	207		Lk	12.6	169	157
	Mt	22.24	221	208		Lk	21.25	232	224
	Mt	23.30	224	215		Lk	23.18	261	259
	Mt	23.37	225	216		Lk	23.33	264	265
	Mt	24.42	236	227		Jn	7.42	//	212
	Mt	24.43	237	227		Jn	19.2	//	263
	Mt	24.51	238	228					
	Mt	25.31	241	230	1365	Mt	16.25	137	131
	Mt	25.41	241	230		Mt	16.27	137	134
	Mt	26.7	244	232		Mt	20.30	207	187
	Mt	26.19	246	236		Mk	10.40	206	186
	Mt	26.42	254	246		Lk	9.47	143	141
	Mt	27.23	261	261					
	Mt	27.40	264	267	1375	Mt	15.37	131	125
	Mt	27.46	265	269		Mt	24.31	232	224
						Mt	26.26	248	239
1296	Lk	19.15	209	190		Mt	27.3	258	256
						Mk	9.32	141	141
1302	Mk	8.16	133	127		Mk	11.2	210	192
						Mk	13.27	232	224
1321	Jn	13.37	//	243		Mk	16.8	268	277
	Jn	19.15	//	262		Lk	8.16	107	92
	Jn	19.18	//	266		Lk	9.29	138	135
	Jn	19.39	//	272		Lk	13.30	179	164
	Jn	20.19	//	280		Lk	19.15	209	190
						Lk	22.17	248	239
1344	Lk	14.5	182	165		Lk	22.22bis	249	241
	Jn	6.71	//	234					
					1396	Mt	8.3	57	45
1346	Mk	7.21	128	122		Mt	8.33	63	49
	Mk	12.14	220	206		Mt	13.3	103	87
	Mk	12.27	221	210		Mt	16.1	132	126
	Jn	19.15	//	262		Mt	17.5	138	136
						Mt	21.3	210	192
1352a	Mk	15.40	265	270		Mt	26.40	254	246
						Mk	2.3	64	49
1354	Mt	20.30[1]	207	187		Mk	9.45	145	144
	Mk	3.2	82	66		Mk	10.47	207	187
	Lk	17.21	197	173		Mk	12.27	221	210
						Mk	12.28	222	210
1355	Mt	9.22	67	56		Mk	13.8	228	219
	Mt	13.32	110	94		Mk	14.6	244	234
	Mt	15.30	130	123		Mk	14.7	244	234
	Mt	22.37	222	210		Lk	8.20	117	96
	Mt	25.41	241	230		Lk	8.32	119	99
						Lk	8.39	119	101
						Lk	9.25	137	131
						Lk	9.54	151	148

[1] Misprinted as 1254.

ms.	Ref.		Pericope	Page	ms.	Ref.		Pericope	Page
1515	Mt	14.3	124	110		Mt	15.37	131	125
	Mt	14.20	125	116		Mt	21.1	210	192
	Mt	14.21	125	117		Mt	22.9	219	205
	Mt	16.13	135	129		Mt	24.46	238	227
	Mt	16.15	135	129		Mt	26.34	253	244
	Mt	17.12	139	138		Mt	27.49	265	269
	Mt	19.26	203	182		Mt	28.2	268	276
	Mt	22.13	219	205		Mt	28.10	269	278
	Mt	24.24	231	223		Mk	7.32	130	124
	Mt	24.43	237	227		Mk	8.8	131	125
	Mt	25.17	240	229		Mk	10.14	202	178
	Mt	27.60	266	273		Mk	10.26	203	181
	Mt	28.1	268	275		Mk	13.3	227	218
	Mk	2.11	64	51		Lk	6.10	82	67
	Mk	9.43	145	144		Lk	8.2ter	97	80
	Mk	10.52	207	188		Lk	9.43a	140	139
	Mk	11.14	213	196		Lk	12.28	171	159
	Mk	11.29	216	200		Lk	20.2	216	199
	Mk	11.30	216	200		Lk	20.14	218	203
	Mk	12.14	220	206					
	Mk	14.32	254	244	1573	Mt	4.21	23	24
	Mk	14.40	254	246		Mt	5.45	39	35
	Mk	15.47	266	273		Mt	15.19	127	122
	Lk	6.6	82	66		Mt	24.46	238	227
						Mt	25.22	240	229
1537	Mk	9.38	144	143		Mt	26.10	244	234
	Lk	12.18	170	158		Mk	12.29	222	210
						Mk	16.10	275	282
1542b	Mk	10.21	203	180		Lk	5.7	29	29
	Mk	10.47	207	187		Lk	11.39	168	156
	Mk	11.29	216	200		Lk	12.8	168	158
	Mk	12.34	222	211		Lk	12.42	172	160
	Mk	13.8	228	219		Lk	12.56semel sic	174	162
	Mk	13.26	232	224		Lk	13.27	179	164
	Mk	14.10bis	245	234f		Lk	17.28	198	174
	Mk	14.12	246	235		Lk	17.30	198	174
	Mk	14.20	247	238		Lk	19.12	209	189
	Mk	14.27	253	243		Lk	20.6	216	200
	Mk	14.51	255	249		Lk	20.36	221	209
	Mk	14.53	256	249					
	Mk	14.61	256	252	1574	Mt	2.19	4	4
	Mk	14.64	256	253		Mt	8.34	63	49
	Mk	14.71	256	255		Mt	9.21bis	67	56
	Mk	15.21	263	264		Mt	11.8	77	61
	Mk	15.36ter	265	269		Mt	12.1	81	64
	Mk	15.39	265	270		Mt	12.26	99	82
	Mk	15.47	266	273		Mt	13.7	103	87
	Mk	16.1	268	276		Mt	13.21	106	90
						Mt	13.31	110	94
1546	Mk	1.21	24	24		Mt	16.26	137	134
	Mk	5.27	120	102		Mt	17.20	140	140
						Mt	19.4	201	176
1547	Mk	7.28	129	123		Mt	19.9	201	177
						Mt	20.23	206	186
1555	Mt	12.36bis	99	83		Mt	21.2bis	210	192
	Mt	13.23	106	91		Mt	21.23	216	199
	Mt	14.15	125	113					

ms.	Ref.	Pericope	Page	ms.	Ref.	Pericope	Page
	Mt 21.27	216	201		Lk 18.23	203	180
	Mt 24.21	230	222		Lk 18.26	203	181
	Mt 25.23	240	229		Lk 18.31	205	184
	Mt 26.56	254	244		Lk 20.23	220	206
	Mt 27.42	264	267		Lk 20.40^{bis}	221	210
	Mt 28.10	269	278		Lk 21.10	228	219
	Mt 28.15	270	278		Lk 21.37	242	231
	Mk 1.11	18	17		Lk 22.2	243	232
	Mk 1.22	24	24		Lk 22.24	250	241
	Mk 1.32	26	26		Lk 23.16	261	258
	Mk 2.19	66	54		Lk 23.31	263	264
	Mk 3.35	102	86		Lk 23.39	264	268
	Mk 5.6	119	98				
	Mk 5.18	119	101	1579	Mt 9.35	70	56
	Mk 6.39	125	115		Mt 10.14	70	57
	Mk 7.9	128	121		Mt 12.35	99	83
	Mk 7.32	130	124		Mt 18.24	150	147
	Mk 8.7	131	125		Mt 24.31	223	212
	Mk 8.27	135	128		Mt 24.30	232	224
	Mk 8.30	135	130		Mt 24.31	232	224
	Mk 9.9^{bis}	139	137		Mk 3.29	99	83
	Mk 9.29	140	140		Mk 6.51	126	118
	Mk 11.6	210	193		Mk 14.25	248	240
	Mk 11.13	213	195		Mk 14.47	255	248
	Mk 12.23	221	209		Mk 15.1	257	256
	Mk 12.42	226	216		Mk 15.16	262	263
	Mk 13.14	230	221		Lk 9.48	143	142
	Mk 14.16	246	236		Lk 12.59	175	162
	Mk 14.18	247	237		Lk 16.16	190	170
	Mk 14.25^{bis}	248	241		Lk 19.1	208	189
	Mk 14.43	255	247		Lk 24.40	273	280
	Mk 14.44	255	247		Lk 24.44	273	281
	Mk 14.47	255	248		Jn 19.18	/ /	266
	Mk 14.49	255	249				
	Mk 14.50	255	249	1588	Mt 10.14	70	57
	Mk 14.69	256	254		Mk 2.9	64	50
	Mk 15.12^{bis}	261	260		Mk 2.11	64	51
	Mk 15.16	262	263		Mk 5.27	120	102
	Mk 15.33	265	268		Mk 13.20	230	222
	Mk 15.46	266	273		Mk 14.45	255	247
	Lk 3.16	17	16		Mk 14.71	256	255
	Lk 3.22	19	18				
	Lk 6.9	82	67	1610	1 Cor 11.25	/ /	240
	Lk 7.22	94	78				
	Lk 7.32	95	79	1635	Mt 26.39	225	216
	Lk 7.33	95	79				
	Lk 8.16	107	92	1642	Lk 1.9	6	5
	Lk 9.5	122	108		Lk 6.4	81	65
	Lk 9.26	137	134		Lk 6.10	82	68
	Lk 9.45^{bis}	141	141		Lk 7.6	92	77
	Lk 9.47	143	142		Lk 8.15	106	91
	Lk 9.60^{bis}	152	148				
	Lk 10.14	153	150	1646	Mt 19.29	203	182
	Lk 10.36	158	151				
	Lk 15.4	186	168	1654	Mk 10.47^{bis}	207	187
	Lk 18.21	203	180		Lk 4.17	22	22

ms.	Ref.	Pericope	Page	ms.	Ref.	Pericope	Page
1661	Mk 6.47	126	117		Mk 10.26	203	181
					Mk 10.48	207	188
1739	I Cor 11.24	/ /	239		Lk 3.8	·14	14
					Lk 5.28	65	52
1790[1]	Mk 1.31	25	26		Lk 6.21	86	72
					Lk 9.3	122	107
1831	I Cor 11.25	/ /	240		Lk 16.12	188	170
					Lk 17.31	198	174
1838	Ac 1.13	/ /	71		Lk 19.46	214	197
					Lk 20.25	220	207
1891	Ac 1.13	/ /	71		Jn 13.36	/ /	243
1898	Ac 1.13	/ /	71	2148	Mt 7.14	52	42
					Mk 15.39	265	270
2145	Mt 11.19	77	62		Jn 1.42	/ /	71
	Mt 13.12	104	88		Jn 16.4	/ /	223
	Mt 13.32	110	94	2355	Lk 1.77	9	8
	Mt 18.6	145	144				
	Mt 19.29	203	182	2533	Lk 4.34	24	25
	Mt 21.13	212	195		Lk 4.39	25	26
	Mt 21.21	215	198		Lk 5.19	64	49
	Mt 21.25	216	200		Lk 5.33	66	54
	Mt 24.15	230	221		Lk 6.7	82	66
	Mt 24.31	232	224		Lk 6.21	86	72
	Mt 24.36	234	226		Lk 7.19	94	78
	Mt 24.40	234	226		Lk 9.5	122	109
	Mt 26.14	245	234		Lk 9.46	143	141
	Mt 26.46	254	246		Lk 10.11	153	149
	Mk 2.4	64	49		Lk 11.13	162	153
	Mk 4.3	103	87		Lk 12.28	171	159
	Mk 5.7	119	99		Lk 13.27	179	164
	Mk 8.30	135	130		Lk 19.45	214	196
					Lk 22.61	256	250
					Lk 23.23	261	261
					Lk 23.55	266	273

[1] Misprinted as 1970.

(b) Lectionaries

ms.	Ref.	Pericope	Page	ms.	Ref.	Pericope	Page
l 1	Lk 2.51[bis]	12	11		Mk 6.7	122	106
	Lk 8.31	119	99		Lk 8.32	119	99
l 2	Mt 23.26	224	215	l 4	Mk 15.34	265	269
	Mk 3.31	102	85		Lk 11.13	162	153
	Mk 5.1	119	98				
	Mk 5.6	119	98	l 5	Mt 6.3	40	36
	Lk 11.29	166	155		Mt 19.7[mg]	201	177
	Lk 18.31	205	184		Mt 19.16	203	179
	Lk 19.4	208	189		Mt 19.22	203	180
l 3	Mt 6.3	40	36		Lk 6.4	81	65

ms.	Ref.		Pericope	Page	ms.	Ref.		Pericope	Page
	Lk	9.5	122	109		Lk	19.42	211	194
	Lk	10.25	157	151	*l* 11	Lk	6.49	91	77
	Lk	21.8	228	219		Lk	8.52	120	104
l 6	Mt	23.35	224	216		Lk	9.5	122	109
	Mt	26.63	256	252		Lk	9.41	140	139
	Mk	14.40	254	246	*l* 12	Mt	6.3	40	36
	Mk	16.18	275	283		Mt	12.47	102	85
	Lk	22.14	247	237		Mt	13.13	104	89
	Lk	22.22	249	241		Mt	13.55	121	105
l 7	Mt	6.3	40	36		Mt	18.11bis	147	145
	Mt	10.12	70	57		Mt	22.30	221	209
	Mt	10.14	70	57		Mt	23.26	224	215
	Mt	28.15	270	278		Mk	4.5	103	87
	Mk	6.2	121	105		Mk	4.24	107	92
	Mk	9.29	140	140		Mk	4.37	118	97
	Mk	10.6	201	176		Mk	7.28	129	123
	Mk	11.1	210	191		Mk	10.7	201	177
	Mk	14.19	247	237		Mk	10.16	202	178
	Mk	14.45	255	247		Mk	11.1	210	191
	Mk	14.70	256	254		Mk	11.25	215	199
	Mk	15.1	257	256		Mk	11.28	216	199
	Lk	3.16	16	15		Mk	12.8	218	203
	Lk	5.2semel *sic*	29	29		Mk	12.16	220	207
	Lk	13.9	176	162		Mk	13.27	232	224
	Lk	21.10	228	219		Mk	14.14	246	236
	Lk	23.26	263	263		Mk	14.19	247	237
l 8	Mk	4.1	103	86		Mk	14.45	255	247
	Mk	5.1	119	98		Mk	15.1	257	256
l 9	Mk	4.41	118	98		Lk	5.26	64	51
	Mk	12.3	218	202		Lk	7.6	92	77
	Mk	12.16	220	207		Lk	7.11	93	78
	Mk	13.27	232	224		Lk	7.22	94	78
	Mk	14.19	247	237		Lk	8.2	97	80
	Mk	14.22	248	239		Lk	8.45	120	102
	Mk	15.1	257	256		Lk	9.1	122	106
l 10	Mt	7.14	52	42		Lk	9.35	138	136
	Mt	18.11bis	147	145		Lk	9.41	140	139
	Mt	22.23	221	207		Lk	9.56	151	148
	Mk	3.29	99	83		Lk	10.25cbis	157	151
	Mk	4.1	103	86		Lk	11.13	162	153
	Mk	4.24	107	92		Lk	13.15	178	163
	Mk	4.37	118	97		Lk	15.1	186	168
	Mk	5.1	119	98		Lk	15.4	186	168
	Mk	10.19	203	179		Lk	16.19	191	171
	Mk	10.25	203	181		Lk	18.36	207	187
	Mk	11.25	215	199		Lk	18.40	207	188
	Mk	12.3	218	202		Lk	18.43	207	188
	Mk	14.4	244	233		Lk	21.8	228	219
	Mk	14.19	247	237		Lk	21.12	229	219
	Mk	14.45	255	247	*l* 13	Mt	6.3	40	36
	Mk	15.10	261	259		Mt	23.35	224	216
						Mk	5.1	119	98
						Mk	9.3	138	135

ms.	Ref.	Pericope	Page
	Mk 9.7	138	137
	Mk 10.34	205	185
	Mk 11.1	210	191
	Mk 11.2	210	192
	Mk 12.23	221	209
	Mk 12.37	223	212
	Mk 13.6	228	218
	Mk 14.24	248	240
	Mk 14.54	256	250
	Mk 14.64	256	253
	Mk 14.70	256	254
	Mk 15.1	257	255
	Mk 15.10	261	259
	Mk 15.12	261	260
	Mk 15.24	264	265
	Mk 15.35	265	269
	Mk 15.37	265	269
	Mk 15.46	266	272
	Lk 5.2	29	29
	Lk 6.10	82	68
	Lk 7.18	94	78
	Lk 10.25	157	151
	Lk 13.9	176	162
	Lk 16.16	190	170
	Lk 16.18	190	170
	Lk 20.34	221	209
	Lk 21.8	228	218
	Lk 21.10	228	219
	Lk 21.33	234	226
	Lk 22.3	259	257
l 14	Mk 5.1	119	98
	Mk 11.1	210	191
	Mk 12.20	221	208
	Mk 14.19	247	237
	Mk 14.64	256	253
	Mk 14.67[bis]	256	253
	Mk 15.1	257	256
	Lk 2.51	12	11
	Lk 3.30	19	18
	Lk 6.10	82	68
	Lk 7.18	94	78
	Lk 10.25	157	151
	Lk 17.21	197	173
	Lk 20.34	221	209
	Lk 21.8	228	218
	Lk 21.10	228	219
l 15	Mk 9.28	140	140
	Mk 11.2	210	192
	Mk 12.31	222	211
	Mk 13.32	234	226
	Mk 15.12	261	260
	Mk 15.13	261	260
	Mk 15.16	262	263
	Lk 7.18	94	78

ms.	Ref.	Pericope	Page
	Lk 10.25	157	151
	Lk 11.13	162	153
	Lk 14.3[bis]	182	165
	Lk 20.34	221	209
	Lk 22.11	246	236
l 16	Mt 24.23	231	223
	Lk 3.24	19	18
	Lk 10.25	157	151
	Lk 19.4[bis]	208	189
l 17	Mk 5.1	119	98
	Mk 8.29	135	129
	Mk 12.31	222	211
	Mk 14.19	247	237
	Mk 14.45	255	247
	Mk 14.54	256	250
	Mk 14.64	256	253
	Mk 14.67[bis]	256	253
	Mk 14.68	256	254
	Mk 14.70	256	254
	Mk 15.1	257	256
	Mk 15.35	265	269
	Mk 15.37	265	269
	Lk 4.7	20	20
	Lk 5.2	29	29
	Lk 6.10	82	68
	Lk 7.18	94	78
	Lk 9.7	123	109
	Lk 10.25	157	151
	Lk 13.9	176	162
	Lk 14.8	183	166
	Lk 16.16	190	170
	Lk 16.18	190	171
	Lk 19.2	208	189
	Lk 19.4[bis]	208	189
	Lk 20.34	221	209
	Lk 22.40	254	244
l 18	Mk 3.31	102	85
	Mk 4.5	103	87
	Mk 4.37	118	97
	Mk 5.2	119	98
	Mk 5.14	119	100
	Mk 6.9	122	108
	Mk 7.18	128	122
	Mk 7.28	129	123
	Mk 8.7	131	125
	Mk 8.8	131	125
	Mk 8.9	131	125
	Mk 8.19	133	127
	Mk 8.27	135	129
	Mk 8.30	135	130
	Mk 9.2	138	135
	Mk 9.42	145	143
	Mk 9.47	145	145

ms.	Ref.		Pericope	Page	ms.	Ref.		Pericope	Page
	Mk	10.4	201	176	*l* 19	Mt	10.1	70	57
	Mk	10.16	202	178		Mk	3.31	102	85
	Mk	10.19	203	180		Mk	4.5	103	87
	Mk	10.21^{bis}	203	180		Mk	4.37	118	97
	Mk	10.27	203	181		Mk	5.2	119	98
	Mk	10.46	207	187		Mk	5.6	119	98
	Mk	10.47	207	187		Mk	5.14	119	100
	Mk	10.49	207	188		Mk	5.22	120	101
	Mk	11.15	214	196		Mk	6.9	122	108
	Mk	11.18	214	197		Mk	7.18	128	122
	Mk	11.25	215	199		Mk	7.28	129	123
	Mk	12.8	218	203		Mk	8.7	131	125
	Mk	12.9	218	204		Mk	8.9	131	125
	Mk	12.14^{ter}	220	206		Mk	8.19	133	127
	Mk	12.18	221	208		Mk	9.2	138	135
	Mk	12.23	221	209		Mk	9.35	138	136
	Mk	12.34	221	209		Mk	9.42	145	143
	Mk	12.43	224	217		Mk	9.46	145	143
	Mk	13.5	228	218		Mk	9.47	145	145
	Mk	13.9	229	220		Mk	10.16	202	178
	Mk	13.25	232	224		Mk	10.21^{bis}	203	180
	Mk	14.14	246	236		Mk	10.27	203	181
	Mk	14.22	248	239		Mk	10.47	207	187
	Mk	14.24	248	240		Mk	10.49	207	188
	Mk	14.43	255	247		Mk	10.51	207	188
	Mk	14.45	255	247		Mk	11.15	214	196
	Mk	14.62	256	252		Mk	11.18	214	197
	Mk	15.11	261	259		Mk	11.25	215	199
	Lk	4.16	22	22		Mk	12.3	218	202
	Lk	4.44	28	28		Mk	12.8	218	203
	Lk	5.14	57	45		Mk	12.9	218	204
	Lk	6.20	86	72		Mk	12.14^{bis}	220	206
	Lk	6.49	91	77		Mk	12.18	221	208
	Lk	7.13	93	78		Mk	12.43	226	217
	Lk	7.18	94	78		Mk	13.5	228	218
	Lk	7.22	94	78		Mk	13.9	229	220
	Lk	7.28	95	79		Mk	13.25	232	224
	Lk	7.33	95	79		Mk	13.27	232	224
	Lk	8.45	120	102		Mk	14.14	246	236
	Lk	9.49	145	143		Mk	14.22	248	239
	Lk	11.13	162	153		Mk	14.37	254	246
	Lk	11.29	166	155		Mk	14.43	255	247
	Lk	12.29	171	159		Mk	14.45	255	247
	Lk	12.31	171	159		Mk	14.62	256	252
	Lk	12.43	172	161		Mk	14.67	256	253
	Lk	13.21	178	163		Lk	4.38	25	26
	Lk	15.1	186	168		Lk	6.20	86	72
	Lk	18.29	203	182		Lk	6.49	91	77
	Lk	18.31	205	184		Lk	7.18	94	78
	Lk	18.40	207	188		Lk	7.22	94	78
	Lk	18.43	207	188		Lk	7.28	95	79
	Lk	19.38	210	194		Lk	8.45	120	102
	Lk	20.15	218	204		Lk	8.52	120	104
	Lk	21.10	228	219		Lk	9.41	140	139
	Lk	22.4	245	235		Lk	9.49	144	143
	Lk	23.26	263	264		Lk	9.59	152	148

ms.	Ref.		Pericope	Page	ms.	Ref.		Pericope	Page
	Lk	3.5	14	13		Mk	11.18	214	197
	Lk	4.34	24	25		Mk	12.37	223	212
	Lk	5.20	64	50		Lk	4.8	20	20
	Lk	5.22	64	50		Lk	4.44	28	28
	Lk	5.29	65	52		Lk	5.20	64	50
	Lk	6.3	81	65					
	Lk	6.5	81	66	*l* 36	Mt	26.36	254	244
	Lk	6.8	82	67		Mk	1.33	26	27
	Lk	6.10	82	68		Mk	2.22	66	55
	Lk	7.6	92	77		Mk	3.31	102	85
	Lk	7.11	93	78		Mk	10.6	201	176
	Lk	7.44	96	80		Mk	10.16	202	178
	Lk	8.9	104	88		Mk	10.17	203	179
	Lk	8.10	104	88		Mk	10.21	203	180
	Lk	8.16	107	92		Mk	10.46	207	187
	Lk	8.31	119	99		Mk	11.2^{ter}	210	192
	Lk	8.32	119	99		Mk	11.8	210	194
	Lk	8.33	119	100		Mk	11.28	216	199
	Lk	8.52	120	104		Mk	12.7	218	203
	Lk	8.54	120	104		Mk	12.21	221	208
	Lk	9.1	122	106		Mk	13.32	234	226
	Lk	9.5	122	109		Mk	14.19	247	237
	Lk	9.41	140	139		Mk	14.22	248	239
	Lk	9.42	140	139		Mk	14.45	255	247
	Lk	9.59	152	148		Mk	14.46	255	248
	Lk	10.25^{bis}	157	151		Mk	14.67^{bis}	256	253
	Lk	10.32^{bis}	158	151		Mk	15.27	264	266
	Lk	11.13	162	153		Mk	15.31	264	267
	Lk	12.5	169	157		Lk	8.45	120	102
	Lk	13.15	177	163		Lk	9.50	144	143
	Lk	13.21	178	163		Lk	10.15	153	150
	Lk	14.11	183	166		Lk	13.21	178	163
	Lk	14.21	184	167		Lk	18.20	203	180
	Lk	16.19	191	171		Lk	18.25	203	181
	Lk	17.10	195	172		Lk	19.4	208	189
	Lk	17.12	196	172		Lk	19.22	209	190
	Lk	18.21	203	180		Lk	22.6^{bis}	245	235
	Lk	18.22	203	180					
	Lk	18.25	203	181	*l* 37	Lk	10.42	159	152
	Lk	18.36	207	187					
	Lk	18.39	207	188	*l* 38	Lk	18.31	205	184
	Lk	18.43	207	188					
	Lk	19.4	208	189	*l* 39	Lk	12.18	170	158
l 33	Mk	5.27	120	102	*l* 40	Lk	8.16	107	92
	Mk	11.25	215	199		Lk	8.52	120	104
	Lk	1.17	6	5		Lk	9.5	122	109
	Lk	4.16	22	22		Lk	9.31	138	135
	Lk	6.3	81	65		Lk	22.34	251	242
	Lk	8.24	118	97					
	Lk	9.5	122	107	*l* 42	Lk	15.26	187	169
	Lk	13.21	178	163					
	Lk	19.4	208	189	*l* 44	Mt	6.5	41	36
						Mt	21.23	216	199
l 34	Mk	1.13	20	20		Mt	26.36	254	244
	Mk	1.15	21	22		Mt	26.63	256	252

ms.	Ref.	Pericope	Page
	Mk 1.10	18	17
	Mk 5.34^bis	120	103
	Mk 6.7	122	107
	Mk 6.11	122	109
	Mk 6.23	124	111
	Mk 8.44	135	129
	Mk 9.38^bis	144	143
	Mk 10.34^bis	205	185
	Mk 15.24	264	265
	Mk 15.26	264	266
	Lk 1.17	6	5
	Lk 1.28	7	6
	Lk 2.40	11	10
	Lk 4.17	22	22
	Lk 5.22	64	50
	Lk 5.24	64	51
	Lk 5.31	65	53
	Lk 6.3	81	65
	Lk 6.4	81	65
	Lk 7.13	93	78
	Lk 8.15	106	91
	Lk 8.16	107	92
	Lk 8.18	107	92
	Lk 13.21	178	163
	Lk 15.26	187	169
	Lk 17.14	196	172
	Lk 21.8	228	219
	Lk 21.27	232	224
	Lk 22.11	246	236
	Lk 22.25	250	241
	Lk 22.34	251	242
	Lk 24.10	268	277
	Lk 24.12	268	277
l 46	Mt 6.3	40	36
	Mk 11.25	215	199
	Lk 8.18	107	92
l 47	Mt 7.14	52	42
	Mt 8.7	58	46
	Mt 9.5	64	50
	Mt 9.27	68	56
	Mt 10.18	71	58
	Mt 12.31	99	83
	Mt 17.22	141	140
	Mt 18.26	150	147
	Mt 24.6	228	219
	Mt 24.14	229	221
	Mt 27.1	257	255
	Mt 27.15	261	259
	Mt 27.23	261	261
	Mt 27.33	264	264
	Mt 27.37	264	264
	Mk 1.10	18	17
	Mk 1.11	18	18
	Mk 1.38	27	27

ms.	Ref.	Pericope	Page
	Mk 5.34^bis	120	103
	Mk 6.18	124	111
	Mk 9.38^bis	144	133
	Mk 15.1	257	255
	Mk 15.6^semel sic	261	259
	Mk 15.10	261	259
	Mk 15.16	262	263
	Lk 2.26	11	9
	Lk 3.16	16	15
	Lk 5.20	64	50
	Lk 5.24	64	51
	Lk 5.25	64	51
	Lk 5.26	64	51
	Lk 5.31^bis	65	53
	Lk 6.3	81	65
	Lk 6.4	81	65
	Lk 7.13	93	78
	Lk 8.15	106	91
	Lk 8.17	107	92
	Lk 8.18	107	92
	Lk 8.42	120	102
	Lk 9.5	122	108
	Lk 9.34	138	136
	Lk 9.35	138	136
	Lk 12.10	169	158
	Lk 13.21	178	163
	Lk 18.39	207	188
	Lk 18.43	207	188
	Lk 19.2	208	189
	Lk 19.4	208	189
	Lk 23.35	264	267
	Lk 23.47	265	270
	Lk 24.12	268	277
	Jn 19.4	/ /	260
l 48	Mt 5.29	35	33
	Mt 5.39	38	34
	Mt 5.47	39	35
	Mt 12.8	81	66
	Mt 12.12	82	67
	Mt 12.13	82	68
	Mt 12.48	102	85
	Mt 16.12	133	127
	Mt 16.25	137	131
	Mt 21.6	210	193
	Mt 21.20	215	197
	Mt 21.21	215	198
	Mt 21.25	216	200
	Mt 24.14	229	219
	Mt 24.15	230	221
	Mt 24.16	230	221
	Mt 24.18	230	222
	Mt 24.24	231	223
	Mt 24.45	238	227
	Mt 25.7	239	228
	Mt 26.7	244	232

ms.	Ref.	Pericope	Page	ms.	Ref.	Pericope	Page
Mt	26.42	254	246	Mk	8.19	133	127
Mt	26.59	256	251	Mk	8.20	133	127
Mt	27.38	264	266	Mk	8.34	135	130
Mt	27.54	265	270	Mk	9.2	138	135
Mt	27.56	265	271	Mk	9.3	138	135
Mk	1.13	20	21	Mk	9.4	138	135
Mk	1.16	23	20	Mk	9.7	138	136
Mk	1.21^{bis}	24	24	Mk	9.8	138	137
Mk	1.25	24	25	Mk	9.11	139	137
Mk	1.27	24	25	Mk	9.45	145	144
Mk	1.28	24	25	Mk	10.4	201	176
Mk	1.33	26	27	Mk	10.7^{bis}	201	176f
Mk	1.36	27	27	Mk	10.21	203	180
Mk	2.4	64	49	Mk	10.47	207	187
Mk	2.22	66	55	Mk	10.48	207	188
Mk	3.21	98	81	Mk	10.49^{bis}	207	188
Mk	3.27	99	82	Mk	10.51	207	188
Mk	3.29	99	83	Mk	10.52	207	188
Mk	4.5	103	87	Mk	11.1	210	191
Mk	4.7	103	87	Mk	11.2	210	192
Mk	4.24	107	92	Mk	11.3^{bis}	210	192
Mk	4.31	110	94	Mk	11.6^{bis}	210	193
Mk	4.38	118	97	Mk	11.27^{bis}	215	199
Mk	4.41	118	98	Mk	12.2	218	202
Mk	5.6	119	98	Mk	12.3	218	202
Mk	5.7	119	99	Mk	12.4	218	202
Mk	5.9	119	99	Mk	12.5	218	203
Mk	5.10	119	99	Mk	12.7	218	203
Mk	5.11	119	99	Mk	12.16	220	207
Mk	5.13	119	100	Mk	12.20	221	208
Mk	5.14	119	100	Mk	12.35	223	212
Mk	5.18	119	101	Mk	12.37	223	212
Mk	5.23	120	101	Mk	13.8	227	219
Mk	5.24	120	102	Mk	14.51	255	249
Mk	5.27	120	102	Mk	15.3	259	257
Mk	5.33	120	103	Mk	15.4	259	257
Mk	5.34^{bis}	120	103	Mk	15.11	261	259
Mk	5.35	120	103	Mk	15.14	261	261
Mk	5.37	120	103	Mk	15.26	264	266
Mk	5.40	120	104	Mk	15.29	264	267
Mk	5.42	120	104	Lk	4.8^{bis}	20	20
Mk	5.52	120	104	Lk	4.16	22	22
Mk	5.54	120	104	Lk	4.39	25	26
Mk	6.3	121	105	Lk	4.44	28	28
Mk	6.8	122	107	Lk	5.22	64	50
Mk	6.9	122	108	Lk	5.31	65	53
Mk	6.11	122	109	Lk	6.3	81	65
Mk	6.45	126	117	Lk	6.40	89	75
Mk	6.47	126	117	Lk	7.25	95	78
Mk	6.49	126	118	Lk	7.33	95	79
Mk	7.3	128	120	Lk	8.16	107	92
Mk	7.4	128	120	Lk	8.42	120	102
Mk	7.16	128	121	Lk	8.45	120	102
Mk	7.18	128	122	Lk	9.3	122	108
Mk	8.7^{bis}	131	125	Lk	9.33^{bis}	138	136
Mk	8.9	131	125	Lk	9.35	138	136

ms.	Ref.	Pericope	Page	ms.	Ref.	Pericope	Page
	Mk 10.32	205	184		Lk 9.49	144	143
	Mk 10.46	207	187		Lk 9.50	144	143
	Mk 10.47	207	187		Lk 11.11	162	153
	Mk 10.49	207	188		Lk 11.13	162	153
	Mk 10.51	207	188		Lk 11.29	166	155
	Mk 10.52	207	188		Lk 12.5	169	157
	Mk 11.1^{bis}	210	191		Lk 12.29	171	159
	Mk 11.18	214	197		Lk 12.43	172	161
	Mk 12.2	218	202		Lk 12.51	174	161
	Mk 12.3	218	202		Lk 14.3	182	165
	Mk 12.7	218	203		Lk 15.1	186	168
	Mk 12.9	218	204		Lk 15.4	186	168
	Mk 12.14^{bis}	220	206		Lk 18.29	203	182
	Mk 12.16	220	207		Lk 18.31	205	184
	Mk 12.20	221	208		Lk 18.40	207	188
	Mk 12.25	221	209		Lk 18.43^{bis}	207	188
	Mk 12.27	221	210		Lk 19.22	209	190
	Mk 12.35	223	212		Lk 20.10	218	202
	Mk 12.43^{bis}	226	217		Lk 20.33	221	209
	Mk 12.44	226	217		Lk 20.34	221	209
	Mk 13.8	227	219		Lk 20.35	221	209
	Mk 13.9	229	220		Lk 21.8	228	219
	Mk 13.25	232	224		Lk 21.21	230	221
	Mk 13.28^{bis}	233	225		Lk 22.11	246	236
	Mk 13.32	234	226		Lk 22.17	248	239
	Mk 14.3	244	234		Lk 22.25	250	241
	Mk 14.8	244	234		Lk 22.42	254	245
	Mk 14.14	246	236		Lk 23.19	261	260
	Mk 14.37	254	246		Lk 23.25	261	262
	Mk 14.43	255	247		Lk 23.53	266	273
	Mk 14.51	255	249		Lk 24.10	268	277
	Mk 14.62	256	252		Jn 1.49	/ /	130
	Mk 14.67	256	253		Jn 18.11	/ /	248
	Mk 14.70	256	254				
	Mk 15.3	259	257	*l* 50	Mt 8.10	58	46
	Mk 15.15	261	261		Mt 9.2	64	50
	Mk 15.17	262	263		Mt 9.10	65	52
	Mk 15.32^{bis}	264	267		Mt 9.27	68	56
	Mk 15.36	265	269		Mt 27.15	261	259
	Lk 4.8	20	20		Mk 4.4	103	87
	Lk 4.16	22	22		Mk 5.34^{bis}	120	103
	Lk 4.23	22	22		Lk 5.27	65	52
	Lk 5.17	64	49		Lk 6.4	81	65
	Lk 5.26	64	51		Lk 7.8	92	77
	Lk 6.20	86	72		Lk 8.32	119	99
	Lk 6.29^{bis}	88	73		Lk 9.31	138	135
	Lk 6.49	91	77		Lk 13.21	178	163
	Lk 7.22	94	78		Lk 18.22	203	180
	Lk 7.28	95	79		Lk 18.43	207	188
	Lk 8.13	106	90		Lk 21.8^{bis}	228	218f
	Lk 8.15	106	91				
	Lk 8.42	120	102	*l* 51	Mt 19.22	203	180
	Lk 8.45	120	102		Mk 4.4	103	87
	Lk 9.25	137	131		Mk 6.9	122	108
	Lk 9.35	138	136		Mk 6.34	125	113
	Lk 9.41	140	139		Lk 4.7	20	20

ms.	Ref.		Pericope	Page	ms.	Ref.		Pericope	Page
_l_ 52	Mt	27.33	264	265		Lk	12.55	174	162
	Mt	27.54	265	270	_l_ 64	Jn	14.14	/ /	198
	Lk	19.4	208	189		Jn	16.4	/ /	223
_l_ 53	Mt	26.59	256	251					
	Mt	28.2	268	276	_l_ 67	Mk	15.16	262	263
	Mt	28.6	268	277					
	Mt	28.9	269	278	_l_ 68	Mk	6.2	121	105
	Mk	1.36	27	27					
	Mk	6.17	124	110	_l_ 69	Mt	13.55	121	105
	Mk	6.28	124	112		Mt	18.11[bis]	147	145
	Mk	9.19	140	138		Mt	23.26	224	215
	Mk	9.24	140	139		Mk	2.10	64	51
	Lk	4.23	22	22		Mk	7.8	128	121
	Lk	8.16	107	92		Mk	9.35	138	136
	Lk	9.27	137	134		Mk	11.26	215	199
	Lk	12.10	169	158		Lk	9.56	151	148
	Lk	21.27	232	224		Lk	11.13	162	153
						Jn	16.4	/ /	223
_l_ 54	Mt	1.11	1	1					
	Mt	2.19	4	4	_l_ 70	Mt	13.13	104	89
	Mt	8.4	57	45		Mt	18.11[bis]	147	145
	Mt	24.28	231	223		Mt	23.26	224	215
	Mt	27.1	257	255		Mk	2.10	64	51
	Mt	27.15	261	258		Mk	9.45	145	144
	Mt	27.33	264	265		Mk	11.26	215	199
	Mt	27.54	265	270		Lk	11.13	162	153
	Mt	28.6	268	277					
	Mk	6.14	123	109	_l_ 72	Mk	10.40	206	186
	Mk	6.18	124	111					
	Mk	10.32	205	184	_l_ 76	Mt	7.14	52	42
	Mk	16.3	268	276		Mt	8.25	62	48
	Lk	3.14	14	16		Mt	9.5	64	50
	Lk	7.42	96	80		Mt	18.21	149	147
						Mt	18.26	150	147
_l_ 55	Mt	8.26	62	48		Mt	20.30	207	187
	Mt	27.48	265	269		Mt	22.30	221	209
	Mk	6.22	124	111		Mt	23.14	224	214
	Lk	6.21	86	72		Mk	1.27	24	25
	Lk	13.9	176	162		Mk	2.10	64	51
	Lk	19.4	208	189		Mk	6.41	125	116
	Jn	15.20	/ /	75		Mk	7.8	128	121
						Mk	8.7	131	125
_l_ 60	Mt	6.32	57	39		Mk	12.23	221	209
	Mk	2.10	64	51		Mk	14.30[bis]	253	244
	Mk	10.40	206	186		Mk	14.68	256	254
	Lk	5.20	64	49		Lk	9.47	143	141
	Lk	5.24	64	51		Lk	9.56	151	148
	Lk	12.42	172	160		Lk	19.38	210	194
	Lk	23.58[bis]	264	267		Jn	16.4	/ /	223
_l_ 63	Mk	14.16	246	236	_l_ 77	Lk	10.25	157	151
	Mk	15.16[bis]	262	263					
	Lk	12.40	172	160	_l_ 80	Mt	13.13	104	89
	Lk	12.42	172	160		Mt	18.11[bis]	147	145
	Lk	12.51	174	161		Mt	21.31	217	201

ms.	Ref.		Pericope	Page	ms.	Ref.		Pericope	Page
	Mt	22.30	221	209	l 158	Mk	1.33	26	27
	Mt	23.26	224	215	l 181	Mt	26.59	256	251
	Mk	3.20	98	81					
	Mk	11.25	215	199	l 183	Mt	3.16	18	17
	Lk	5.2	29	29		Mt	6.32	47	39
	Lk	6.4	81	65		Mt	7.12	51	41
	Lk	6.10	82	68		Mt	8.23	62	48
	Lk	6.33	88	74		Mt	9.22	67	56
	Lk	9.59	152	148		Mt	9.27	68	56
	Lk	13.15	177	163		Mt	21.18	213	195
	Lk	15.1	186	168		Mt	21.25	216	200
	Lk	15.4	186	168		Mt	22.21	220	209
	Lk	16.19	191	171		Mt	23.34	224	215
	Lk	17.10	195	172		Mt	24.6	228	219
	Lk	18.36	207	187		Mt	24.21	230	222
	Lk	18.40	207	188		Mt	26.18	246	236
	Lk	21.8	228	219		Mt	26.71	256	252
						Mt	27.1	257	255
l 88	Lk	10.15	153	150		Mt	27.33	264	265
						Mt	27.37	264	266
l 108	Lk	10.25	157	151		Mt	27.41	264	267
						Mt	27.54	265	270
l 124	Mk	12.14	220	206		Mt	27.56	265	271
	Mk	12.44	226	217		Mt	28.17	271	279
						Mk	1.11	18	18
l 130	Lk	10.25	157	151		Mk	5.34	120	103
						Mk	6.7	122	107
l 134	Mk	1.13	20	21		Mk	6.8	122	107
						Mk	6.18	124	111
l 135	Jn	19.15	/ /	262		Mk	9.31	141	140
	Jn	19.16bis	/ /	263		Mk	12.30	222	211
	Jn	19.17	/ /	265		Mk	12.31	222	211
	Jn	19.19	/ /	266		Mk	13.9	229	220
						Mk	13.11	229	220
l 148	Mt	5.37	37	33		Mk	15.16bis	262	263
	Lk	18.39	207	188		Mk	15.26	264	266
						Mk	15.33	265	268
l 150	Mt	8.25	62	48		Mk	15.46	266	272
	Mt	10.4	70	57		Mk	16.9	275	282
	Mk	2.10	64	51		Lk	4.16	22	22
	Mk	8.9	131	125		Lk	5.2	29	29
	Mk	8.13	132	126		Lk	5.24	64	51
	Mk	8.17ter	133	127		Lk	6.3	81	65
	Mk	8.19	133	127		Lk	7.25	95	78
	Mk	8.21	133	127		Lk	7.26	95	79
	Mk	10.27	203	181		Lk	7.46	96	80
	Mk	14.30bis	253	244		Lk	8.25	119	98
	Mk	14.47	255	248		Lk	8.42	120	102
	Lk	6.4	81	65		Lk	9.34	138	136
	Lk	13.13	104	89		Lk	9.35	138	136
	Lk	16.14	189	170		Lk	12.7	169	157
	Lk	18.25	203	181		Lk	13.27	179	164
	Lk	21.19	229	221		Lk	13.34	181	165
	Lk	23.50	266	272		Lk	14.11	183	166
	Jn	18.5	/ /	247		Lk	18.18	203	179
	Jn	21.4	/ /	29					

ms.	Ref.	Pericope	Page
	Lk 17.35	198	174
	Lk 17.37	198	175
	Lk 18.6	199	175
	Lk 18.31	205	184
	Lk 18.32	205	184
	Lk 18.36	207	187
	Lk 19.4^{bis}	208	189
	Lk 19.42	211	194
	Lk 19.44	211	195
	Lk 19.46	214	197
	Lk 19.48	214	197
	Lk 20.5	216	200
	Lk 20.10	218	202
	Lk 20.24	220	207
	Lk 20.30	221	208
	Lk 20.34	221	209
	Lk 20.35	221	209
	Lk 20.40	221	210
	Lk 21.10	228	219
	Lk 21.11	228	219
	Lk 21.13	229	220
	Lk 22.40	254	244
	Lk 22.42	254	245
	Lk 22.43	254	245
	Lk 22.52	256	249
	Lk 23.8	260	258
	Lk 23.12	260	258
	Lk 23.14	261	258
	Lk 23.25	261	262
	Lk 23.26	263	263
	Lk 23.43	264	268
	Lk 23.44	268	260
	Jn 5.46	/ /	171
	Jn 14.14	/ /	198
	Jn 16.4	/ /	223
	Jn 18.11	/ /	248
	Jn 20.12	/ /	278
l 185	Mt 5.32	36	33
	Mt 5.44	39	35
	Mt 8.23	62	48
	Mt 8.25	62	48
	Mt 10.3	70	57
	Mt 16.12	133	127
	Mt 18.11^{bis}	147	145
	Mt 21.25	216	200
	Mt 22.23	221	207
	Mt 22.30	221	209
	Mt 25.30	240	229
	Mt 26.27	248	240
	Mk 2.12	64	51
	Mk 3.29	99	83
	Mk 5.37	120	103
	Mk 6.22	124	111
	Mk 6.39	125	115
	Mk 6.41	125	116

ms.	Ref.	Pericope	Page
	Mk 9.43	145	144
	Mk 10.4	201	176
	Mk 10.7	201	176
	Mk 10.20	203	180
	Mk 14.4	244	233
	Mk 15.24	264	266
	Lk 9.35	138	136
	Lk 9.56	151	148
	Lk 11.13^{bis}	162	153
	Lk 12.43	172	161
	Lk 17.35^{bis}	198	174
	Lk 18.31	205	184
	Lk 19.32	210	193
	Lk 22.10	246	236
	Lk 22.22	249	241
	Lk 23.16	261	258
	Lk 23.50	266	272
	Jn 12.4^{bis}	/ /	233
	Jn 16.4	/ /	223
	Jn 18.11	/ /	248
l 187	Mt 6.33	47	40
l 195	Mk 3.7	84	69
l 196	Lk 5.24	64	51
	Lk 6.4	81	65
	Lk 7.13	93	78
l 211	Mt 3.16	18	17
	Mt 8.8	57	46
	Mt 13.55	121	105
	Mt 16.12	133	127
	Mt 18.11^{bis}	147	145
	Mt 24.6	228	219
	Mk 1.40	57	44
	Mk 2.10	64	51
	Mk 3.20	98	81
	Mk 7.8	128	121
	Mk 12.23	221	209
	Mk 14.25	248	240
	Lk 7.28	95	79
	Lk 9.35	138	136
	Lk 11.13	162	153
	Lk 13.35	181	165
	Lk 22.42	254	245
	Jn 12.4^{bis}	/ /	233
l 219	Jn 14.14	/ /	198
l 238	Lk 19.20	209	190
l 241	Lk 23.23	261	261
l 246	Mk 6.14	123	109

ms.	Ref.		Pericope	Page	ms.	Ref.		Pericope	Page
l 251	Mk	1.10	18	17		Mk	15.32^{quater}	264	267
	Mk	2.6	64	50		Mk	15.46^{bis}	266	273
	Mk	4.5	103	87		Mk	16.1	268	275
	Mk	4.10	104	88		Mk	16.18	275	283
	Mk	4.11	104	88		Lk	2.48	12	11
	Mk	4.22	107	92		Lk	6.23	86	72
	Mk	5.23	120	101		Lk	22.43	254	245
	Mk	5.28	120	101		Lk	24.50	274	281
	Mk	8.19	133	127		Jn	6.17	/ /	117
	Mk	8.21	133	127		Jn	12.4	/ /	233
	Mk	9.2	138	135		Jn	18.5	/ /	247
	Mk	9.3	138	135		Jn	19.4	/ /	260
	Mk	9.8	138	137		Jn	20.16	/ /	278
	Mk	9.32^{bis}	141	141		Jn	20.21	/ /	281
	Mk	9.45	145	144					
	Mk	10.16	202	178	*l* 258	Mk	8.31	136	132
	Mk	10.21	203	180		Lk	4.17	22	22
	Mk	10.43^{bis}	206	186		Lk	10.25	157	151
	Mk	11.1^{bis}	210	191					
	Mk	11.18	214	197	*l* 259	Mk	14.37	254	246
	Mk	11.27	216	199		Lk	5.24	64	51
	Mk	12.7	218	203		Lk	7.13	93	78
	Mk	12.8	218	203		Lk	10.25	157	151
	Mk	12.9	218	204					
	Mk	12.20	221	208	*l* 260	Mt	28.9	269	278
	Mk	12.43	226	217		Mk	4.5	103	87
	Mk	12.44	226	217		Mk	8.6	131	125
	Mk	13.11	229	220		Mk	8.19	133	127
	Mk	13.27	232	224		Mk	9.44	145	144
	Mk	13.28^{bis}	233	225		Mk	9.45^{bis}	145	144
	Mk	14.7	244	234		Mk	9.47	145	145
	Mk	14.45	255	247		Mk	10.1	201	176
	Mk	14.67^{bis}	256	253		Mk	10.21	203	180
	Mk	14.71	256	255		Mk	11.18	214	197
	Mk	15.16	262	263		Mk	11.27	216	199
	Mk	15.17	262	263		Mk	12.7	218	203
	Lk	4.16	22	22		Mk	12.8	218	203
	Lk	10.25	157	151		Mk	12.25	221	209
	Jn	12.3	/ /	233		Mk	13.11	229	220
	Jn	12.4	/ /	233		Mk	14.37	254	246
	Jn	18.13	/ /	249		Mk	14.45	255	247
						Mk	15.16	262	262
l 253	Mt	17.9	139	137		Mk	15.26	264	266
	Mt	27.41	264	267		Mk	16.3	268	276
	Mk	1.10	18	17		Lk	4.16	22	22
	Mk	2.15	65	52		Jn	19.16	/ /	263
	Mk	2.16	65	52		Jn	20.2	/ /	276
	Mk	3.2	82	66					
	Mk	3.4	82	67	*l* 299	Mt	8.25	62	48
	Mk	5.24	120	102		Mt	13.13	104	89
	Mk	6.14	123	109		Mt	18.11	147	145
	Mk	6.23	124	111		Mt	22.30	221	209
	Mk	8.28^{bis}	135	129		Mt	26.27	248	240
	Mk	8.29	135	129		Mk	2.10	64	51
	Mk	15.24	264	265		Mk	6.2	121	105
	Mk	15.26	264	266		Mk	14.4	244	233

ms.	Ref.	Pericope	Page		ms.	Ref.	Pericope	Page
l 302	Mk 2.16	65	53			Lk 9.1	122	106
						Lk 9.5	122	109
l 303	Mt 6.4	40	36			Lk 9.41	140	139
	Mt 6.5	41	36			Lk 10.25	157	151
	Mt 13.55	121	105			Lk 13.15	177	163
	Mt 18.11 bis	147	145			Lk 13.21	178	163
	Mt 22.23	221	207			Lk 14.5	182	165
	Mt 22.30	221	209			Lk 15.1	186	168
	Mt 23.26	224	215			Lk 15.4	186	168
	Mt 28.17	271	279			Lk 16.19	191	171
	Mk 1.40	57	44			Lk 18.40	207	188
	Mk 2.10	64	51			Lk 18.43	207	188
	Mk 7.8	128	121			Lk 21.8	228	219
	Mk 11.26	215	199					
	Lk 6.4	81	65		l 360	Mk 13.32	234	226
	Lk 7.6	92	77					
	Lk 7.11	93	78		l 374	Mt 6.18	43	37
	Lk 8.15	106	91			Mt 18.11 bis	147	145
	Lk 8.45	120	102			Mt 23.26	224	215
	Lk 8.52	120	104			Mk 11.26	215	199
	Lk 9.1	122	106			Lk 7.11	93	78
	Lk 9.11	125	113			Lk 8.15	106	91
	Lk 9.23	137	131			Lk 8.28	119	99
	Lk 9.41	140	139			Lk 8.45	120	102
	Lk 10.25 bis	157	151			Lk 9.1	122	106
	Lk 13.15	177	163			Lk 9.41	140	139
	Lk 13.21	178	163			Lk 10.25 bis	157	151
	Lk 15.1	186	168					
	Lk 15.4	186	168		l 382	Lk 18.36	207	187
	Lk 16.19	191	171					
	Lk 18.36	207	187		l 490	Mt 24.36	234	226
	Lk 18.40	207	188					
	Lk 18.43	207	188		l 543	Jn 6.10	//	115
	Lk 21.8	228	219					
					l 823	Mt 24.36	234	226
l 305	Mt 19.9	201	177					
					l 845	Mt 19.9	201	177
l 309	Mt 15.26	129	123					
					l 850	Mt 13.13	104	89
l 313	Mt 9.5	64	50			Mt 13.55	121	105
	Mk 6.41	125	116			Mt 18.21	149	147
	Mk 8.7	131	125			Mt 23.26	224	215
	Mk 11.26	215	199					
					l 854	Lk 9.56	151	148
l 331	Lk 9.56	151	148					
					l 861	Mt 22.23	221	207
l 333	Mt 6.18	43	37					
	Mt 8.23	62	48		l 871	Mt 5.44	39	34
	Mt 13.55	121	105					
	Mt 18.21	149	147		l 883	Mt 8.23	62	48
	Mt 23.26	224	215			Mt 8.25	62	48
	Mk 2.10	64	51			Mt 9.5	64	50
	Mk 11.26	215	199			Mt 13.54	121	105
	Lk 6.33	88	74			Mt 24.6	228	219
	Lk 7.6	92	77			Mk 2.10	64	51
	Lk 8.45	120	102			Mk 3.7	84	69

ms.	Ref.		Pericope	Page		ms.	Ref.		Pericope	Page
	Mk	4.24	107	92			Lk	2.2[2]	10	8
	Mk	6.2	121	105			Lk	2.5[2]	10	8
	Mk	6.41	125	116			Lk	2.15bis [2]	10	9
	Mk	7.8	128	121			Lk	11.27	165	154
	Mk	8.7	131	125						
	Mk	10.19	203	179		l 1084	Mt	13.13	104	89
	Lk	1.9[1]	6	5			Mt	13.55	121	105
	Lk	9.56	151	148						
						l 1127	Mt	21.31	217	201
l 932	Lk	1.55	8	7			Mt	22.30	221	209
							Mt	22.32	221	210
l 950	Mt	6.18	43	37			Mt	23.26	224	215
	Mt	8.13	58	47			Mk	2.10	64	51
	Mt	8.23	62	48			Mk	7.8	128	121
	Mt	8.25	62	48			Lk	9.35	138	136
	Mt	13.13	104	89			Lk	9.56	151	148
	Mt	18.11	147	145			Lk	11.13ter	162	153
	Mt	19.22	203	180			Lk	19.38	210	194
	Mt	20.23	221	207			Jn	12.4bis	/ /	233
	Mt	22.30	221	209			Jn	16.4	/ /	223
	Mt	23.26	224	215						
	Mt	24.6	228	219		l 1231	Mt	6.18	43	37
	Mt	28.17	271	279			Mt	8.25	62	48
	Mk	3.7	84	69			Mt	27.24	261	262
	Mk	7.8	128	121			Mt	28.17	271	279
	Mk	10.19	203	179			Mk	4.24	107	92
	Mk	14.25	248	240			Lk	4.44	28	28
	Mk	14.30bis	253	244			Lk	6.33	88	74
	Lk	8.43	120	102			Lk	7.11	93	78
	Lk	9.35	138	136			Lk	8.14	106	90
	Lk	9.56	151	148			Jn	14.14	/ /	198
	Lk	17.35	198	174						
	Lk	19.38	210	194		l 1345	Lk	1.55	8	7
	Lk	21.6	227	218			Lk	1.77	9	8
	Lk	23.38	264	267						
						l 1346	Lk	1.55	8	7
l 952	Mk	1.40	57	44			Lk	1.77	9	8
l 956	Mk	1.40	57	44		l 1347	Lk	1.55	8	7
l 997	Mt	13.55	121	105		l 1348	Lk	1.55	8	7
	Mt	22.30	221	209			Lk	1.77	9	8
l 1043	Mt	3.16	18	17		l 1349	Lk	1.55	8	7
	Mt	7.14	52	42						
	Mt	7.18	53	42		l 1350	Lk	1.55	8	7
	Mk	6.21[2]	124	111			Lk	1.77	9	8
	Mk	6.22[2]	124	111						
	Mk	6.24[2]	124	111		l 1353	Mt	16.13	135	129
	Mk	6.27bis [2]	124	111			Mk	1.3	13	13
	Mk	6.29[2]	124	112			Mk	1.4	13	13
							Mk	1.5	13	13
							Mk	1.6	13	13

[1] Only here is l 883 given its correct number
(l 1761).
[2] Mistakenly given as l 1596.

ms.	Ref.	Pericope	Page
	Mk 1.8	13	16
	Mk 12.35	223	212
	Mk 12.36^bis	223	212
	Mk 12.37	223	212
l 1354	Mt 3.16	18	17
l 1355	Mt 4.5	20	20
l 1536	Mt 18.11	147	145
l 1564	Mt 6.18	43	37
	Lk 5.20	64	50
	Lk 5.24	64	51
	Lk 5.30	65	52
	Lk 7.11	93	78
	Lk 7.13	93	78
l 1578	Lk 7.28	95	79
l 1579	Mt 5.32	36	33
	Mt 8.28	62	48
	Mt 13.55	121	105
	Mt 16.8	133	127
	Mt 23.26	224	215
	Mk 11.26	215	199
	Lk 9.56	151	148
	Lk 14.5	182	165
	Lk 17.35^bis	198	174
	Lk 21.4	226	217
l 1599	Mt 8.25	62	48
	Lk 6.33	88	74
	Lk 8.32	119	99
	Lk 9.1	122	106
	Lk 9.3	122	107
	Lk 9.5	122	109
	Lk 10.25^bis	157	151
	Lk 11.13	162	153
	Lk 13.15	177	163
	Lk 15.1	186	168
	Lk 15.4	186	168
	Jn 19.16^ter	//	263f
	Jn 19.17^bis	//	264f
l 1602	Mk 16.2^ter	268	276
	Mk 16.6	268	277
	Mk 16.9^quater	275	282
	Lk 24.9	268	277
	Lk 24.10	268	277
l 1604	Mt 8.8	58	46
l 1623	Lk 6.33	88	74
l 1627	Mt 3.16	18	17

ms.	Ref.	Pericope	Page
	Mt 6.3	40	36
	Mt 7.14	52	42
	Mt 8.13	58	47
	Mt 8.25	62	48
	Mt 9.5	64	50
	Mk 1.40	57	44
	Mk 11.26	215	199
	Lk 5.20	64	50
	Lk 5.27	65	52
	Lk 5.30	65	52
	Lk 6.4	81	65
	Lk 7.8	92	77
	Lk 7.11	93	78
	Lk 8.10	104	88
	Lk 8.16	107	92
	Lk 8.27	119	98
	Lk 8.32	119	99
	Lk 8.43	120	102
	Lk 8.49	120	103
	Lk 8.52	120	104
	Lk 9.1	122	106
	Lk 9.5	122	109
	Lk 10.25^bis	157	151
	Lk 16.19	191	171
	Lk 19.4	208	189
	Lk 28.33	234	226
l 1629	Mk 15.18	262	263
l 1632	Mt 6.3	40	36
	Mk 1.39	28	28
l 1634	Mt 6.5	41	36
	Mt 26.27	248	240
	Mt 28.17	271	279
	Lk 6.33	88	74
	Lk 7.6	92	77
	Lk 7.11	93	78
	Lk 8.45	120	102
	Lk 8.52	120	104
	Lk 9.1	122	106
	Lk 9.5	122	109
	Lk 9.41	140	139
	Lk 10.25^bis	157	151
	Lk 13.21	178	163
	Lk 15.4	186	168
	Lk 16.19	191	171
	Lk 18.36	207	187
	Lk 18.43	207	188
	Lk 21.8	228	219
l 1642	Mt 13.55	121	105
	Mt 18.11^bis	147	145
	Mt 22.23	221	201
	Mk 8.7	131	125
	Mk 9.35	138	136
	Mk 9.43	145	144

ms.	Ref.		Pericope	Page	ms.	Ref.		Pericope	Page
	Mk	10.19	203	179		Lk	16.19	191	171
	Lk	8.19	117	96		Lk	17.14	196	172
	Lk	8.52	120	104		Lk	18.25	203	181
	Lk	9.1	122	106		Lk	18.36	207	187
	Lk	9.3	122	107		Lk	18.43	207	188
	Lk	9.5	122	109		Lk	19.4	208	189
	Lk	9.42	140	139		Lk	20.47	224	214
	Lk	9.56	151	148		Lk	21.4^{bis}	226	217
	Lk	10.25^{bis}	157	151					
	Lk	10.32	158	151	*l* 1693	Lk	21.8	228	219
	Lk	12.39	172	160					
	Lk	13.21	178	163	*l* 1749	Lk	11.27	165	154
	Lk	14.11	183	166					
	Lk	16.19	191	171	*l* 1837	Mt	28.2	268	276
	Lk	17.10	195	172					
	Lk	18.37	207	187	*l* 1963	Mt	6.3	40	36
	Lk	18.40	207	188		Mt	6.5	41	36
	Lk	19.4[1]	208	189		Mt	6.14	42	37
	Lk	21.8	228	219		Mt	25.31	241	230
	Lk	21.33	234	226		Mt	25.40	241	230
						Mt	25.45	241	230
l 1663	Mt	6.3	40	36		Lk	5.25	64	51
	Mt	6.14	42	37		Lk	7.6	92	77
	Mt	6.17	43	37		Lk	7.8	92	77
	Mt	6.18	43	37		Lk	7.11	93	78
	Mt	8.25	62	48		Lk	7.13	93	78
	Mt	25.45	241	230		Lk	8.15	106	91
	Mk	2.10	64	51		Lk	8.16	107	92
	Lk	2.15	10	9		Lk	8.27	119	98
	Lk	5.24	64	51		Lk	8.28	119	99
	Lk	7.6	92	77		Lk	8.31	119	99
	Lk	7.11^{bis}[2]	93	78		Lk	8.42	120	102
	Lk	8.16[2]	107	92		Lk	9.1^{bis}	122	106
	Lk	8.42	120	102		Lk	9.3^{bis}	122	107f
	Lk	8.47	120	103		Lk	9.5	122	108
	Lk	9.1	122	106		Lk	9.59	152	148
	Lk	9.3	122	107		Lk	10.25^{bis}	157	151
	Lk	9.5	122	108		Lk	10.27	157	151
	Lk	9.35	138	136		Lk	12.40	172	169
	Lk	10.25^{bis}	157	151		Lk	13.22	179	164
	Lk	10.27	157	151		Lk	15.26	187	169
	Lk	15.17	187	169		Lk	16.19	191	171
						Lk	18.25	203	181
						Lk	18.36	207	187
						Lk	18.43	207	188
						Lk	21.4	226	217

[1] Misprinted as *l* 1692.
[2] Misprinted as 1633.

APPENDIX II

Most editors of a Greek New Testament take the evidence of the early
versions seriously and this is especially true of the Old Latin. Not all editors
include the same Old Latin mss. in their apparatus. Two reasons explain this:
one is that the number of manuscripts that may confidently be assigned as Old
Latin (rather than mixed Old Latin and Vulgate, or predominantly Vulgate) is
disputed; the other is due to the inevitable idiosyncrasies of the compilers of a
critical apparatus. The number of Old Latin mss. therefore varies from edition
to edition.

This Appendix attempts to plot which edition of the Greek New Testament
used which Old Latin mss., and is companion to an article I have written on the
use made of Greek New Testament mss.[1] For the purpose of this survey seven
Greek testaments published since 1947 are included, together with three gospel
synopses.

These are as follows:

1. A. Souter, *Novum Testamentum Graece*, 2nd edition (Oxford 1947) (=
   Souter)
2. **Η ΚΑΙΝΗ ΔΙΑΘΗΚΗ**, British and Foreign Bible Society, 2nd edition
   (London 1958) (= BFBS²)
3. H. J. Vogels, *Novum Testamentum Graece et Latine*, 4th edition (Freiburg
   1955) (= Vogels⁴)
4. A. Merk, *Novum Testamentum Graece et Latine*, 9th edition (Rome 1964)
   (= Merk⁹)
5. *The Greek New Testament*, United Bible Societies (New York, London,
   Amsterdam, Edinburgh, Stuttgart), 1st edition (1966), 2nd edition (1968),
   3rd edition (1975) (= UBS¹⁻³)
6. J. M. Bover and J. O'Callaghan, *Nuevo Testamento Trilingüe* (Madrid 1977)
   (= B–O'C)
7. Nestle-Aland, *Novum Testamentum Graece*, 26th edition (4th revised
   printing (Stuttgart 1981)) (= N–A²⁶). Occasionally the previous edition of
   the text is referred to (as N–A²⁵).

The synopses are:

1. K. Aland, *Synopsis Quattuor Evangeliorum*, 10th edition (Stuttgart 1978)
   (= Syn¹⁰). Occasionally the diglot edition *Synopsis of the Four Gospels*, 3rd
   edition (United Bible Societies 1979) is referred to (as Greek-English Syn³).
   In the Old Latin Syn¹² = Syn¹⁰.

---

* Published originally in *Novum Testamentum* XXVI, 3(1984), pp 225–48.

2.   A. Huck, *Synopse der drei ersten Evangelien*, 13th edition revised by
      H. Greeven (Tübingen, 1981) (= H–G¹³)
3.   B. Orchard, *A Synopsis of the Four Gospels* (Edinburgh 1983) (= Orchard)

In addition I have included information from the apparatus to Luke prepared by
the International Greek New Testament Project, of which I am executive editor
(= IGNTP). Part I was published by Oxford University Press in 1984; part II
in 1987.

In order to test which Old Latin mss. are used, the Greek apparatus to each
edition has been searched and this has yielded some surprising results. It is not
sufficient to accept the introductory list of mss. found in each edition as
definitive. Sometimes mss. included in these lists are never to be found in an
apparatus (except arguably subsumed under a general siglum such as lat), and
sometimes Old Latin mss. are cited in the apparatus without being included in
the introductory list. We may draw two conclusions from these findings. One is
that there seems no point in including a ms. in an introductory list if a reader is
not to encounter that ms. in the apparatus. Conversely, the second point is that
it is unfortunate if a reader encounters a ms. in an apparatus the details of which
are not to be found in the introduction. I am indebted to the Revd. J. I. Miller of
Bury St. Edmunds for the meticulous care and attention he has given in assisting
my preparation of this article, and in preparing Tables II–XI which give this
information.

In addition to the Greek texts, I have also included in Table I columns for the
major Latin editions of the New Testament that give prominence to Old Latin
mss. These are J. Wordsworth, H. J. White and H. F. D. Sparks, *Novum
Testamentum Latine* (Oxford 1889–1954) (= WW) and the editions prepared
especially to show the evidence of Old Latin witnesses: A. Jülicher, *Itala* (edited
by W. Matzkow and K. Aland (Berlin and New York: Matthew 2nd edition
1972; Mark 2nd edition 1970; Luke 2nd edition 1976; John 1963)) and the
volumes of the *Vetus Latina* edition (Freiburg) that have appeared before 1982.
These are 24/1 Ephesians (1962–4); 24/2 Philippians and Colossians (1966–71);
25 (fascicles 1–9) 1, 2 Thessalonians, 1, 2 Timothy (1975–82); 26/1 Catholic
epistles (1956–69). Both the *Itala* volumes and the *Vetus Latina* volumes are
combined under the heading VL. It is not to be assumed that mss. found in B.
Fischer's list in B. M. Metzger, *Early Versions*, 461–464 (see below) but absent
from the *Itala* volumes are heavily contaminated with Vulgate readings. The
apparatus to these Latin texts has not been examined: it is assumed that all the
mss. listed in the introductions to these editions have been made use of in the
apparatus, and that there are no extra mss. found in the apparatus.

As well as monitoring the accuracy of the introductory lists of Old Latin mss.
in the printed editions of the Greek testaments, this present survey is intended to
show which editions make fullest use of Old Latin mss. With the aid of Table I
comparison between all the editions is possible. Certain editors have obviously
kept their apparatus up-to-date by including recently discovered or published,
Old Latin texts — others seem merely to repeat information found in earlier

apparatuses. Some mss. will be seen in Table I to have been included by only one or two editors. Editors also differ in their inclusion as Old Latin witnesses of mss. that are mixed texts. The statistics resulting from Table I are set out in Tables II–XI.

TABLE I

Column one contains the traditional siglum of the ms. followed in column two by the Beuron number. With the exception of editions from Beuron these numbers have generally not found favour in recent critical apparatuses even though this classification unambiguously refers to one ms. only, thus avoiding the confusion sometimes occurring with the traditional sigla (e.g. see q and r). Where the letter in column one is bracketed this ms. is known only by its Beuron number in the lists of Old Latin mss. in B. M. Metzger, *The Early Versions of the New Testament* (Oxford 1977) (cited hereafter as *Versions*) pp. 296–311 and 461–4. When the superscript number following the letter is bracketed (e.g. ff$^{(1)}$) the ms. is known to some editors as ff, to other editors as ff^1 as explained in a subjoined footnote.

Column three gives the contents of the mss. divided, where applicable, into the normal sub-divisions of the New Testament (e = Gospels, a = Acts, p = Pauline epistles (including Hebrews), c = Catholic epistles, r = Revelation). A cross in this column indicates the ms. if fragmentary. If the ms. is also referred to by a name or title this is given in column four.

In each subsequent column an oblique line indicates that the ms. is found in the edition named at the head of the column. Where the oblique is enclosed in square brackets this indicates that I have been unable to locate a citation of the ms. in the apparatus. If any observant reader discovers this ms. in the apparatus I would be grateful to be informed. When an oblique is enclosed in round brackets this means that the editor brackets the ms. in his introductory list of Old Latin mss. usually in order to cast doubt about the validity of including such a ms. or section of ms. as a witness to the Old Latin. S (= Sundry) indicates that the ms. has been located in the apparatus of the appropriate section of the New Testament but is not included in the introductory lists. Tables II–XI give details where the sundry mss. are located.

The number of mss. in this table includes all the mss. listed in the introductory lists of the editions covered in the survey. In addition I have added (a) all the Old Latin mss. listed in Metzger, *Versions*, not found in any Greek testament (b) all the Old Latin mss. included in the New Testament fascicles of *Vetus Latina* published before 1982. Manuscripts included in *Vetus Latina* 1/1 have not been added unless they have subsequently been cited in a text fascicle of *Vetus Latina* or in a Greek testament. Some mss. included in the table are not clear witnesses to the pre-Jerome text in all parts. Where the Old Latin element is disputed or absent a reference is given in the footnote usually on the authority of Metzger, *Versions*, or F. G. Kenyon, *The Text of the Greek Bible* (3rd edition revised by A. W. Adams, London 1975) (= Adams). I gratefully acknowledge the assistance given by H. J. Frede of Beuron.

TABLE I

				NA[26]	B-O'C	UBS[1-3]	Merk[9]	Vogels[4]	BFBS[2]	Souter[2]	W-W	VL Jülicher	IGNTP	Syn[3] = Syn[10]	H-G[13]	Orchard
												INDIVIDUAL BOOKS		SYNOPSES		
a	3	e	Vercellensis	/	/	/	/	/	/	/	/	/	/	/	/	/
(a)	[2]61	e	Armagh	/	/	[/]	/	/	/	/	/		/	/	/	/
		a				/										
		p		/		/										
		c		/		/						/				
		r		/		/										
a²	[3]16	e⁺	Curiensis	/	/	/	/	(/)	/	/	/	/	/	/	/	/
aur	[4]15	e	Aureus	/	/	/	/	/	/	/	/	/	/	/	/	/
b	4	e	Veronensis	/	/	/	/				/	/	/	/	/	/
b	89	p	Budapestiensis	/		/					/					
β	26	e⁺	Carinthianus	/		/	/	/	/	/	/	/	/	/	/	/
c	[5]6	e	Colbertinus	/		/	/		/	/	/	/	/	/	/	/
		a			s	/	s		s	(/)	/					
		p		s		/	s		s	(/)	/					
		c				/			s	[(/)]	/	/				
		r				/			s		/					
d	5	e	Cantabrigiensis	/	/	/	/	/	/	/	/	/	/	/	/⁶	/
		a⁺		/		/	/		/							
		c⁺		s		/	/	/	/	[/]						

TABLE I (continued)

				NA²⁶	B-O'C	UBS¹⁻³	Merk⁹	Vogels⁴	BFBS²	Souter²	W-W	VL Jülicher	IGNTP	Syn³ =Syn¹⁰	H-G¹³	Orchard
d	75	p	Claromontanus	/	/		/	/	/	/	/	/		/	/	
dem	⁷59	a	Demidovianus			[/]					/	/		/	/	
		p							s		/	/				
		c					s				/	/				
		r							s		/	/				
div	-	p	Divionensis			/	s		s		/	/				
		c									/	/				
		r									/	/				
δ	⁸27	e	Sangallensis	/	/	/	/	/	/	s	/	/	/	/⁹	/⁹	/
e	2	e	Palatinus	/	/	/	/	/ /	/	/	/	/	/	/	/	/
e	50	a	Laudianus	/	/	/	/	/	s	/	/	/	/			/
e	¹076	p	Sangermanensis	¹¹	[/]	/	/	/	/	/	/	/	/			/
f	¹210	e	Brixianus	/	/	/	/	(/)	/	(/)	/	/	/	/	/	/
f	¹078	p	Augiensis	/	/	/	/	(/)	/	/	/	/	/	s	/	/
ff^(1)	¹39	e+	Corbeiensis I	/	/	/	/	/	/	(/)	/	/	/	/	/	/
ff²	¹48	e	Corbeiensis II	/	/	/	/	/	/	/	/	/	/	/	/	/
ff	66	c+	Corbeiensis	/	/	/	/	/	/	/	/	/	/	/	/	/

264

TABLE I (continued)

		NA²⁶	B-O'C	UBS¹⁻³	Merk⁹	Vogels⁴	'BFBS²	Souter²	W-W	VL Jülicher	IGNTP	Syn³ = Syn¹⁰	H-G¹³	Orchard
[fu	Fuldensis]													
g⁽¹⁾ 157	eapcr Sangermanensis	/			/	/	/	s	/	/(p, c)	/	/	/	/
	a			[/					/					
	p			[/					/					
	c			[/					/					
	r			[/										
g ¹⁰⁷⁷	p Boernerianus	/	/				/		/			/		/
g² 29	e Sangermanensis		s	/	/	/	/	/	/			/	/¹⁶	
g² 52	a⁺ Fragmenta Mediolanensia		s			(/)			/					/
gat ¹⁰³⁰	e Gatianus	¹⁷							/			/		
g(ig) ¹⁸⁵¹	e Gigas	/		[/	/	/	/	(/)	/				/¹⁶	/
	a						/		/					
	p		[/	[/	[/		/	[/]	/	/	/	/¹⁹		
	c		[/		/		/		/	/				
	r						/		/					
gue ²⁰⁷⁹	p⁺ Guelferbytanus	/				/	/	/	/		/			
h ²¹¹²	e⁺ Claromontanus	/				/	/	/	/			/	/	/
h ²²⁵⁵	a⁺ Floriacensis	/				/	/	/	/			/¹⁹		

TABLE I (continued)

siglum	no.	book	name	NA²⁶	B-O'C	UBS¹⁻³	Merk⁹	Vogels⁴	BFBS²	Souter²	W-W	VL Jülicher	IGNTP	Syn³ = Syn¹⁰	H-G¹³	Orchard
haf		c⁺	Hafnianus	/	/	/	/	[/]	/	/	/					
		r⁺		/	/	/	/	s	/	/	/					
i	17	r	Vindobonensis	/	/	/	/	/	/	/	/	/				/
j	²³22	e⁺	Sarzanensis	/	/	/	/	/	/	/	/	/	/	/	/	/
k	1	e⁺	Bobiensis	/	/	/	/	/	/	/	/	/	/	/	/	/
l	11	e⁺	Rehdigeranus	/	/	/	/	/	/	/	/	/	/	/	/	/
l	²⁴67	e	Legionensis	/	/	/					/	/				
		a			/	[/]										
		p			/	/					/					
		c⁺			/	[/]										
		r			/											
λ	–	e⁺	Fragmentum Rosenthal	/	/	[/]	/	/	/	/	/			/	/	/
m	²⁵	e			[/]	/	/	/	/	/	/			/	/	
		a			[/]	/	/	s	/	/	/					
		p			/	/	/	[/]	/	s	/					
		c			/		/	[/]	/			s				
		r			[/]	/	/		/							
(m)	²⁶86	p⁺	Monza	/						(/)		/	/			
mm	²⁷	e														

TABLE I (continued)

| | | | | INDIVIDUAL BOOKS | | SYNOPSES | | |
			NA²⁶	B-O'C	UBS¹⁻³	Merk⁹	Vogels⁴	BFBS²	Souter²	W-W	VL Jülicher	IGNTP	Syn³ = Syn¹⁰	H-G¹³	Orchard
μ	⁸35	e⁺	Mulling	/²⁸					/			/		/	/	/
(μ)	⁸2	p⁺	Fragmenta Monacensia	/		/	/		/	/		/		/	/	/
n	²⁹16	e⁺	Sangallensis	/	s	/	/	[/]	/		/	/		/	/	
o	²⁹16	e⁺	Sangallensis	/		/	/	s	s		/	/		/	[/]	
p	20	e⁺	Sangallensis	/		/	/				/	/				
p	³⁰54	e	Perpinianensis	/	s	/	/		/	/	/	/		/¹⁹		
		a				[/]				/						
		p			s	/			s³¹	[/]						
		c				[/]					/	/				
		r										/				
p (ph)	³²30	p⁺	Heidelberg	[/]	/	/	/		/	/	/	/		/	/	/
	63	a				/			/	/	/	/		/	/	/
π	⁸18	e⁺	Fragmenta Stuttgartensia	/	/	/	/		/	/	/	/		[/]	/	/
q	13	e	Monacensis	/	/	/	/		/	/	/	/		/	/	
q	³³64	p⁺		/	/	/	/		s	/	/	/				
q	³⁴64	c⁺	Fragmenta Frisingensia	/	/	/	/	[/]	/	/	/	/				
r⁽¹⁾	³⁵14	e	Usserianus I	/	/	/	/	/	/	/	/	/	/	/	/	/

TABLE I (continued)

				NA²⁶	B-O'C	UBS¹⁻³	Merk⁹	Vogels⁴	BFBS²	Souter²	W-W	INDIVIDUAL BOOKS		SYNOPSES		
												VL Jülicher	IGNTP	Syn³ = Syn¹⁰	H-G¹³	Orchard
r²	³⁶28	e	Usserianus II	³⁷	s	[/]	/	(/)	/	/	/			[/]	/	/
r	³⁸57	a+	Schlettstadtensis	/		/	/	/	/	/						
r	³⁹62	e	Rodensis	/		/	/	/	/	/	/					
		a										/				
		p										/				
		c		/							/	/				
		r		/							/	/				
r	⁴⁰64	p+	Fragmenta Frisingensia	/		/	/	/	/	/	/	/				/
		c+		/		/	/	/				/				
r²	64	p+	Fragmenta Frisingensia	/		/	/	/		/	/	/				
r³	64	p+	Fragmenta Frisingensia	/		/	/	/		/	/	/				
ρ	24	e+	Ambrosianus Fragmentum	/		[/]	/	/		/	/	/		[/]		
ρ	88	p+	Basilense	/		/	/	/		/	/	/				
s	21	e+	Ambrosianus	/		/	/	/		/	/	/	/	/	/	/
s	⁴¹53	a+	Bobiensis	/		/	/	/	s	/	/	/	/	/	/	/
		c		/		/	/	/	/	/	/	/				
sin	74	a+	Fragmentum Sinaiticum	/		/	/	/	s	/	/	/				
		r+		/		/	/	/		/	/	/				
t	19	e+	Fragmenta Bernensia	/		/	/	/		/	/	/	/	/	/	/

TABLE I (continued)

				NA²⁶	B-O'C	UBS¹⁻³	Merk⁹	Vogels⁴	BFBS²	Souter²	W-W	INDIVIDUAL BOOKS VL Jülicher	IGNTP	SYNOPSES Syn³ = Syn¹⁰	H-G¹³	Orchard
t	⁴²56	e	Liber Comicus	/	/	/	/	/			/				/	/
		a⁺	Toletanus		[/]	[/]	[/]		s	/	/	/	/			
		p⁺			[/]	[/]	/				/	/				
		c⁺			[/]	[/]	[/]				/					
		r⁺			/	/	/		s	[/]	/	/				
[tepl]		e	Teplensis]⁴³		/	/	/	/			/				/	/
		a			/	-	-				/	/				
		c			[/]	/	[/]				/					
v	25	e⁺	Vindobonensis	/	/	/	/	/			/			/	/	/
v	81	p⁺	Fragmentum Veronense Weiss.	/		/			s							
(w)	32	e	Guelferbytanus	/								/	/			
		a														
		p														
		c⁺														
w¹		e⁺	Wirceburgensis				/									
w²		e⁺	Wirceburgensis				/									
w³		e⁺	Wirceburgensis			/	[/]									
w⁴		e⁺	Wirceburgensis				/									
w	⁴⁴58	e	Wernigerodensis									/	/			

TABLE I (continued)

			NA²⁶	B-O'C	UBS¹⁻³	Merk⁹	Vogels⁴	BFBS²	Souter²	W-W	**INDIVIDUAL BOOKS** VL Jülicher	IGNTP	**SYNOPSES** Syn³ = Syn¹⁰	H-G¹³	Orchard
w	79	a⁺	= gue	/	/		/	/	/	/		/				
(w)	83	p		/				/	/	/						
		c						/								
		r						/								
x¹		p⁺	Waldeccensis	[/]	[/]	[/]	[/]			/		/				
x⁴⁵		a	Bodleianus													
x		p	Bodleianus			/					/					
z	15	ap	Bodleianus		[/]						/					
z	22	e	= aur													
z	⁴⁶65	e	= j													
		p⁺	Harleianus	/	[/]	/	/	/				/			/	/
		c⁺		/	/	/	s					/				
		r		/		/	s									
	23	e⁺	Aberdonensis		[/]							/			[/]	
	⁴⁷31	e	Ordo Scrutiniorum		[/]										/	

TABLE I (continued)

		NA²⁶	B-O'C	UBS¹⁻³	Merk⁹	Vogels⁴	BFBS²	Souter²	W-W	VL Jülicher	IGNTP	Syn³ = Syn¹⁰	H-G¹³	Orchard
Fi³³	4833 e⁺	Parisiensis										/		
	34 e⁺	Cryptoferratensis												
	36 e⁺	Giessenense											/	
	37 e⁺	Hieronymus in Matthaeum											/	
	38 e⁺	Hieronymus in Matthaeum											/	
	39 e⁺	Pictaviensis											[/]	
	40 e⁺	Vennessenus											[/]	
	41 e	Lectionarium Veronense											[/]⁺⁹	
	⁵⁰42 e	Juv. Cantabrigiensis											[/]	
	43 e	Book of Dimma											[/]	
	60 a⁺													
	63 a													
	68 p⁺	Fragmenta Toletana (τ⁶⁸)									/				
	c⁺										/				
	⁵¹69 e	Liber Comicus Legionensis (τ⁶⁹)													
	a													
	p										/				
	c														
	r										/				

INDIVIDUAL BOOKS

SYNOPSES

TABLE I (continued)

		NA[26]	B-O'C	UBS[1-3]	Merk[9]	Vogels[4]	BFBS[2]	Souter[2]	W-W	VL Jülicher	IGNTP	Syn[3] = Syn[10]	H-G[13]	Orchard
										INDIVIDUAL BOOKS		**SYNOPSES**		
5270	e Liber Comicus Aemilianensis (τ[70])													
	a									√				
	p									√				
	c									√				
	r									√				
71	p+ Fragmenta Parisina (τ[71])													
	c+													
72	e Missale Toletanum (τ[72])													
	a													
	p									√				
	c									√				
	r													
73	e Missale Silense (τ[73])													
	a									√				
	p													
	c													
	r													
74	a Fragmentum Sinaiticum													
	r													

TABLE I (continued)

		NA²⁶	B-O'C	UBS¹⁻³	Merk⁹	Vogels⁴	BFBS²	Souter²	W-W	INDIVIDUAL BOOKS		SYNOPSES		
										VL Jülicher	IGNTP	Syn³ = Syn¹⁰	H-G¹³	Orchard
84	p⁺													
85	p⁺													
87	p⁺ Fragmentum Basilense													
88	p⁺									/				
⁵³91										/				
92														
93										/				
94										/				
95										/				
100										/				
175										/				
250										/				
⁵⁴251	p c									/				
262	e a p c									/				

TABLE I (continued)

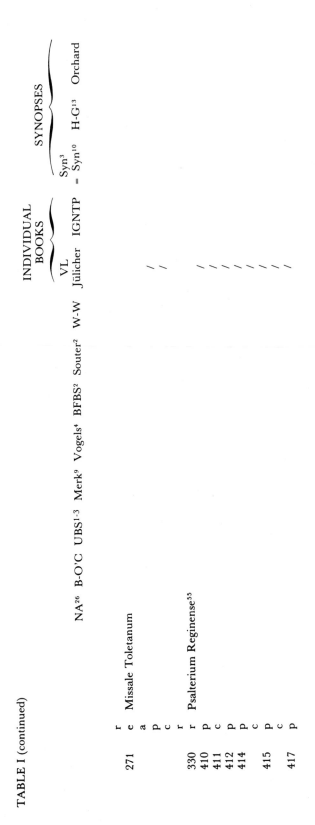

	NA²⁶	B-O'C	UBS¹⁻³	Merk⁹	Vogels⁴	BFBS²	Souter²	W-W	INDIVIDUAL BOOKS VL Jülicher	IGNTP	SYNOPSES Syn³ = Syn¹⁰	H-G¹³	Orchard
271 r e a p c r Missale Toletanum													
330 r Psalterium Reginense⁵⁵										✓ ✓			
410 p										✓			
411 c										✓			
412 p										✓			
414 p c										✓			
415 p c										✓			
417 p										✓			

Tables II–XI

The following tables show the number of mss. used by each of the editions in this survey. Unused mss. are those mss. represented in Table I above by an oblique within square brackets: these mss. have not been found in the apparatus despite their inclusion in the introductory list of mss. in the edition. Used mss. are mss. found in both the introductory list and the critical apparatus. Sundries are mss. noted as S in Table I: details of where these mss. are cited are included below.

Table II

Nestle-Aland, *NOVUM TESTAMENTUM GRAECE (26th Edition)*

	e	a	p	c	r
MANUSCRIPTS USED	28	11	13	9	5
MANUSCRIPTS UNUSED	–	–	1	–	–
TOTAL	28	11	14	9	5
% of Non-Use	–	–	7.1	–	–

Unused ms.   p:p

Table III

J. M Bover-J. O'Callaghan, *NUEVO TESTAMENTO TRILINGÜE*

	e	a	p	c	r
MANUSCRIPTS USED	28	8	4	7	2
MANUSCRIPTS UNUSED	1	2	6	3	3
TOTAL	29	10	10	10	5
% of Non-Use	3.4	20.0	60.0	30.0	60.0
SUNDRIES	3	1	2	1	–

Sundries
- e: g² Matt 6:13; 25:17.
- υ Mark 16:14.
- r² Luke 5:5; 10:24.
- a: g² Acts 6:9.
- p: c 1 Cor 3:3.
- p 1 Cor 3:3.
- c: d 3 John 14.

Unused mss.
- e: 23
- a: m, x
- p: e, m, t, w, x, z
- c: gig, t, w
- r: m, t, z

Table IV

United Bible Societies, *GREEK NEW TESTAMENT*, 3rd EDITION

	e	a	p	c	r
MANUSCRIPTS USED	27	13	17	14	10
MANUSCRIPTS UNUSED	4	2	4	2	3
TOTAL	31	15	21	16	13
% of Non-Use	12.9	13.3	19.0	12.5	23.1

Unused mss: e: ar, gig, m, r² [56]
               a: dem, g¹ [57]
               p: g¹, l, p, w
               c: d, g¹
               r: g¹, l, p

Errata

r¹ and r² are described in the introduction as gospel mss. only, but the following occur

r¹ Rom 14:10, 12, 16, 19, 23; 15:7.
    1 Cor 1:4, 8, 13; 2:1, 4, 10, 14, 15, 33; 6:11, 20; 7:5; 16:24.
    2 Cor 1:6, 15; 2:1, 7, 9; 5:17; 9:12; 10:13; 11:3; 12:15bis; 13:4.
    Gal 2:12bis, 20; 3:14, 17; 4:6.
    Eph 1:1, 14, 15.
    Phil 1:11.
    1 Tim 6:5, 7.
    Heb 10:1bis, 11; 11:10.
r² Phil 4:16, 23.
    1 Thess 1:1.

Presumably r³ (64) is intended throughout. r³ is used in the apparatus.

Insofar as Metzger's *Commentary*[58] (= MC) is the companion volume to UBS³ it may be worth noting that Metzger does not add any Old Latin mss. to those listed in UBS³, although the *Commentary* betrays some errata. r without a numerical suffix occurs at John 2:3 (MC p. 201) — r¹ is intended (r² is not extant here). In the Pauline Epistles r occurs without numerical suffix in the following places:

    Rom 1:7; 14:22.
    1 Cor 1:20; 2:12; 6:11; 16:23, 24.
    2 Cor 2:7; 4:5; 5:17; 12:15.
    Gal 2:9, 12bis; 3:1; 6:15.
    Phil 1:14; 4:23.
    1 Thess 1:1, 7.
    1 Tim 2:7; 6:7.
    Heb 10:34, 38; 11:4.

As with UBS³, r³ (64) is probably intended. MC unlike UBS³ cites m as Speculum throughout. The siglum p² at Acts 10:26 (MC p. 375) is not explained in MC or UBS³ and probably represents a corrector of Perpinianensis (54).

Table V

A. Merk, *NOVUM TESTAMENTUM GRAECE ET LATINE*, 9th edition

	e	a	p	c	r
MANUSCRIPTS USED	28	10	8	8	8
MANUSCRIPTS UNUSED	1	–	–	3	–
TOTAL	29	10	8	11	8
% of Non-Use	3.4	–	–	27.27	–
SUNDRIES	–	1	1	2	1

Sundries: a: c Acts 3:11; 17:19; 24:7; 27:19; 28:24, 29.
             p: c Rom 1:1; 8:35.
                    1 Cor 14:2, 5; Col 1:10.
             c: dem 1 John 4:7.
               z Jas 1:18; 1 John 3:10, 13.
             r: z Rev 1:13, 16; 2:2; 8:9; 9:4bis; 10:10; 13:6; 14:8.

Certain Vulgate mss. (Amiatinus, Cavensis, Dublinensis, Fuldensis, Oxoniensis and Toletanus) occur in the apparatus to the Greek text abbreviated in a different way from the abbreviation used in the Latin apparatus. These are not to be thought of as sundry Old Latin mss. although Fuldensis e.g. seems to be so used in Souter's apparatus (see *infra*): z is also included in the list of Vulgate mss. although it is abbreviated as Z or harl there. Nevertheless z could possibly be intended as a Vulgate witness here in c r.

Unused mss.   e: w³

c: gig, t, w

Teplensis included in Merk's lists of Old Latin mss. is in fact not Latin but Middle High German.[43] It is cited there as extant for e a c but has been located only in a. It has been included in the above table neither where it is used nor where it is apparently not cited. Where teplensis is found e.g. in the apparatus to Acts 3:11 it is not printed as if it were a witness to the Old Latin.

Table VI

H. J. Vogels, *NOVUM TESTAMENTUM GRAECE ET LATINE*, 4th edition

	e	a	p	c	r
MANUSCRIPTS USED	23	9	5	2	1
MANUSCRIPTS UNUSED	1	–	–	3	1
TOTAL	24	9	5	5	2
% of Non-Use	4.2	–	–	60.0	50.0
SUNDRIES	1	–	1	–	1

Sundries: e: p Joh 11:33.

p: m Rom 6:4; 8:10; 13:5; 1 Cor 8:4, 5; 2 Cor 5:4; Gal 4:8.

r: h Rev 12:5; 15:4.

Unused mss.   e: o (Beuron ms. 16 is found in the apparatus to Mark 16 subsumed under the siglum n, but siglum o has not been removed from the Explanatio p. XII.)

c: h, m, q.

r: m.

Table VII

British and Foreign Bible Society: H ΚΑΙΝΗ ΔΙΑΘΗΚΗ, 2nd edition

	e	a	p	c	r
MANUSCRIPTS USED	24	10	6	6	2
MANUSCRIPTS UNUSED	–	–	–	–	–
TOTAL	24	10	6	6	2
% of Non-Use	–	–	–	–	–
SUNDRIES	3	2	4	3	3

Sundries: e: p   John 11:33.

s   Luke 17:9, 29; 19:24, 29.

t   Mark 1:11; 2:26.

a: c   Acts 1:18, 20; 5:39; 6:3; 15:33, 41; 16:1, 10; 21:20; 22:12; 23:24; 24:8, 25; 26:15; 28:19, 24, 29, 30.

e   Acts 1:23, 25; 2:14, 37; 3:1, 8, 13, 14bis, 22; 4:10, 31, 32, 33; 5:16, 17, 24, 28, 34, 36, 37, 39; 6:3, 8, 10; 7:16, 17, 18bis, 21, 24, 29, 30bis, 43bis; 9:4, 22; 10:24, 33, 41; 11:28; 12:14, 25; 13:5, 6, 12, 18, 27, 31, 42, 43, 44, 45, 48, 50; 14:1, 2, 19, 25; 15:18, 24bis, 26, 33; 16:1, 9, 11, 12, 13, 16, 18, 23; 17:23, 26bis, 27, 34; 18:27; 19:1, 10, 14, 16; 20:3, 13, 27; 21:25, 26; 22:7; 23:6; 24:8, 10; 25:18.

p: c   Rom 1:1, 18; 2:16; 3:26; 4:18, 19; 5:8, 13; 6:13; 7:3; 8:34, 38; 9:4; 13:9; 16:7, 20.

  1 Cor 1:14; 3:5; 5:5; 7:14, 34; 9:7; 11:24bis; 12:3; 16:15, 19.
  2 Cor 4:11; 5;14; 6:15; 7:8; 11:17; 12:6.
  Gal 1:9.
  Eph 5:17.
  Phlm 6.
  Heb 7:4.
dem Rom 4:18; 5:13.
t   Rom 2:16; 6:13; 8:23; 12:13.
    1 Cor 1:8; 6:14; 7;14, 34; 9:7; 10:23; 11:24bis; 12:3bis.
    2 Cor 6:15; 11:17.
    Gal 4:6, 26.
    2 Tim 3:16.
    Heb 1:1, 12; 9:14; 10:38.
v   Heb 1:1; 4:2.
c: c   Jas 4:9.
        1 Pet 1:22, 24; 3:18.
        2 Pet 3:10.
        1 John 1:4; 2:25; 5:1.
        2 John 9.
        3 John 10.
        Jude 25.
    p   Jas 2:20, 3:6; 5:20.
        1 Pet 1:22, 24; 2:23; 3:8.
        2 Pet 2:9; 3:6.
        1 John 5:1, 6.
        2 John 9.
        3 John 10.
        Jude 15, 25.
    q   1 John 6:13, 20.
r: c   Rev 7:3; 16:1; 20:3.
    dem Rev 16:1; 18:12.
    t   Rev 1:3, 9; 2:17, 20; 4:1; 14:4; 19:6.

Errata
r without numerical suffix occurs at John 1:21, where r¹ is expected. q occurs at Rev 1:8.

Table VIII

A. Souter, *NOVUM TESTAMENTUM GRAECE*, 2nd edition

	e	a	p	c	r
MANUSCRIPTS USED	19	11	6	6	2
MANUSCRIPTS UNUSED	–	–	–	5	–
TOTAL	19	11	6	11	2
% of Non-Use	–	–	–	45.45	–
SUNDRIES	1	–	1	–	1

Souter's Introduction p. xix does not separate a from c. The mss. used in c include w (58) but exclude p (54).

Sundries: e: δ   John 10:9.
             r: m   Rev 14:10; 18:4; 22:19.

  It is not certain if the Vulgate ms. Fuldensis cited as fu at 1 Tim 6:7 is intended as an Old Latin witness. No other edition in this survey takes it as an Old Latin ms. — on the contrary it is usually cited as a Vulgate ms. (e.g., see Syn¹⁰, p. xxix: vg^{fuld}).

Unused mss   c: c, d, p, t, gigas. Souter's Introduction, p. xix, brackets c
probably because the Old Latin content of this ms. outside a and r
is minimal. gigas is also predominantly Vulgate outside the
gospels. p. xix is ambiguous regarding the contents of p.

Table IX[59]

K. Aland, SYNOPSIS QUATTUOR EVANGELIORUM, 10th edition

MANUSCRIPTS USED   = 34 (incl. 3 cited outside the gospels)
MANUSCRIPTS UNUSED   = 3
TOTAL   = 37
% of Non-Use   = 8.1
SUNDRY   = 1

Sundry

Non-gospel ms. f (78) is found in the apparatus to 1 Cor 11:24 (see p. 437, *ad* Mark
14:22–25 par).

Unused mss.

π r² ρ

Erratum

r at Mark 7:19 (p. 218) lacks a superscript number. The UBS apparatus *ad loc* shows
that r¹ is intended.

Table X

A. Huck, SYNOPSE DER DREI ERSTEN EVANGELIEN, 13th edition revised by
H. Greeven

MANUSCRIPTS USED   = 44
MANUSCRIPTS UNUSED   = 7
TOTAL   = 51
% of Non-Use   = 13.7

Unused mss.

p (20), 23, 39, 40, 41, 42, 43.

Table XI

B. Orchard, *SYNOPSIS* does not provide an introductory list of mss. so it is inappro-
priate to check for non-use or sundries. 27 different mss. are in fact found in the
apparatus.

Notes

[1] J. K. Elliott, 'The Citation of Manuscripts in Recent Printed Editions of the Greek
New Testament', *NT* 25, 1983, pp. 97–132.
[2] Known as ar in UBS. For UBS contents see UBS³, p. xxxii, footnote 1. Known
only by Beuron number in H–G¹³. Old Latin only in a, p and r (VL 26/1 pp 21 * f.). Listed
as Vulgate ms. D by BFBS² (and WW).
[3] See also n (16) and o (16). Vogels⁴ notes that a² = n and that n = a² but keeps both
sigla in the apparatus.
[4] Cited as z in BFBS² Merk⁹ H–G¹³ (and N–A²⁵) and by its Beuron number by
Orchard.
[5] Vulgate in a p c r (*Versions*). Mark and Luke are Old Latin, the rest of the NT is
mixed (Adams).

[6] Cited only when differing from Greek D.

[7] Known only by its Beuron number in H–G[13]. Vogels[4] lists it among its Vulgate mss. Old Latin elements in a c p (*Versions*), but cf. *Biblica* 54 (1973), pp. 516–536. The ms. is now lost, which may explain its absence from N–A[26] and B–O'C. Ms. divionensis (following) is also a Vulgate ms.

[8] Known only by its Beuron number in Orchard.

[9] Cited only when different from Greek Δ or from the Vulgate.

[10] Known only by its Beuron number in H–G[13].

[11] Used in N–A[25] as an Old Latin ms. A copy of d(75)e is an independent witness only in Rom 1:1–7 and 1 Cor 14:8–18 (cf. H. J. Frede, *Altlateinische Paulushandschriften* (Freiburg 1964), 34 ff.). w (83) is also a copy of 75 (cf. ibid, 47 ff.).

[12] Mixed text (Adams).

[13] All editions except Souter use ff[1]. Souter uses both ff and ff[1]. This ms. exists only in Matthew — UBS[3] contents are wrong. Vogels[4] and Merk[9] list this ms. among their Vulgate mss. B–O'C lists ff for ac on p. LX, which should be understood as ff (66) extant only in c.

[14] Souter gives ff as an alternative siglum (Introduction, xix) but note that he also uses ff for ff[1] (see, e.g., the apparatus to Matt. 15:40).

[15] For UBS contents see footnote 2 above. Only Souter uses the siglum ǵ for this ms. Merk (and WW) use g[1] only for Matthew: elsewhere the ms. is cited as Vulgate ms. G. See B. Fischer, 'Das Neue Testament in lateinischer Sprache', in *Die alten Übersetzungen des Neuen Testaments . . .*, ed. K. Aland (= ANTF 5) (Berlin and New York 1972), 36 ff.

[16] Cited only where it differs from the Vulgate.

[17] Used in N–A[25] as an Old Latin ms. Vogels[4] and Merk[9] list this ms. among their Vulgate mss.

[18] Known as g in Vogels[4], Merk[9], BFBS[2], B–O'C and by its Beuron number in Orchard. *Versions* and Adams state the ms. is Old Latin only in a r. For UBS contents see footnote 2 above.

[19] Used by Syn[10] — not by the English-Greek Synopsis.[3]

[20] Known as w in Merk[9], B–O'C.

[21] Listed as Old Latin only for Matthew in Vogels[4]. Adams states Matthew is a mixed text: the rest of the gospels is Vulgate.

[22] This ms. was known to Tischendorf as reg.

[23] This ms. was known to Tischendorf as z.

[24] Old Latin in a c, the rest of the NT is Vulgate (*Versions*). For the contents in UBS see footnote 2 above and note that the card insert shows that l (67) is not cited in e.

[25] Cited as Speculum Ps-Augustine by Vogels and Speculum by Merk. *Vetus Latina* lists it as a Patristic witness (PS-AU spe) and it is so used by N–A[26].

[26] Known as mon in UBS.

[27] Listed as a Vulgate ms. in Syn[10]. Used as an Old Latin ms. in N–A[25].

[28] In N–A[26], Jülicher, Syn, H–G μ = Munich Fragments of Matthew *not* the Book of Mulling.

[29] a[2] and n are fragments of one ms. to which o, a rewritten portion, belongs. (See de Bruyne, *Les Fragments de Freising* (Rome 1921), xi, note 1.) Vogels[4] cites n in Mark 16 despite the Explanatio, xii. Merk uses n for n + o.

[30] Old Latin only in a. For the text in c, see *VL* 26/1, 13* ff. For UBS contents see footnote 2 above: the card insert shows that p (54) is not cited in e.

[31] See E. S. Buchanan, 'An Old Latin Text of the Catholic Epistles', *JTS* xii (1911), 497–534.

[32] Known as r[4] (*Versions*).

[33] This ms. is listed as a separate ms. in *Versions*. For Paul, editions of the Greek New Testament use r. See also r[2].

[34] This is the same ms. as r 64 in the Catholic epistles. Some editors use q, some r (*q.v.*). Merk's q (monac.) is presumably the same as his r (fragm frising.) for the Catholic epistles. Both sigla are found in his apparatus to c.

[35] r[1] in the apparatus to Paul in UBS = r[3]. Souter (and WW) refer to r[1] as r.

[36] A mixed text. The strongest Old Latin elements occur in Matthew (Adams).

[37] N–A[25] used r[2] as an Old Latin witness. G. D. Kilpatrick (*TLZ* 106, 1981), col. 656, complains that N–A[26] neglects this ms.

[38] According to *Versions* this ms. is also known as scel.

[39] *Versions* states this is a Vulgate Bible with some Old Latin elements in Acts. Merk lists this ms. among its Vulgate mss. and uses it in Acts as such. Cited as κ[p] in *VL* 25 (see p. 78).

[40] Known as r[3] in UBS. Beuron 64 = r + r[2] + r[3] + q. *Versions* has r[1] as part of 64 on pp. 305, 311 but not on p. 309. *VL* 24 p. 11 * uses r for r[2] and r[3].

[41] A mixed text (Adams).

[42] For UBS contents see footnote 2 above: the card insert eliminates t(56) from e. Only a p c r are Old Latin (*Versions*). Vogels[4], ix, lists this ms. among its Vulgate mss., but see p. xiii. Known only by its Beuron number in H–G[13]. N–A[26] replaces Beuron number with τ: this symbol is used also for other Spanish liturgical mss., e.g. 68, 69, 70, 71, 72, 73, 251.

[43] Although this ms. is listed by Merk among its Old Latin mss. it is written in Middle High German. (See H. J. Frede, *VL* 24/2, 288 f.) Textually the ms. is close to w(58).

[44] Only a c are Old Latin (*Versions*). *VL* 1/1 has only a as Old Latin.

[45] x[1] according to *Versions*, p. 304, contains Acts, x[2] Paul. B–O'C combines both x[1] and x[2] under the siglum x. UBS cites only x[2] but uses the siglum x. The Pauline ms. is a descendant of V (see *VL* 25, p. 47).

[46] Known by Beuron number in H–G[13]. Mainly Vulgate outside Heb, 1 Peter, 1 John. Listed as a Vulgate ms. by Merk.

[47] Lectionary with some Old Latin and some Vulgate readings.

[48] Unequivocally a Vulgate ms. This ms. is unlettered in *Versions*. It is known as 33 in Syn[3].

[49] Although this lectionary seems not to have been cited in the apparatus, Greeven uses it in his special example (H–G[13], xx)!

[50] The Old Latin text is found in marginal glosses in a ms. of Juvencus.

[51] This is the León ms. described in *VL* 26/1, p. 45*.

[52] Old Latin readings may be found in all these Toledo mss.

[53] Mss. 91–95 contain glosses in a Spanish Vulgate ms. They occur in readings from c in *VL* 26: mss. 100 and 175 occur in *VL* 26.

[54] This lectionary occurs in *VL* 24, 25, 26.

[55] Rev 15:3–4 occurs in an Old Latin text as a canticle.

[56] The card insert explains that l(67) p (54) and t(56) are not cited for e.

[57] g[1] (and possibly others in this list) are probably not intended to be classed as Old Latin outside the Gospels (see UBS[3], p. xxxii, footnote 1). The absence of d from the Catholic Epistles is due to there being no *v.l.* for the portion of 3 John where d is extant.

[58] Bruce M. Metzger, *A Textual Commentary on the Greek New Testament* (United Bible Societies 1971).

[59] A table has not been included for IGNTP. This is because all 19 Old Latin mss. included in the introduction are used throughout Luke. There are no sundries.